W9-ANJ-396

The Yellowstone Wolf

A Guide and Sourcebook

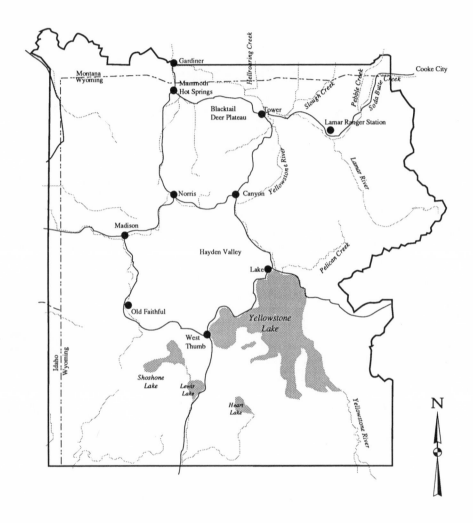

Yellowstone National Park, map by Renee Evanoff, Yellowstone Center for Resources.

Edited by Paul Schullery

The Yellowstone Wolf

A Guide
and Sourcebook

High Plains Publishing Company

All royalties from this book
go to the Yellowstone wolf project

High Plains Publishing Company, Inc.
Post Office Box 1860
Worland, Wyoming 82401

Cover illustration: A detail from
"High Ridge," ©1995, Daniel Smith.
Courtesy of the artist and
Mill Pond Press, Inc., Venice, FL 34292.

Dedicated to all those who have worked
to restore wolves to Yellowstone

Contents

Contents

Foreword

Our ancestors came to the New World prepared only to conquer, and conquer they did. But each succeeding generation became increasingly aware that conquest takes its toll. One of the dearest of those tolls has been the loss of some of the world's most spectacular predators. Places like the Greater Yellowstone Ecosystem, with its vast tracts of wild land, now provide us with an opportunity to make timely mid-course corrections in our treatment of this land's ecological character.

The Yellowstone wolf recovery program is a milestone project, demonstrating that our society has matured to the point where we recognize that humans share the earth with many other species as deserving of existence as we are. Through projects like this one, we learn not only to appreciate animals we once abused in ignorance, but also to use the planet's natural resources in ways that sustain rather than exhaust them.

The year 1995 began with one of the more memorable events in my lifetime. It took place in the heart of Yellowstone National Park, in January, a time when a layer of deep, pure snow blanketed the first protected landscape in America. But for all its beauty, over the previous 60 years this landscape had been an incomplete ecosystem; by the 1930s, government-paid hunters had systematically eradicated the predator at the top of the food chain: the American gray wolf.

I was there on that day, knee-deep in the snow, because I had been given the honor of carrying the first wolves back into that landscape. Through the work of conservation laws, I was there to restore the natural cycle, to help make Yellowstone complete once again.

The first wolf was an Alpha female, and after I set her down in the transition area, I looked through the grate into the green eyes of this magnificent creature, within this spectacular landscape, and was profoundly moved by the elevating nature of America's conservation laws.

But my experience was only a single, brief fragment. Paul Schullery's book, with its gathering of many voices from many times, tells you the whole story, from the days when wolves roamed the primitive Yellowstone wilderness, through the hard struggle to eliminate them, to a more tolerant age, when we realized that wolves have much to offer the human spirit.

I encourage you to read this story with humility for what we were so slow to learn, with pride for the course we have charted, and with hope for all we have yet to gain from our relationship with wolves.

Bruce Babbitt
Secretary of the Interior

Introduction

T he story of the wolves of
Yellowstone has become one of the most dramatic sagas in American
conservation history, rich in a symbolism that has proven irresistible
to journalists, historians, and activists (both wolf lovers and wolf hat-
ers) beyond counting. I have put this book together to make sure that
the original, authentic voices heard during the history of Yellowstone
wolf management are also heard today. Those historical and historic
voices speak in this book, in all their glorious disagreement, ignorance, intuition, and foresight. The only voice missing is that of the
wolf itself, and if you want to hear it you must first ensure that it
survives to be heard, and then you must come here and listen for
yourself. I have already heard it, and I tell you that it has changed a
landscape I thought I knew into a landscape of wondrous new possibilities.

Part One documents the "social history" of the Yellowstone wolf.
Following John Weaver's landmark overview of Yellowstone wolf history and management, we hear some representative and often influential voices from Yellowstone's past, and through their words we may
see the wolf as a symbol of change. When Yellowstone National Park
was created, in 1872, the wolf had no friends. Its slaughter was relent-
less, and even the new national park provided no sanctuary; the historical evidence summarized in Chapter 2 suggests that the wolves of
Yellowstone were greatly reduced, if not nearly eliminated, by 1880,

long before the federal government launched the formal predator-eradication programs of the early 1900s. But by the early 1900s, even as federal wolf-killing geared up, the discipline of ecology gained students and public attitudes matured, so that predators were no longer reviled by everyone. As wildlife managers got a generation or two of practical experience under their belts, they noticed that predators seemed to matter more than anybody had realized. As American society became increasingly urban, and wild country correspondingly less common and threatening, people had more tolerance and enthusiasm for remote wild things. As the conservation movement likewise matured, and the national park idea evolved, wolves became recognized too late as legitimate inhabitants of wild lands.

Part Two documents our most recent attempts to understand the wolf—not only the animal in its wilderness habitat but its relationships with other predators, its effects on its prey, and, perhaps most far–reaching for the wolf restoration program, its relationship with human society. As we watch various stereotypes and simplistic traditions dissolve in the face of ever more penetrating analysis, we may see the wolf as a symbol of complexity. Once viewed as nothing more than an evil force in an otherwise benign natural setting, predators have passed through a series of public images. For a long time after they had shed much of their demonic image, they were still respected only begrudgingly, as necessary evils placed on earth to serve as balance wheels in some intricate and clock-like natural machine. More recently, they have been viewed as furry, four-legged people—likeable, family-loving predators who had the good taste to dispose only of the unfit among their prey populations. These and other stereotypes are perhaps too easy to belittle today; without our having passed through these stages of understanding, we could not appreciate the real wolf as well as we do. Besides, it would be arrogant, even among late-twentieth century humans, to assume that our modern understanding of predators won't cause future naturalists to shake their heads in wonder at our naïveté.

Part Three documents the convoluted but essential path by which our laws and policies translated all these emotions, opinions, and science into a new way of managing wolves, from the days when all Yellowstone predators were most often enjoyed as moving targets to a time when Congress proclaimed that wolves matter. We might best see in this story the wolf as a symbol of social process: the animal as the vehicle by which our most Byzantine political bureaucracy grinds into action to change some small element of American life. The interplay of social mores and legislative action is almost always a diffuse and tangled business; by their caution, their equivocation, and indeed by their occasional brilliance, these expressions of policy and law mirror the tumultuous dialogue through which America came to reconsider not only wolves but the entire idea of conservation.

Part Four documents the most immediate effects of the past century of the human-wolf relationship in Yellowstone, the recovery program of recent years and the arrival of the first new wolves in January 1995. It is necessarily the least complete part of the story, because the project has just begun. Society has taken a kind of control over the wilderness unimagined a century ago and has put that control to a use never imagined by the park's founders. By bringing back the first wolves we have embarked on a period of experimentation and learning in which the wolves themselves will be our primary teachers. And so it may be that in this launching of a new wolf population, the wolf will serve as a symbol of conservation in a swiftly changing and often rather frightening world.

All of this symbolism is a lot to ask of an animal, or, more specifically, to ask of the few wolves that are currently exploring, hunting, and making themselves at home in Yellowstone. We have placed an enormous burden on these animals with all our expectations, fears, and hopes. Perhaps the thing that makes all this most wonderful is that the wolves do not care in the least; they will just go out and be wolves, with no regard for the consequences to any of us. That freedom, that utter remoteness from human needs, is probably the quality we should most treasure in them.

For all its size, I must warn you that a documentary treatment like this, depending as it does on what has been written in the past, has a different purpose than a narrative history. This book will give you a good idea of what many, many participants in the Yellowstone wolf story have said, but no one book can tell it all.

For example, to fully understand the recovery process, you must read most or all of the 1980 Recovery Plan, its 1987 revision, the draft Environmental Impact Statement and its revised final version, and quite a few other documents that are too long to be fully represented here. For another example, to fully understand the legal complications and subtleties of wolf recovery, you need to read not only the relevant laws and regulations, and not only the transcripts of the recent court cases relating to wolf restoration, but also the legal scholarship that has grown up around this issue. For reasons like these, I include a list of suggested additional readings at the end of the book.

Part I

History

 hen Yellowstone National Park was established in 1872, America was passionately absorbed in the conquest of a continent. At every turn, native culture and wild nature were being subdued, and natural resources were exploited and wasted at a phenomenal rate. The decade following the creation of the park saw the destruction of the last great bison herds, and the near-destruction of many other Western wildlife populations. Although its founders had only the faintest understanding of the park's eventual values, Yellowstone shone as one of the few bright lights in the conservation movement that was just then beginning. Established to protect strange geological and geothermal wonders, the park very quickly became a wildlife reserve of unprecedented scope. Ever since, Yellowstone has been one of the foremost laboratories in the world for learning how to manage not only wildlife but also wildlife habitat and wilderness landscapes.

As these readings demonstrate, management philosophy and policy have evolved continuously since the park was created. That evolution continues today. Fires, once viewed as almost satanically evil, are now accepted as a necessary part of the ecological system; relatively few people seem to have developed a new esthetic that embraces the stark beauty of a burned forest, but more and more people are at least willing to admit that fires must occur. Hot springs, once viewed as opportunities for intrusive plumbing systems to move warm water to bath houses and swimming pools, are now allowed to express themselves as they will; their mineral deposits, once chipped off by the ton as souvenirs, are now admired solely as marvels of geological architecture. Fish, once stocked and transplanted aggressively to create the best possible fishing with no regard for native species distribution, are now recognized as wild animals in their own right; managers now invest most of their energy in trying to protect or restore the native species to some semblance of their earlier role in the park's ecosystem. And predators, subjected to a persecution of almost religious intensity in the park's early decades, are now prized as both beautiful animals and important elements of a complex ecological community of life.

Yellowstone provided us with the opportunity to learn by doing. Each generation of park managers, visitors, supporters, and opponents wrestled with the park's management dilemmas. Because of the underlying goal of the park as a place where nature would somehow be preserved (and who could agree on what *that* meant?), we never took control of Yellowstone in the way we did most other landscapes. After the first decade or so, we left the forests unharvested, the meadows unplowed, the game animals unhunted. Our confusion over fire, fish, predators, and other things seemed to entangle us in ever more complicated questions about what preserving nature involved.

Few things are more illustrative of the intellectual and emotional struggles we've endured than are the wolves. As our attitude toward wolves shifted away from pure hate and toward begrudging acceptance and eventual admiration, the wolf gave us one of our most valuable lessons in humility. We learned the lesson too late to save those early wolves in Yellowstone, but as the modern wolf recovery movement shows, we learned the lesson well. I read these accounts of Yellowstone's original wolves with a mixture of sadness and anger, but I also find some comfort in them, because they prove we can learn, and we can change.

CHAPTER 1
THE WOLVES OF YELLOWSTONE
JOHN WEAVER

Biologist John Weaver was hired by the National Park Service in 1975 to study the park's wolf situation, and his report was published in 1978. It represented the first scientific attempt to gather all available information on the wolves of Yellowstone and to make a concerted effort in the field to determine if wolves still inhabited the park. It was also the first systematic attempt to reconstruct what was known about the habits and behavior of the wolves of Yellowstone, and it was the first publication of many historical records of wolf sightings, gathered by Weaver and by National Park Service biologist Mary Meagher. The vast amount of subsequent research on Yellowstone wolves, summarized in Part Two of this book, has expanded or improved on all aspects of our understanding. But this report was the beginning, and it serves as an excellent overview of wolves in Yellowstone history.

ABSTRACT

Historical records and intensive field surveys 1975–77 provided information on the population history, ecology, and current status of wolves (*Canis lupus*) in Yellowstone National Park and vicinity. Wolves occurred in unknown but seemingly low densities during the latter 1800's in several areas of Yellowstone where they were controlled periodically until 1926. Populations apparently began increasing about 1912, primarily in the northeast, and may have reached nonequilibrium levels of 30–40 animals (postwhelping). Intensive control 1914–26 removed at least 136 wolves, including about 80 pups. During this period Yellowstone wolves characteristically lived in packs of 3–16 members, some of which followed the ungulates in their seasonal migrations. Litters averaging 7.8 were born in late March and April, primarily in the north central sector of the park. Limited evidence suggests that elk (*Cervus elaphus*) were important food for wolves during all seasons. Wolves either survived the control era or moved in shortly thereafter for singles, pairs, and a pack of

SOURCE: J. Weaver. 1978. *The wolves of Yellowstone, history, ecology, and status.* Natural Resources Report Number 14, National Park Service, 38 pp.

3

four were reported the following decade. Resident wolf packs, however, were eliminated from Yellowstone National Park by the 1940's. Large canids have been sighted intermittently to the present, but their identity has not been established. Singles and pairs comprised 89% of 116 "probable" reports over the past 50 years. Speculation about factors limiting the Yellowstone wolf population considers its relative geographic isolation from viable wolf populations and possible genetic problems (including wolf-coyote hybridization) associated with prolonged minimal population status. A transplant of wolves from British Columbia or Alberta, or perhaps Minnesota, is recommended to restore a viable population of this native predator to Yellowstone National Park.

INTRODUCTION

Wolves historically occupied a wide range of habitats throughout much of North America north of the 20th parallel in southern Mexico (Goldman 1944), but their geographical range in the contiguous United States today has been reduced by nearly 99% (Mech 1971). The Northern Rocky Mountain Wolf (NRMW) (*Canis lupus irremotus*), one of 23 subspecies recognized by Goldman, once roamed the backbone of the continent from southern Idaho and Wyoming to southeastern British Columbia and southern Alberta (Fig. 1). Wolves throughout this area, including Yellowstone National Park, were reduced drastically by the 1930's by government and private control. In 1973 the Secretary of the Interior placed the NRMW on the Endangered Species List.

The primary purpose of administration of natural areas by the National Park Service is to preserve natural environments and native plant and animal life while providing for enjoyment by visitors in ways which maintain natural conditions (USDI National Park Service 1968). Mission-oriented research involves determining the completeness of park ecosystems and developing management procedures to prevent or compensate for departures caused by human actions (Cole 1969a). Lack of ecological completeness, for example, might stem from unnatural reduction or elimination of predator populations.

In recent years personnel and visitors in Yellowstone National Park have reported sightings of large canids (Cole 1971). No intensive field research, however, had been conducted specifically on wolves there. Mech (1971) stated:

For the wolves reported from Yellowstone Park, an immediate and

4

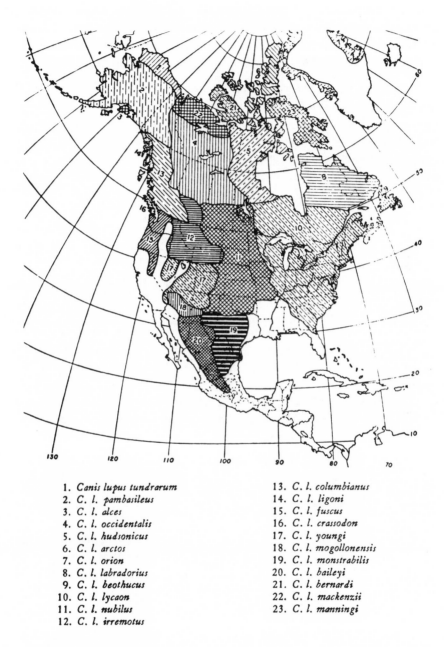

1. *Canis lupus tundrarum*
2. *C. l. pambasileus*
3. *C. l. alces*
4. *C. l. occidentalis*
5. *C. l. hudsonicus*
6. *C. l. arctos*
7. *C. l. orion*
8. *C. l. labradorius*
9. *C. l. beothucus*
10. *C. l. lycaon*
11. *C. l. nubilus*
12. *C. l. irremotus*
13. *C. l. columbianus*
14. *C. l. ligoni*
15. *C. l. fuscus*
16. *C. l. crassodon*
17. *C. l. youngi*
18. *C. l. mogollonensis*
19. *C. l. monstrabilis*
20. *C. l. baileyi*
21. *C. l. bernardi*
22. *C. l. mackenzii*
23. *C. l. manningi*

FIGURE 1. *North American distribution of subspecies of* Canis lupus *(from Goldman 1944).*

concerted program is necessary. Intensive efforts should be made to determine the extent of populations . . . both in terms of numbers and area occupied. Special attention should be given to determine whether breeding and successful reproduction are taking place.

In August 1975, I was contracted as an independent research biologist by the National Park Service to survey the status of wolves in Yellowstone National Park. Objectives of the study were to compile the historical information on wolves in Yellowstone and to determine their present distribution, abundance, and reproductive success.

STUDY AREA

A 19,151 km^2 (7,481 mile^2) area, encompassing Yellowstone National Park and a 16–24 km strip around its perimeter in northwestern Wyoming and adjacent parts of Montana and Idaho (Fig. 2), was selected for the wolf survey. Much of the area is designated or de facto wilderness, and developments such as roads, buildings, and campgrounds occupy less than 1% of the park.

Quaternary volcanic deposits which have undergone three glaciations cover most of the area (Keefer 1972). Elevations range from about 1,500 m to over 3,400 m, but forested rhyolite plateaus at 2,100–2,600 m are extensive.

Winters are usually long and cold while summers are short and cool (Dirks 1976; Houston 1976). Most of the annual precipitation of 34.5–96.5 cm falls as snow. In general, temperatures are lower and precipitation higher in the central and southern parts of the area.

About 79% of the terrestrial area of Yellowstone is forested, with lodgepole pine (64%) and subalpine fir–Engelmann spruce (6%) predominating. Despain (1973) and Houston (1976) have described the vegetation.

Distribution and estimated abundance of bison (*Bison bison*) (Meagher 1973), elk (Cole 1969b; Craighead et al. 1972; Houston 1974), moose (*Alces alces*), mule deer (*Odocoileus hemionus*), pronghorn antelope (*Antilocapra americana*), and bighorn sheep (*Ovis canadensis*) (Barmore in prep.) have been reported (Table 1). Ecology of the coyote (*Canis latrans*) (Murie 1940) and grizzly bear (*Ursus arctos*) (Craighead et al. 1974; Mealey 1975; Cole 1976; Knight et al. 1977) has been presented. Houston (1973) commented upon the status of mountain lions (*Felis concolor*) and wolverines (*Gulo gulo*) in the park.

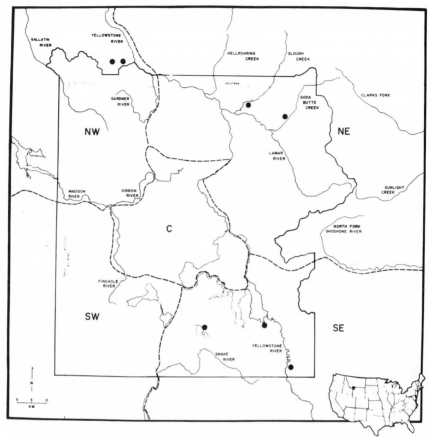

FIGURE 2. Location of the Yellowstone wolf study area. Broken lines arbitrarily distinguish five geographical sections to faciltate discussion of reported wolf observations. Shaded circles represent ungulate baits and/or canid scent and time-lapse cameras, February–March 1997.

TABLE 1. Seasonal population estimates of ungulates in Yellowstone National Park; 1977.

Species	Summer	Winter
Elk	20,000–25,000	10,000–13,000
Mule deer	2,000–4,000	500–2,000
Moose	1,500	1,000
Bison	1,100–1,200	1,100–1,200
Bighorn sheep	600	600
Pronghorn antelope	150	150

7

METHODS

Information on the history and ecology of wolves in Yellowstone National Park up to the 1930's was obtained from journals, Army scout diaries, Army station records (extracted by M. Meagher), and from monthly and annual reports of the superintendent, in the Yellowstone National Park Research Reference Library.

Population trends since that time to the present were assessed from nearly 500 reports of wolf-like animals and/or sign. These reports included replies to a questionnaire mailed to 89 big-game outfitters operating on the Gallatin, Shoshone, and Teton National Forests adjacent to the park. A point system was devised for evaluating and categorizing the observations (Table 2). The principal criteria included experience and reliability of the observer, details of the observation, and description of the animal and/or sign which would distinguish it in external appearance from other canids. Reports were categorized as "probable" or "possible" depending upon the number of points received. A "positive" category was reserved for instances where an animal was trapped or killed and verified as a wolf.

This point system was designed to be conservative. For example, an observation of a large gray canid at short range by a person familiar with Western coyotes received a "possible" evaluation. Reports citing a distinctive color, howl, or track rated "probable" if the observer was qualified. All reports were classified independently of any others.

This system remains subjective, however, and with such sources, all reports are questionable to a degree. Some observations, especially those from the 1930's and 1940's, may well have been of wolves but were classified "possible" for lack of details. Some "probable" sightings may have been of large coyotes. Nonetheless, the point system provides consistency for evaluating these observations. All reports were coded on computer-compatible sheets and filed at park headquarters.

I spent 12 months in the field, August–October 1975 and August 1976–April 1977, searching intensively for wolves and/or sign. Since the wolves' reproductive success was an important question, I designed the field study to cover periods of breeding, denning, and rendezvous activity. My field assistants and I traveled approximately 2,700 km on foot, skis, and snowshoes while inspecting government-maintained trails, game trails, ridges, and stream courses for wolves, tracks, and scats.

Tape-recorded and human-imitated wolf howls were broadcast approximately 1,400 times both day and night from elevated spots (Joslin

TABLE 2. *Criteria and point system for categorizing wolf observations.*[a]

Criteria	Points
Observer	
experience with Western coyotes	7
experience with wolves	3
Observation	
distance	
<100 m	3
100–400 m	2
>400 m	1
length of observation time	
>10 seconds	1
optical aid such as binoculars	1
Description of animal and/or sign	
body description	
large body size	4
large and blocky head, short ears, and	
relatively short muzzle	4
relatively large, long, legs	2
color	
solid white or black	10
howl	
distinctively different from coyote	10
track	
>10 cm (4.0 in) long including toenails	
(must include evidence to rule out domestic dog)	10

[a] Reports scoring ≥ points qualified as "probable"; those <16 points, "possible." See text for discussion of system.

1967). A parabolic microphone was available for recording any responses.

Baits of road-killed ungulates and canid scent were placed at seven locations in and near the park (Fig. 2), February–March 1977, and were monitored with time-lapse movie cameras (Diem et al. 1973). Some cameras were preset to expose a single-frame picture at 1.5-minute intervals; others, at 8-minute intervals.

Thirty hours in flight time were spent searching specifically for wolves and/or sign. In addition, approximately 1,800 hours have been logged by other park research biologists since 1964 during wildlife distribution and censusing flights.

Most of the intensive ground search concentrated on the northeast and southeast portions of the study area (Fig. 2), whereas flights were made over most of the park.

THE YELLOWSTONE WOLF

The wolves of Yellowstone—*C. l. irremotus*—probably intergraded with *columbianus* to the north, *nubilus* to the east, and *youngi* to the south (Goldman 1944). Specimens from northwestern Wyoming were considered by Goldman to be "somewhat intermediate" between *irremotus* and *youngi*.

Goldman (1944:404) pointed out that gray wolves ". . . are all very similar in the more essential features and are believed to intergrade through the vast range of the species on the North American mainland." Indeed, taxonomists today, with multivariate statistical techniques, might reduce the number of wolf subspecies or perhaps eliminate them altogether (*see* Nowak 1973; Jolicoeur 1975; Skeel and Carbyn 1977). Although there are reasons to question the validity of the subspecific groupings, I use Northern Rocky Mountain Wolf (NRMW) for convenient reference to this geographical population. Wolf taxonomy and its implications for management will be discussed later.

The NRMW is medium- to large-sized for the species. An adult male from Red Lodge, Montana, measured 1,870 mm (61.4 inches) total length, while two adult females from Soda Springs, Idaho, measured 1,929 and 2,046 mm (Goldman 1944). An adult male taken in Montana in 1968 weighed 42 kg (92 lb) (Gary Day pers. comm.). For wolves in Yellowstone, Bailey (1930) stated: "The male is consistently larger than the female, weighing well over a hundred pounds."

Goldman (1944) described the winter pelage of the NRMW:

Upper parts from nape to rump usually near "light buff" or varying shades of gray, sparingly overlaid with black, becoming nearly white on sides and limbs; short pelage on top of head light buffy white, the hairs tipped with black; ears and upper surface of muzzle light buffy; under parts in general more or less soiled white; tail above light buffy, thinly and inconspicuously overlaid with black, light buffy below to tip, which is a mixture of buff and black all around. Individuals in the black phase appear to be rare.

10

FIGURE 3. *Three wolves killed near Hellroaring Creek (NE) and the den in a rock cave from which six pups were removed, Yellowstone National Park, April 1916 (from Bailey 1916).*

Of 136 wolves killed in the park, three were black and one was white (Fig. 3); two others observed were black. All others were gray. It seems reasonable that most black or white wolves, due to their conspicuousness, would be reported. Neither the reported kills nor the recorded observations substantiate Skinner's (1927) claim that up to 40% of Yellowstone wolves were black.

POPULATION HISTORY

Prior to 1914

Wolves were members of Yellowstone's native fauna. Although few observations were recorded during the 1800's (Appendix I), this could reflect either an actual low density of wolves or simply a lack of records. Some early writers used "wolf" in reference to both true wolves and coyotes ("small prairie wolf" or "medicine wolf" (*see* Haines 1955:129), but reports from about 1880 on usually distinguished the two species. Five accounts of gray wolves were recorded 1869–80.

At least as early as 1877, however, ungulate carcasses in the park were poisoned with strychnine by free-lance "wolfers" for "wolf or wolverine bait" (Supt. Annual Rept. 1877). By 1880, Superintendent Norris stated in his annual report that ". . . the value of their [wolves and coyotes] hides and their easy slaughter with strychnine-poisoned carcasses have nearly led to their extermination." Sightings of single wolves, pairs, and groups of three and six were recorded 1881–1908, primarily in the Geyser Basins (C), Hayden Valley (C), and Lamar (NE) (Fig. 4).

The Yellowstone wolf population apparently began to increase about 1912, at least in the northern sector. In a letter dated 29 July, 1912, Col. L. M. Brett remarked that ". . . several were killed on the Upper Gallatin River but a few miles outside [the park] . . . last spring" (Appendix I). Skinner (1927) observed four wolves in Lamar Valley that same year and believed wolves "were coming in faster." Randall (1966) saw a pack of nine along the Yellowstone River near Hellroaring in spring, 1913.

1914–1926

By 1914, wolves had increased noticeably in northeast Yellowstone Park (Supt. Annual Rept. 1914). They were considered, though, "a decided menace to the herds of elk, deer, mountain sheep, and antelope" (Supt. Annual Rept. 1915) and concerted efforts to "exterminate" (Supt.

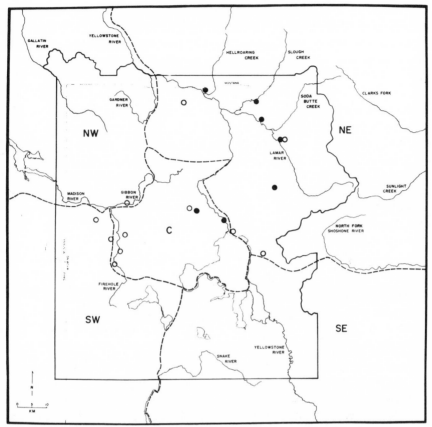

FIGURE 4. *Location of wolf observations in Yellowstone National Park prior to 1914. Open circles represent sightings of pairs; shaded circles, three or more animals together.*

Monthly Rept. February 1919) wolves were mounted. Opposition to this policy was ignored as suggested by the following (Supt. Monthly Rept. May 1922): "It is evident that the work of controlling these animals must be vigorously prosecuted by the most effective means available whether or not this meets with the approval of certain game conservationists."

During 1914–26 a minimum of 136 wolves—including about 80 pups (59%)—were removed from dens, trapped, shot, and probably poisoned within the park (Table 3). This total is slightly higher than Skinner's (1927) and Murie's (1940) due to a more detailed examination of histori-

TABLE 3. Wolf mortality in Yellowstone National Park, 1914–26.

Year	Adults	Pups	Totals[d]	
			Monthly Rpts.	Annual Rpt.
1914	7	–	7	–
1915	3	4	7	"several"
1916	2	8	10	12
1917	2	–	2	–
1918	21	14[a]	35	36
1919	2	–	2	6
1920	6	20+[b]	26+	28
1921	3	11	14	
1922	9	16	25	24[c]
1923	1	5	6	8
1924	–	–	–	–
1925	–	–	–	–
1926	–	2	2	–
Total	56	80	136	114

[a] Report did not distinguish between adults and pups. Nineteen wolves were killed in April and I have assumed that, as for the same month in other years, most of these were pups.
[b] One den with unreported number of pups was closed up.
[c] Combined for 1921 and 1922.
[d] Monthly reports were more detailed and were considered to be the best source.

cal sources. In each of 3 years (1918, 1920, 1922), the toll exceeded 24 animals (mostly pups). In 1918, 21 adult wolves were killed. The annual kill fluctuated throughout this period, indicating either real changes in wolf numbers or varying effort by the control personnel, or both. Certain trends, however, appear evident.

Between 1914 and 1923, 15 (56%) of 27 reports involved three or more wolves together (Appendix II). Four occupied and distinct dens found in 1916 and 1920 suggest at least four different reproductive units those years. The last den destroyed by park personnel was in 1923 near Tower Falls (NE). In the next 3 years, only 3 (21%) of 14 reports mentioned more than two wolves together. Two pups were trapped near Soda Butte (NE) in October 1926 (Fig. 5).

All the reported killing of wolves occurred in the northeast section from near Mammoth east to Soda Butte and south to Pelican Valley (Fig. 6), as did many observations. In addition, one or two wolves were sighted occasionally in the southeast section. Hayden Valley and the Geyser Basins, areas occupied by wolves around the turn of the century, furnished but one record of a single animal during 1914–26.

FIGURE 5. *Wolf pups trapped at bison carcass near Soda Butte (NE), Yellowstone Park, October 1926. (Photo by Scott Riley.)*

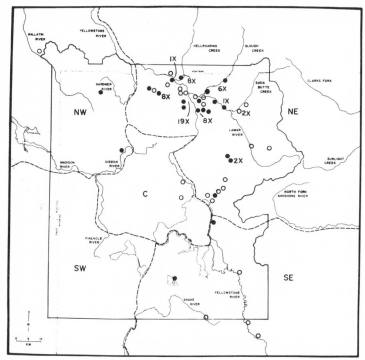

FIGURE 6. *Location of observations and numbers of wolves killed (X) in Yellowstone Park and vicinity, 1914–26. Open circles represent sightings of singles or pairs; shaded circles, three or more animals together.*

15

1927–1966

The population history of wolf-like canids in Yellowstone 1927–66 relies upon reports which have been classified "probable" and Superintendent Monthly Reports up to 1936. Within the recognized subjective nature of the data, this represents my best interpretation of wolf population trends during those years. To facilitate discussion, I grouped reports into 10-year periods.

1927–36. In the decade following intense persecution of wolves in the park, 14 observations of 29 large canids were tallied. Seven reports involving 17 animals were classified "probable" (Fig. 7a) (*see* Appendix III). A pack of four was observed up Tower Creek (NE) in 1934 (Arnold

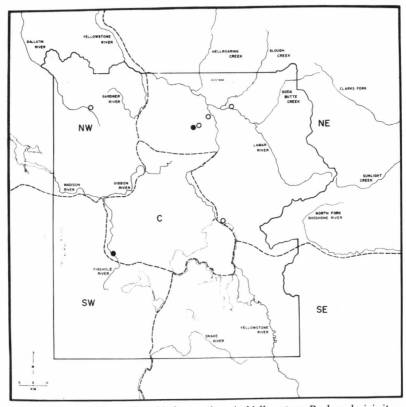

FIGURE 7a. *Locations of canid observations in Yellowstone Park and vicinity, 1927–36. Open circles represent sightings of singles or pairs; shaded circles, three or more animals together.*

1937), but sightings of singles or pairs accounted for five of seven reports.

1937–46. There were 16 reports of 18 large canids for this period; 8 of these involving 10 animals were rated "probable" (Fig. 7b). Three wolves were seen in 1937 on lower Specimen Ridge, a single on Soda Butte Creek in 1938, and another single just north of the park in 1942 (all in NE). A wolf was observed up Mol Heron Creek (NW) the following year. In 1944, single wolves were reported at Heart Lake (SE), Elk Park (NW), and Crevice (NE). Sightings of singles or pairs comprised seven of eight reports.

1947–56. Twenty-six reports of 37 canids were received; six involving 10

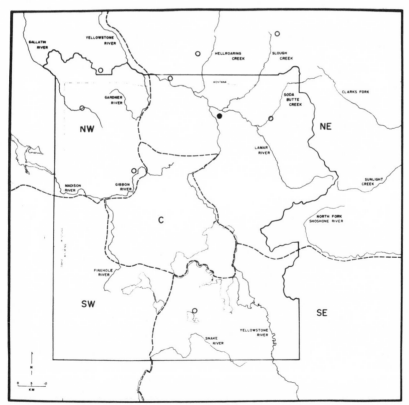

FIGURE 7b. *Locations of canid observations in Yellowstone Park and vicinity, 1937–46. Open circles represent sightings of singles or pairs; shaded circles, three or more animals together.*

animals were classified "probable" (Fig. 7c). Two wolves were observed at Soda Butte in 1947, one near Lost Creek in 1949, and three at Amethyst Creek in 1952 (all in NE). A single, large canid was seen just south of the park in 1950. Along the Madison River, a pair of wolves was seen in 1952 and a single, the following year. Five of these six "probable" reports mentioned only singles or pairs.

1957–66. Thirty-two observations of 42 canids were recorded. Fourteen reports involving 21 animals received a "probable" rating (Fig. 7d). Single wolves were observed in the northeast in 1957, 1958, 1963, and 1965. A large adult canid with three pups was reported there in 1963. Singles were seen near Swan Lake (NW) in 1958 and 1965 and a pack of three on the Gallatin River in 1966. One of two wolves observed up Mol

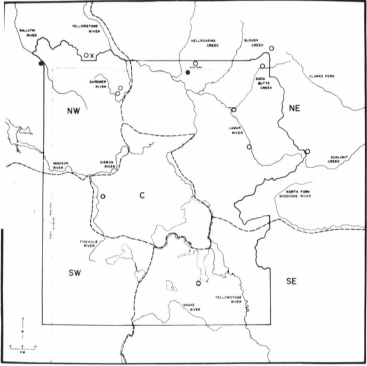

FIGURE 7c. *Locations of canid observations in Yellowstone Park and vicinity, 1947–56. Open circles represent sightings of singles or pairs; shaded circles, three or more animals together.*

18

Heron in 1963 was shot but not recovered. In 1960 one wolf was reported at Grouse Creek (SE) south of Yellowstone Lake and another, along the east boundary near Sunlight Basin (NE). A single wolf was seen near Porcupine Hills (C) in 1963. Sightings of singles and pairs constituted 12 of 14 reports.

Summary. Wolf-like canids either survived the 1914–26 control era in Yellowstone National Park or moved in shortly thereafter. Murie (1940) believed that "the last wolves were eliminated in the twenties although a few have been reported in recent years." Two packs of three to four and five wolves may still have been present in the mid-1930's, but records do not indicate they persisted. During the next 30 years, observations of wolf-like canids—mostly singles and pairs—were reported sporadically from the northwest and northeast sections of the study area.

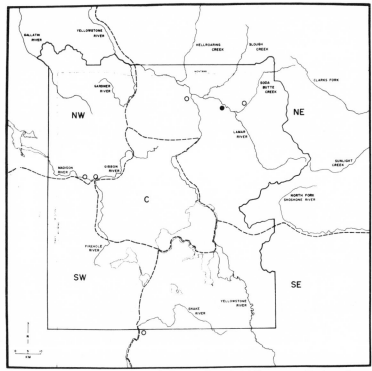

FIGURE 7d. *Locations of canid observations in Yellowstone Park and vicinity, 1957–66. Open circles represent sightings of singles or pairs; shaded circles, three or more animals together.*

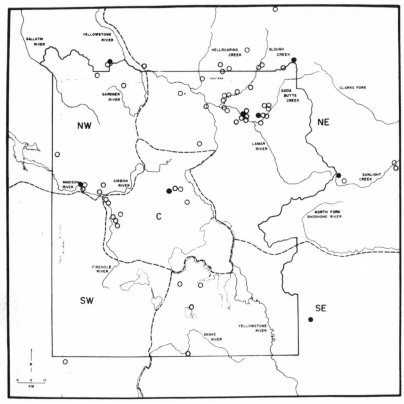

FIGURE 8. Locations of canid observations in Yellowstone Park and vicinity, 1967–April 1977. Open circles represent sightings of singles or pairs; shaded circles, three or more animals together.

POPULATION STATUS

1967–April 1977

During the past decade, 401 reports of 531 canids have been received; 81 involving 109 animals were classified "probable" (Fig. 8). The increase in reports during this period was due partly to a system established in 1968 for recording sightings of wolves (Cole 1971) and to greater awareness of their occurrence in the park.

About 90% of the "probable" observations came from four areas (Fig. 8). Each year throughout this period, one or two wolf–like canids have been seen in the northeast. In Hayden Valley (C), a single wolf was observed in 1969 and 1971. A wolf reportedly was shot in Sunlight Basin east of the park in January 1968, but no remains were found the following summer. Sightings of a large canid in that area were recorded in 1968, 1969, 1971, and 1975. In the northwest section of Yellowstone, one to five wolves were seen in 1968–70, a pair in 1971, and singles in 1972 and 1974. None has been reported from that area since. Sixty (74%) of the "probable" observations occurred during 1968–71. Singles and pairs accounted for 91% of these reports over the entire period.

During approximately 1,800 hours of flight by park biologists over all sections of the park since 1964, only one wolf-like canid has been seen. D. Houston and D. Stradley observed this dark animal in Hayden Valley in 1971, but poor light conditions precluded a positive identification.

During 12 months I found only two separate sets of tracks and heard one series of howls which may have been wolf. All occurred on the Shoshone National Forest, Wyoming, within 20 km of each other and 1–22 km east of the park boundary. Tracks measuring 11.3 cm (4.5 inches) long (including nails) by 9.6 cm (3.8 inches) wide with a 63-cm stride were found in sand near a stream on 7 September 1975. No evidence of human activity or domestic dogs was discovered anywhere in the general area. Tape-recorded wolf howls were broadcast the previous and following nights, but no responses were heard. Two weeks later, one canid howled three separate times in response to a broadcast wolf howl. This occurred about 18 km from the site of the tracks. The animal was in dense timber and never was observed. No measurable tracks were found as the ground was hard and dry. The howls were not recorded, but I am confident the animal was not a coyote. Subsequently, 34 days were spent afield in this area (August–September 1976, April 1977). Canid tracks, identical in measurement to the first set, were found 20 April 1977 about 2 km from the site of the howls. Casts of these tracks are in the park Museum Collection.

No wolves were photographed by time-lapse cameras monitoring the ungulate baits and/or canid scent during February–March 1977, nor were any observed during 30 hours of flight. Unfortunately, winter conditions were very mild and many wildlife species remained scattered throughout the study area.

ECOLOGY

Reproduction

Breeding and Denning Dates. The earliest positive birth date known for wolves in Yellowstone was 26 March (1916) when pups, judged less than 1 week old, were taken (Appendix II). Pups were removed from dens in March 1920 and 1921, but the exact date was not recorded. Skinner (1927) reported "three lots of pups which were born about March 1." Pups of unreported age were taken from other dens 1–8, 16, an 30 April, and 12 May. For wolves in the Bighorn Basin of north-central Wyoming, King (1965) related denning dates of 25 and 29 March and 19 April. Assuming a 63 day gestation (Brown 1936; Woolpy 1968), these dates indicate that Yellowstone wolves bred anytime from January until early March. This breeding season coincides with others reported from a similar latitude (Mech 1970:117).

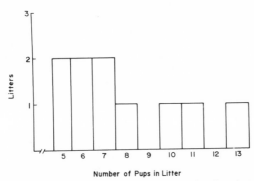

FIGURE 9. *Histogram of litter sizes of wolves in Yellowstone Park, 1916–23.*

Litter Sizes. The size of 10 presumably complete wolf litters extracted from dens averaged 7.8 and ranged from 5 to 13 (Fig. 9). Litters of 11 and 10 were found in 1921 and 1922, respectively, following several years of persecution. Such large litters seem characteristic of exploited wolf populations (Mech 1970).

Dens. Bailey (1930) stated that wolf dens in Yellowstone were usually "situated in caves or hollows among rocks or sometimes, in large burrows on steep hillsides." He described a den near Hellroaring as composed of four or five large burrows dug into the open hillside "which, evidently, had been used for several years." When disturbed by humans, the adults moved the pups to another den in a natural cave about a mile (1.6 km) away (*see* Fig. 3).

Certain physiographic features appear characteristic of these and other wolf den sites described in the literature (Mech 1970:120–121;

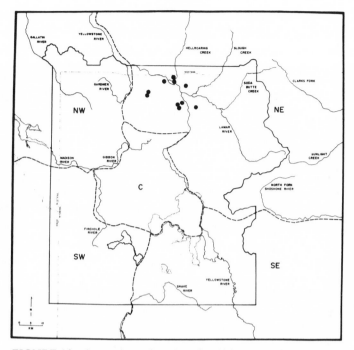

FIGURE 10. *Approximate location of wolf dens in Yellowstone Park, 1916–23.*

Stephenson 1974). Typically, dens are located on south or southwest aspects of moderately steep slopes in well drained soils (or rock caves), at elevations 2–200 m above the surrounding area, and usually within 30–200 m of surface water. All the reported wolf dens in Yellowstone were located in the north central part of the park, from Blacktail Deer Plateau to Specimen Ridge (Fig. 10).

Rendezvous Sites. Murie (1944) used the term "rendezvous" for specific resting and gathering areas occupied by wolf packs during summer after the natal den has been abandoned. These are usually small, open meadows close to wooded cover and surface water (Joslin 1967; Carbyn 1974). In August 1922, Park Ranger Anderson found an apparent rendezvous site of wolves in Yellowstone.

This is a section of the park that is practically inaccessible due to bog holes, rim rock, down timber, and jack pines [sic]. The area is the part of the Mirror Plateau lying near the head of Timothy, Raven, Pelican, and Broad Creeks [Appendix II].

It is possible that this area had been used by wolves for rendezvous in previous years. Nowlin (1912) reported wolves howling at the head of Raven Creek on 25 July 1912. Bailey (1930) found tracks "especially numerous along Pelican and Raven Creeks where at least ten or a dozen wolves hunted in one pack in July and August, 1915."

Pack Size

Wolves characteristically live in packs of three or more individuals (Mech 1970). Although a pack usually functions as an intact unit, members may split off temporarily at any season of the year (Murie 1944; Burkholder 1959; Jordan et al. 1967). Hence, cursory observations of wolves may underestimate true pack size.

Nonetheless, even rough estimates of pack size may provide insight if, as Rausch (1967) proposed, pack size reflects population density. Between 1902 and 1926, wolf packs of 3–16 members were reported for 9 different years. Based upon the number of distinct dens occupied by wolves, three to four reproductive units were present in some years (1916–22) in the northeast. By contrast, between 1927 and 1977, there have been "probable" reports of three to five wolf-like canids together in only 8 years. It is doubtful if more than one group existed in any one year.

Seasonal Distribution and Movements

Some wolves in Yellowstone apparently followed the ungulates in their altitudinal migrations to and from summer and winter ranges. Bailey (1930) reported that "during the summers of 1914 and 1915 they [wolves] . . . were following the elk herds to the high pastures of Mirror Plateau, returning with them in winter to the valleys along the Lamar and Yellowstone Rivers." The Superintendent's Monthly Reports during 1915 state:

> Towards the end of the month [May] the wolves seemed to leave the Specimen Ridge district and have not been much in evidence since. They were considerably in evidence in Slough and Hellroaring Creeks [November].

Although some wolves wintering in the Lamar and Yellowstone valleys moved toward Mirror Plateau and Pelican Valley during summer, others may have headed north out of the park.

Food habits

Kills by wolves and scat contents suggest that elk were important prey both winter and summer for wolves in Yellowstone. Scout McBride found a cow elk killed on 21 December 1914, between Mammoth and Blacktail Deer Creek. Between 16 October and 31 January 1916, Scout Black discovered eight elk killed by wolves (Appendix II). Skinner (1927) wrote that during the winter of 1914–15, two or three wolf packs "harried" the elk on the lower valleys of the park. Bailey (1930) reported that wolf droppings in Pelican Valley collected during July 1915 were made up entirely of elk hair. That same month he also discovered a young elk in Slough Creek which he believed had been killed by wolves.

Studies of food habits of wolves in the Rocky Mountain National Parks of Canada (Cowan 1947; Carbyn 1974) and in Glacier National Park in Montana (Singer 1975) provide an interesting comparison with Yellowstone since similar species of prey inhabit these areas. Cowan (1947) reported that elk hair occurred in 49% of winter scats and 42% of summer ones. Mule deer hair was found in about 15% of scats collected at both seasons. Most wolf kills found by personnel were either elk (54%) or mule deer (23%). Cowan believed the actual kill of elk may have been higher because very few scats were collected in areas where wolves subsisted "almost exclusively on elk." Carbyn (1974) found elk hair in 46% of 1,190 summer scats and 11% of 265 winter scats. Mule deer hair was detected more often (66%) in the winter samples than in the summer (30%). His study area contained more mule deer than other areas of Jasper Park where Cowan (1947) worked. In both Canadian studies, bighorn sheep and mountain goats (*Oreamnos americanus*) were comparatively invulnerable to wolf predation. In Montana's Glacier Park, Singer (1975) reported eight white-tailed deer (*Odocoileus virginianus*), three moose, one elk, one beaver (*Castor canadensis*), and five snowshoe hares (*Lepus americanus*) killed by wolves.

Elk were also important food for Yellowstone wolves during the denning season in late March and April. On 26 March 1916, scouts Black and Stevenson found "a score or more of old elk skulls . . . and one fresh elk head" near a den in Hellroaring. A freshly killed young elk was discovered about 0.5 km from another den in the same area. Scraps of elk meat were in the den with the pups (Appendix II). Considering the abundance of beaver between Hellroaring and Tower Falls around 1920 (Warren 1926) and the reported predilection of wolves for them (Voight et al. 1976), it seems likely they formed a portion of the wolves' diet, too. At two wolf dens in Jasper Park, Cowan (1947) found remains of 12 elk, 2 mule deer, and 2 beaver. Carbyn (1974) reported occurrence of mule deer in 44% and elk in 32% of 312 scats collected at wolf dens. Later in summer at rendezvous sites, 55% of 270 scats contained elk, while 22% had mule deer.

Data on the sex and age of ungulates killed by wolves in the Rocky Mountains are limited but suggest that calves or fawns and individuals 10 years and older may be most vulnerable. Of nine elk killed in Yellowstone and reported by scouts, six were adult cows, two were calves, and one was unidentified. No kills of adult bulls were recorded (Appendix II). In Jasper, Cowan (1947) classified 66 wolf killed elk: very young—20, mature—29, and diseased-senile—17. Carbyn (1974) believed that young individuals less than 3 years old of all ungulates were most vulnerable to wolf predation. Individuals 3–9 years old appeared relatively sure.

DISCUSSION

Wolves inhabited the Yellowstone area in unknown densities when the park was established in 1872 but were subject to early exploitation (1870's) and later control (1914–26). A noticeable population increase about 1912 was met by intense year-round control, especially removal of pups from dens. Estimates of wolf numbers, based upon population stability via reproductive responses to removal of wolves 5 months and older (Rausch 1967; Kelsall 1968; see Mech 1970), cannot be made from the Yellowstone data. Nonetheless, certain comments seem appropriate. Control records (Table 3) and the presence of up to four reproductive units (Appendix II) suggest postwhelping populations of 30–40 wolves around 1920, primarily in the northeast and southeast (Fig. 6). Of 103 wolves observed 1914–23, 83% were in packs of 3 or more. What level the Yellowstone wolf population might have reached had control been minimal remains unknown.

After wolf control ceased within the park in 1926, very few wolves were reported. Whether these were remnant survivors or immigrants, or both, is unknown. Wolf numbers elsewhere in Wyoming and Montana were reduced drastically by this time, too. In Wyoming and South Dakota 508 wolves were killed 1918–23 by government personnel, with the last one taken in 1940 (G. Rost pers. comm.). In Montana, government agents removed 413 wolves during 1918–30 and their last one in 1945 (N. Miner pers. comm.). Yellowstone records do not indicate that any resident wolf packs persisted after the mid-1930's.

Wolf-like canids have been sighted within the study area intermittently to the present, with an increase of "probable" reports 1968–71. Based upon geographical distribution of the sightings and some pelage differences, up to 10 of these canids may have occupied several separate areas around 1970. Observations reflect human distribution and variations in the visibility of animals as well as their actual seasonal ranges. Hence, it is difficult from these cursory reports to determine whether these canids were residents or transients.

The identity of wolf-like canids reported recently in Yellowstone Park has not been established and would require skeletal material. Interpretations include: (1) a remnant population of genetically pure wolves persisted through occasional, successful recruitment; (2) wolves in Canada and Montana immigrated periodically down to Yellowstone; (3) wolves were released into the park; and (4) wolf-like canids occurred through hybridization of various kinds.

The interpretation that a small population of pure wolves survived seems untenable without more consistent evidence of pack activity during the intervening years.

Use of toxicants on surrounding public and private lands would have made journeys hazardous for immigrating wolves. In Glacier National Park, black wolves, more prevalent in *C. l. "columbianus"* (Canadian) than in *"irremotus"* comprised 32% of the wolf observations (Singer 1975). Near Three Forks, Montana (100 km northwest of Yellowstone Park), a wolf with a very large skull was killed in 1941, and both Goldman (1944) and Cowan (1947) believed it a Canadian emigrant. But in Yellowstone from 1966–77, 5% of canids sighted were black, suggesting that few Canadian wolves immigrated as far south as Yellowstone.

Despite suggestions of *sub rosa* releases of wolves (Mech and Rausch 1975), park officials have denied that any were ever transplanted to Yellowstone. Although I found no evidence to the contrary, this allegation has not been fully investigated. The possibility of a surreptitious release of captive wolves by private individuals cannot be totally discounted, but their chances for survival would seem slight.

The prolonged geographical isolation of Yellowstone from wolf population centers suggests the remaining possibility—hybridization. While reproductive isolation between species is usually maintained by geographic and ethological barriers, individuals on the periphery of their species' range may have trouble finding a conspecific mate. In the absence of adequate breeding stimuli, they may respond to inadequate signals and hybridize (Mayr 1963). Recent evidence from several areas of North America suggests that coyotes may hybridize both with gray wolves Kolenosky 1971; Mengel 1971; Kolenosky and Standfield 1975; Lawrence and Bossert 1975; Hilton 1976) and red wolves (*Canis rufus*) (Paradiso and Nowak 1971; Riley and McBride 1972; Gipson et al. 1974; Elder and Hayden 1977). Coyote-dog crosses are considered much less likely in Yellowstone due to its remoteness and the peculiar reproductive timing of such hybrids (Mengel 1971).

Kolenosky (1971, 1977 pers. comm.) reported that F^1 offspring of an Ontario wolf (V) and coyote (M) phenotypically resemble Eastern coyotes but with massive legs and large feet. He suspected that if they were sighted in the wild they would be identified as "normal" Eastern coyotes. However, in external appearance, one of the F^2's is almost identical to an Algonquin-type wolf (*see* Kolenosky and Standfield 1975), with larger head, legs, and feet than other progeny. Some wild canids in Ontario (Kolenosky and Standfield 1975) and Maine (Hilton 1977) appear to be mainly coyotes with some introgression of wolf genes. In Yellowstone we have no cranial material with which to trace such an incursion, if it ever occurred. Yet many reports describe animals phenotypically similar to the F^1 canids observed by Kolenosky. Some of the recorded track measurements (9–11 cm long × 7–9 cm wide) are between typical coyote and wolf in size.

Whatever the identity of some large canids in Yellowstone, the sporadic nature of reports and the high incidence (89% of 116 "probable" sightings) of singles and pairs over the past 50 years do not indicate a viable wolf population in the park.

MANAGEMENT RECOMMENDATIONS

A stated purpose of the National Park Service is to "conserve, perpetuate, and portray as a composite whole the indigenous . . . terrestrial fauna" (USDI National Park Service 1968). A departure from natural conditions exists in Yellowstone National Park because fewer pure wolves, if any, occur now than in the past. Control by humans—both within and outside the park—has brought the Yellowstone wolf to the edge of extinction.

Two options are available for wolf management in Yellowstone National Park: (1) do nothing; or (2) attempt to restore a viable wolf population by introduction. The former alternative has been employed since 1927 when wolf control ceased in the park. Over the next 50 years, a viable population has not reestablished, and the wolf niche appears essentially vacant. Therefore, I recommend restoring this native predator by introducing wolves to Yellowstone.

In proposing a transplant, one must consider the suitability of source stock. The Department of the Interior originally placed *C. l. irremotus* on the Endangered Species List. However, use of trinomens has been questioned for many animals (Wilson and Brown 1953; Brown and Wilson 1954; Hagmeier 1958; Chapman and Morgan 1973), including wolves (Mech 1974; R. M. Nowak pers. com.). Recent multivariate analyses of wolf skulls (Nowak 1973; Jolicoeur 1975; Skeel and Carbyn 1977) have shown few statistically significant differences between many subspecific groupings made by Goldman (1944). Upon consideration of such factors, the U.S. Fish and Wildlife Service has proposed (Federal Register, 9 June 1977:29527) deleting *C. l. irremotus* and listing the entire species (*Canis lupus*) as endangered throughout the 48 contiguous states (except Minnesota).

Perhaps a more important aspect of reintroduction is finding wolves that would have the best chance of adapting to the physiography and prey of Yellowstone. Wolves from the mountains of British Columbia or Alberta would seem suitable, especially if gene flow from that direction has occurred. Wolves from Minnesota are another possible source.

REFERENCES

Arnold, M. 1937. Yellowstone wolves. *Nature Mag.* Yellowstone Natl. Park, Wyo. August:111–112.

Bailey, V. 1930. *Animal life of Yellowstone National Park.* Charles C. Thomas, Baltimore. 241pp.

Barmore, W. J. In prep. Population characteristics, distribution, and habitat relationships of six ungulates in northern Yellowstone National Park.

Black, C. 1916. Scout diary, 1915–16. Yellowstone Natl. Park Arch.

Brown, W. L. and E. O. Wilson. 1954. The case against the trinomen. *Syst. Zool.* 3:174–176.

Burkholder, B. L. 1959. Movements and behavior of a wolf pack in Alaska. *J. Wildl. Manage.* 23:1–11

Carbyn, L. N. 1974. *Wolf predation and behavioral interactions with elk and other ungulates in an area of high prey diversity.* Canad. Wildl. Serv. Rept., Edmonton 233pp.

Chapman, J. A. and R. P. Morgan II. 1973. Systematic status of the cottontail complex in western Maryland and nearby West Virginia. *Wildl. Monogr.* No. 36. 54pp.

Cole, G. F. 1969a. Mission-oriented research in the natural area of the National Park Service. Res. Note 6. Yellowstone Natl. Park. 6pp.

———. 1969b. The elk of Grand Teton and southern Yellowstone National Parks. Res. Rept. GRTE-1. Yellowstone Natl. Park 192pp.

———. 1971. Yellowstone wolves. Res. Note 4. Yellowstone Natl. Park. 6pp.

———. 1976. Management involving grizzly and black bears in Yellowstone National Park, 1970-75. Nat. Res. Rept. No. 9. 56pp.

Cowan, I. M. 1947. The timber wolf in the Rocky Mountain national parks of Canada. *Can. J. Res.* 25:139–174.

Craighead, J. J., G. Atwell, and B. W. O'Gara. 1972. Elk migrations in and near Yellowstone National Park. *Wildl. Monogr.* No. 29. 48pp.

———, J. R. Varney, and F. C. Craighead, Jr. 1974. A population analysis of the Yellowstone grizzly bears. Mont. For. and Conserv. Expt. Sta. Bull. 40. Univ. Montana, Missoula. 20pp.

Despain, D. 1973. Major vegetation zones of Yellowstone National Park. Yellowstone Natl. Park Info. Paper No. 10. 4pp.

Diem, K. L., L. A. Ward, and J. J. Cupal. 1973. Cameras as remote sensors of animal activities. Univ. Wyoming, Laramie. 10pp.

Dirks, R. A. 1976. Climatological studies of Yellowstone and Grand Teton National Parks, continuing studies. Dept. Atmospheric Sciences, Univ. Wyoming.

Elder, W. H. and C. M. Hayden. 1977. Use of discriminant function in taxonomic determination of canids from Missouri. *J. Mammal.* 58:17–24.

Gipson, P., J. A. Selander, and J. E. Dunn. 1974. The taxonomic status of wild *Canis* in Arkansas. *Syst. Zool.* 23:1–11.

Goldman, E. A. 1944. *The wolves of North America*, part II: classification of wolves. Am. Wildl. Inst., Washington, D.C., p 389–636.

Hagmeier, E. M. 1958. Inapplicability of the subspecies concept to the North American marten. *Syst. Zool.* 7:1–7.

Hague, A. 1893. Notebook No. 1. Natl. Arch. (USGS library).

Haines, A. 1955. *Osborne Russell's journal of a trapper.* Oregon Hist. Soc., Portland. 179pp.

———. 1965. *The valley of the Upper Yellowstone. An exploration of the Headwaters of the Yellowstone River in the year 1869.* Univ. Oklahoma Press, Norman. 70pp.

Henderson, A. B. 1870. Narrative of a prospecting expedition to the East Fork and Clark's Fork of Yellowstone. Yellowstone Natl. Park Lib. p 96.

Hilton, H. 1976. Physical characteristics, taxonomic status and food habits of the eastern coyote in Main. M. S. Thesis, Univ. Maine, Orono. 76pp.

Hough, E. 1894. Forest and Stream's Yellowstone Park Expedition of 1894. Newspaper Acct. Yellowstone Natl. Park Lib.

Houston, D. B. 1973 (Rev.) Cougar and wolverine in Yellowstone National Park. Res. Note 5. Yellowstone Natl. Park. 22pp.

———. 1974. The northern Yellowstone elk, parts I & II: History and demography. Yellowstone Natl. Park. 185pp.

————. 1976. The northern Yellowstone elk, parts III & IV: Vegetation and habitat relations. Yellowstone Natl. Park. 444pp.

Jolicoeur, P. 1975. Sexual dimorphism and geographical distance as factors of skull variation in the wolf *Canis lupus* L. Pages 54–61 in M. F. Fox, ed. *The Wild Canids*. Van Nostrand Reinhold, New York.

Jones, W. A. 1875. *Report on the reconnaissance of northwestern Wyoming, including Yellowstone National Park, made in the summer of 1873.* Government Printing Office, Washington, D.C. 331pp.

Jordan, P. A., P. C. Shelton, and D. A. Allen. 1967. Numbers, turnover, and social structure of the Isle Royale wolf population. *Am. Zool.* 7:233–252.

Joslin, P. W. B. 1967. Movements and home sites of timber wolves in Algonquin Park. *Am. Zool.* 7:279–288.

Keefer, W. R. 1972. *The Geologic story of Yellowstone National Park.* U.S. Geol. Surv. Bull. 1347. 92pp.

Kelsall, J. P. 1968. *The migratory barren-ground caribou of Canada.* Can. Wildl. Serv. Monogr. No. 3. Ottawa. 340pp.

King, C. L. 1965. *Reasons for the decline of game in the Bighorn Basin of Wyoming.* Vantage Press. New York. 161pp.

Knight, R. R., J. Basile, K. Greer, S. Judd, L. Oldenburg, and L. Roop. 1977. Annual Rept. Interagency Grizzly Bear Study Team, 1976. 75pp.

Kolenosky, G. B. 1971. Hybridization between a wolf and a coyote. *J. Mammal.* 52:446–449.

————, and R. O. Standfield. 1975. Morphological and ecological variation among gray wolves (Canis lupis) of Ontario, Canada. Pages 62–72 in M. F. Fox, ed. *The Wild Canids*. Van Nostrand Reinhold, New York.

Lawrence, B. and W. H. Bossert. 1975. Relationships of North American Canis shown by multiple character analysis of selected populations. Pages 73–86 in M. F. Fox, ed. *The Wild Canids*. Van Nostrand Reinhold, New York.

Mayr, E. 1963. *Animal species and evolution.* Harvard Univ. Press, Cambridge. 797pp.

McBride, J. 1914. Scout diary. Yellowstone Natl. Park Arch.

Meagher, M. M. 1973. *The Bison of Yellowstone National Park.* NPS Sci. Monogr. Ser. No. 1. 161pp.

Mealey, S. P. 1975. The natural food habits of free ranging grizzly bears in Yellowstone National Park, 1973–74. M.S. Thesis, Montana State Univ., Bozeman. 158pp.

Mech, L. D. 1970. *The wolf: the ecology and behavior of an endangered species.* Natural History Press, New York. 389pp.

————. 1971. Where the wolves are and how they stand. *Nat. Hist.* 80(4):26–29.

————. 1974. *Canis lupis.* Mammalian Species No. 37, p 1–6. Am. Soc. Mammalogists, New York.

————, and R. A. Rausch. 1975. The status of the wolf in the United States—1973. *In* Wolves. IUCN Suppl. Paper No. 43. Morges, Switzerland. 145pp.

Mengel, R. M. 1971. The study of dog-coyote hybrids and implications concerning hybridization in Canis. *J. Mammal.* 52:316–336.

Murie, A. 1940. *Ecology of the coyote in the Yellowstone.* Fauna of the Natl. Parks, No. 4. Government Printing Office, Washington, D.C. 206pp.

————. 1944. *The wolves of Mount McKinley.* Fauna of the Natl. Parks, No. 5. Government Printing Office, Washington, D.C. 238pp.

Nowak, R. M. 1973. North American quaternary Canis. Ph.D. Thesis, Univ. Kansas, Lawrence. 380pp.

Nowlin. D. C. 1912. Report on wild buffalo and elk, Yellowstone Park, July 22–30. 5pp. *In* File no. 21 & 22, Yellowstone Natl. Park Arch.

Paradiso, J. L. and R. M. Nowak. 1971. A report on the taxonomic status and distribution of the red wolf. USDI Spec. Sci. Rept. Wildl. 145:1–36.

Randall, L. W. 1966. *Footprints along the Yellowstone.* The Nayor Co., San Antonio. 186pp.

Rausch, R. A. 1967. Some aspects of the population ecology of wolves, Alaska. *Am. Zool.* 7:253–265.

Riley, G. A. and R. T. McBride. 1972. A survey of the red wolf *Canis rufus.* USDI Spec. Sci. Rept. Wildl. 162:1–15.

Singer, F. J. 1975. Status and history of timber wolves in Glacier National Park, Montana. Symp. Wolf Behavior and Ecology, Wilmonton, N.C. 17pp.

Skeel, M. A., and L. N. Carbyn. 1977. The morphometric relationship of grey wolves (*Canis lupus*) in national parks of central Canada. *Can. J. Zool.* 55:737–747.

Skinner, M. P. 1927. The predatory and fur-bearing animals of the Yellowstone National Park. *Roosevelt Wildl. Bull.* 4(2):163–281.

Stephenson, R. O. 1974. Characteristics of wolf den sites. Final Rept. Job 14.6 R, Alaska Dept. Fish & Game, Juneau. 27pp.

Stevenson, D. 1916. Scout diary, 1915–16. Yellowstone Natl. Park Arch.

USDI National Park Service. 1968. *Administrative Policies for Natural Areas of the National Park System.* Government Printing Office, Washington, D.C.

Voight, D. R., G. B. Kolenosky, D. H. Pimlott. 1976. Changes in summer foods of wolves in central Ontario. *J. Wildl. Manage.* 40(4):663–668.

Walworth, L. 1971. Interview with E. R. Hall, Univ. Kansas, Lawrence. Yellowstone Natl. Park Biol. Off. files.

Warren, E. R. 1926. A study of beaver in the Yancey Region of Yellowstone National Park. *Roosevelt Wildl. Ann.* 1:1–191.

Wilson, E. O., and W. L. Brown. 1953. The subspecies concept and its taxonomic application. *Syst. Zool.* 2:97–111.

Woolpy, J. H. 1968. The social organization of wolves. *Nat. Hist.* 77:46–55.

ACKNOWLEDGMENTS

This study was funded by the National Park Service, National Audubon Society, Boone & Crockett Club, Wyoming Environmental Institute, N. J. Bellegie, M.D., and J. F. Turner through the NPS Cooperative Park Studies Unit, Utah State University, Logan, and the Environmental Research Institute, Moose, Wyoming. Drs. Thadis Box (USU), Douglas Houston (NPS), and Frank Craighead (ERI) assisted with administrative matters. Yellowstone Park personnel were very helpful and supportive, especially Douglas Houston, Mary Meagher, Glen Cole, Vicky Kurtz, Richard Knight, and the Ranger Division. Mary Meagher generously permitted use of her unpublished notes from archival material. All the material in the appendixes, except monthly and annual reports of the Superintendent and published references, were extracted by Dr. Meagher. The Gallatin and Shoshone National Forests provided logistical support. Kirk Knudsen, Jan Peterson, and Marguerite Deimel ably assisted in the field. Dave and Roger Stradley, Gallatin Flying Service, provided excellent flight service. Susan Sindt prepared the figures and Carol Snow drew the cover for this publication. Drs. I. M. Cowan, F. C. Craighead, Jr., D. B. Houston, F. F. Knowlton, and M. M. Meagher read the manuscript and made helpful suggestions. To each of you, my sincere gratitude.

APPENDIX I

Summary of Wolf Reports Prior to 1914, Yellowstone National Park

Source	Date	Report
Haines (1955)	1836	Trapper Osborn Russell heard a howl near the outlet of Yellowstone Lake (could be either wolf or coyote.)
Haines (1965)	1869, 16 September	Howl heard at Cache Creek
Henderson (1870)	1870	Group (wolves) seen at junction of Cache Creek with Lamar River.
Jones (1875)	1873	*Doleful howl of a large wolf*—near Pelican Meadows.
Supt. Annual Report (1877)	1877	Ungulate carcasses poisoned with strychnine for wolves
Supt. Annual Report (1880)	1880	Hides of wolves taken in late fall. *The large ferocious gray or buffalo wolf, the sneaking, snarling coyote, and a species apparently between the two of a dark-brown or black color, were once exceedingly numerous in all portions of the Park, but the value of their hides and their easy slaughter with strychnine-poisoned carcasses of animals have nearly led to their extermination.*
Supt. Annual Report (1881)	1881	Howl heard in Hayden Valley
Hague (1893)	1886–87	Wolf in Upper Geyser Basin
Hough (1894)	1894, March	Billy Hofer saw wolves in Hayden Valley.

Soda Butte Station Record	1899, 1 June	Wolf seen near Slough Creek.
	3 June	Wolf seen near Slough Creek.
	13 June	One wolf seen on northeast side of Slough Creek just above Buffalo Creek.
	29 June	Three wolves seen on southwest side Slough Creek.
Fountain Station Record	1901, 13 November	Wolf tracks seen at Lower Geyser Basin.
	19 November	Wolf tracks seen at Bear Park.
Lake Station Record	1902, 20 September	Six wolves seen between Lake and Mud Geyser.
Fountain Station Record	1902, 1 November	One wolf seen at Goose Lake.
	3 November	Two wolves seen at north end of Mesa Road on the Gibbon River.
	18 November	One wolf seen at 8-mile post between Fountain and Riverside.
Soda Butte Station Record	1904, 21 April	Two wolves between Fort Yellowstone and Yancey's.
Sylvan Pass Station Record	1907, 3 September	Two wolves seen between Sylvan and Lake.
	4 September	One wolf seen between Lake and Sylvan.
Upper Basin Station Record	1908, 10 August	One wolf seen between Upper Basin and Excelsior.
Letter from W. B. Sheppard to Col. L. M. Brett, dated 29 Jan. 1912	1911, Late August	*Gray wolves, of which latter I saw two, and considerable sign . . .*
Letter from Col. L. M. Brett to Wm. J. Hornaday	1912, 29 July	*McBride has been in the Park for many years, and is not convinced that there have ever been any gray wolves here. Statements have been made that they have been seen, but none have ever been killed or captured inside of the Park though several were killed on the Upper Gallatin River but a few miles outside in the state of Montana, last spring.*
Nowlin (1912)	1912, 25 July	Wolves howling at head of Raven Creek.

Walworth (1971)	1912, December	Tracks of 3–4 wolves seen at Buffalo Ranch (Lamar).
Supt. Annual Report (1912)	1912	*It is claimed that gray wolves have been heard and that their tracks have been seen in the Park, but up to this time none have ever been killed, and there is no absolute proof that they exist within the limits of the reservation, though they have been taken not many miles outside on the cattle ranges in Montana.*
M. P. Skinner (1927)	1912	*In 1912, I saw four [wolves] near Lamar Valley. After that, signs of their presence increased and I believed they were coming in faster.*
Randall (1966)	1913, Spring	Randall saw pack of nine (wolves) along Yellowstone River trail near Hellroaring Creek.

APPENDIX II

Summary of Wolf Reports 1914–26, Yellowstone National Park.

Source	Date	Report
James McBride (1914)	1914, 29 January	Tracks of three wolves between Mammoth and 10 miles west.
Lake Station Record	1914, 25 April	One wolf seen between Lake and Pelican Creek.
Skinner (1927)	1914, 7 September	. . . When I found an extraordinarily bold pack of eleven big fellows [wolves] in the Pelican Valley
Letter of transmittal from F. T. Arnold, Captain 12th Cavalry, to Sec. of Interior	1914, 3 December	*Four wolves killed by Ranger Henry Anderson on Slough Creek. Wolves have become rather numerous along the north line of the Park during the past two or three years, and have been seen frequently, but this is the first instance where anyone has been able to capture them or get close enough to shoot them.*
McBride (1914)	1914, 21 December	One cow elk killed by wolves between Mammoth and Blacktail Deer Creek.
Letter of transmittal from F. T. Arnold, Captain 12th Calvary, to Sec. of Interior	1914, 31 December	*Three more wolves have been killed in the Park during the month making a total of seven killed, and there are indications that they are present in considerable numbers and are destroying much game.*
Supt. Annual Report (1914)	1914	*Gray wolves have made their appearance in the Park in considerable numbers, having been seen traveling in packs of ten or less. While efforts have been made to kill*

		them, thus far none have been taken inside of the Park although a few have been killed just outside, along the northern border . . . efforts will be made to kill them.
Skinner (1927)	1914–15	*That winter, two or three packs harried the elk on the lower, open valleys of the Park. . . . They began to increase about 1914, soon numbered about sixty . . .*
Vernon Bailey (1930)	1914 and 1915, Summer	*During the summers of 1914 and 1915 they [wolves] . . . were following the elk herds to the high pastures of Mirror Plateau, returning with them in winter to the valleys along the Lamar and Yellowstone Rivers. In the summer of 1915, Mr. Frazier, at the Buffalo Ranch [Lamar], told me that wolves had been very trouble some during the preceding winter and had killed many elk. During June of that year, Mr. Frazier killed two half grown wolf pups and caught two more, which were kept chained up at the ranch. During July and August, 1915, I found where a family of wolves had killed and eaten a young elk in Slough Creek Valley and found wolf tracks along Slough Creek and Lamar Valleys up to the mouth of Mist Creek, also along Pelican Creek, and later a few tracks on Fox Creek at the southern edge of the Park. Tracks were especially numerous along Pelican and Raven Creek where at least ten or a dozen wolves hunted in one pack.*
Vernon Bailey (1930)	1915, July	*On this same trip I found big wolves common, feeding their young on elk, and probably also on buffaloes, as they were right in the midst of the buffalo ranges. This*

		probably accounted for the slow rate of increase of the herd, for after the wolves were trapped out of this section the following winter by Donald Stevenson, the herd began to make rapid increase.
Bailey (1930)	1915, November	*Donald Stevenson counted nine separate tracks, where a band of wolves had crossed a sandbar on Pelican Creek, but at that time they were leaving that section of the Park and following the elk herds to lower levels.*
Bailey (1930)	1915	*On Pelican Creek, along the trails which they [wolves] were constantly using, their droppings were made up entirely of elk hair, and a scarcity of elk calves was very noticeable among the herds in that section.*
Bailey, Letter to YNP Supt.	1915, 13 August	*Band of apparently 8 or 10 large wolves ranging on the upper part of Pelican Creek. . . . There are also some wolves along Slough Creek and some old and young along Lamar River. There seem to be very few elk calves left where these wolves range.*
Tower Station Record	1915, 3 September	One wolf seen 9 miles east of Tower.
Cruse Black (1915–16)	1915, 10 October	One black wolf seen between Tower Falls and Buffalo Ranch (Lamar).
	10 October	Two-year-old cow elk killed by wolves between Buffalo Ranch (Lamar) and west Lamar Canyon.
Donald Stevenson (1915–16)	1915, 19 October	One wolf track between Lake and Pelican Cabin.
Black	1915, 23 October	Trapped one female wolf (Rose Creek area).

	24 October	One elk killed by wolves between Buffalo Ranch (Lamar) and Blacktail.
	28 October	Killed one black female wolf up Slough Creek.
	30 October	Killed one black male wolf in Slough Creek.
Stevenson	1915, 2 November	Tracks of nine wolves up Pelican Creek from cabin.
	3 November	A few tracks seen in Pelican and Raven Creeks.
Black	1915, 3 November	One elk calf killed by wolves between Buffalo Creek and Specimen Ridge.
Stevenson	1915, 22 November	One wolf track seen 5 miles down valley from Pelican Cabin.
Black	1915, 6 December	One cow elk killed by gray wolves.
Supt. Annual Report (1915)	1915	Gray wolves are increasing and have become a decided menace to the herds of elk, deer, mountain sheep, and antelope. Several were killed in the Park last winter, and an effort will be made the coming winter to capture or kill them.
Stevenson	1916, 6 January	Saw three wolves in Geode Creek Canyon. Killed one.
Black	1916, 7 January	Tracks of three wolves between Tower and Buffalo Ranch (Lamar).
	17 January	Wolf tracks on Specimen Ridge. One adult cow elk killed by wolves.
	18 January	Followed tracks of four wolves for 10 miles on Specimen Ridge and found one adult cow elk killed by them.
Tower Station Record	1916, 18 January	One wolf seen between Tower and Slough Creek.
Stevenson	1916, 20 January	Tracks of two wolves in the Blacktail area.

Black	1916, 31 January	One *old* cow elk killed by wolves.
Bailey (1930)	1916, January	*In January, 1916, they [wolves] were found in the Lamar and Yellowstone Valleys, where Stevenson and Black secured four of the old wolves and, later, a family of seven.*
Tower Station Record	1916, 13 February	Two wolves seen between Tower and lower Yellowstone River.
Stevenson	1916, 14 February	Tracks of two wolves seen in Blacktail area.
	19–20 March	Wolf tracks between Blacktail Cabin and Hellroaring Cabin.
	22 March	Wolf tracks between Hellroaring and Buffalo Ranch (Lamar).
	26 March	Hunted wolf dens. One wolf tracked to den near Hellroaring . . . female seen.
Bailey (1930)	1916, 26 March	*One [den] found by Stevenson and Black on the rough slope near Hellroaring Creek on March 26, watched for some days in an effort to shoot the old wolves, which finally became suspicious and carried the pups away to another location farther up the side of the mountain. The den was described as composed of four or five large burrows dug into the open hillside and had evidently been used for several years as a score or more of old elk skulls were lying about, and one fresh elk head that had recently been brought in was found.*
Stevenson	1916, 27 March	One wolf seen near Hellroaring.
	28 March	Two wolves howling near Hellroaring.
	30 March	One large white wolf seen near Hellroaring.
	14 April	Dug out wolf den in the Hellroaring area but they had moved.
	15 April	Found wolf den.

	16 April	One wolf seen and six pups caught.
Bailey (1930)	1916, 16 April	*On April 14 [sic], this family of wolves was located about a mile from the first den in a natural cave among some loose rocks. Back about eight feet from the entrance of the cave seven wolf pups estimated to be three weeks old were secured. A freshly killed young elk was found about a half mile from the den and there were pieces of elk meat in the den with the pups. The old wolves were very shy and kept well out of sight while the den was being watched but were frequently heard howling and answering each other from different points and the old male was several times seen guarding the den from a point high above. The male is consistently larger than the female, weighing well over a hundred pounds.*
Stevenson	1916, 19 April	Wolf tracks between Tower and Blacktail.
	29 April	Wolf den found near Hellroaring, and one old wolf shot.
	30 April	One pup dug out.
	1 May	Tracks near Hellroaring Creek.
	5 May	Tracks near Yancey's.
	10 May	Den found between Slough Creek Cabin and Hellroaring Cabin.
	12 May	Den found between Yancey's and the Buffalo Ranch (Lamar). One wolf pup dug out.
Supt. Annual Report (1916)	1916	*From October 6, 1916 to June 30, 1916, two United States Biological Survey hunters killed 12 wolves . . . skulls sent to the National Museum. Two young male wolves captured in the spring of 1915 by the employee at the buffalo farm [Lamar] were shipped alive on*

		November 16 to the National Zoological Park.
Supt. Monthly Report	1917, December	*Wolves not numerous . . . two killed by lion hunter Elkins.*
Supt. Monthly Report	1918, January	*Wolves reported in several different sections of the Park.*
	February	Pack of *about* 16 wolves on Specimen Ridge.
	March	Signs of wolves on Specimen Ridge.
	April	Nineteen wolves killed, with indications of *many more* on Specimen Ridge and Hellroaring.
	May	Seven wolves killed. *Towards the end of the month the wolves seemed to leave the Specimen Ridge district and have not been much in evidence since.*
	June	Four wolves killed.
	July	One large gray wolf killed.
	August	Sign of two wolves in the upper Yellowstone area reported by Biological Survey hunter Clemons.
	September	One gray wolf trapped and shot.
	October	Three gray wolves killed.
	November	No wolves killed but *they were considerably in evidence on Slough and Hellroaring Creeks.*
	December	No wolves killed but sign found along north line.
Supt. Annual Report (1918)	1918	Thirty-six wolves killed in the park that year.
Supt. Monthly Report	1919, January	No wolves killed, sign along north line.
	February	Two wolves killed. *Signs indicate presence of several ranging from Mammoth to Soda Butte . . . efforts are being made to exterminate them.*
	November	Reports received of wolves present.

Supt. Annual Report (1919)	1919	Six wolves killed in the park.
Supt. Monthly Report	1920, January	Three wolves, including two females, killed.
	March	Nine wolves killed . . . one in the northeast and eight (including seven pups) in Blacktail.
	April	At least 14 wolves killed . . . one adult in the northeast, eight pups in a den near Tower Falls, and one den with pups closed up solid on Blacktail Deer Creek.
	November	Pack of nine wolves and tracks seen near Tower Falls.
Supt. Annual Report (1920)	1920	Twenty-eight wolves killed by two rangers.
Supt. Monthly Report	1921, January	Forty coyotes and wolves (not distinguished) killed.
	February	Two black wolves seen in Slough Creek and Specimen Ridge.
Supt. Monthly Report (continued)	March	Several wolf dens located and kept under surveillance.
	April	One den dug out and male (largest ever) and 11 pups destroyed.
	October	One wolf killed by Anderson.
	November	One wolf killed, and many tracks seen in Mammoth and Blacktail Districts.
	December	A *few wolves* identified from signs.
Supt. Annual Report (1922)	1921–22	Twenty–four wolves killed.
Supt. Monthly Report	1922, February	One wolf killed during the winter.
	April	Wolf dens located first week of April between Blacktail and Hellroaring, and adult female killed and 10 pups captured alive. Thirteen (sic) wolves taken to date.
	May	One wolf den discovered on Specimen Ridge, destroyed both adults and six pups. Felt that this

was the pair ranging in Lamar Valley for several years—21 (sic) wolves killed to date. *It is evident that the work of controlling these animals must be vigorously prosecuted by the most effective means available whether or not this meets with the approval of certain game conservationists.*

July — Three wolves killed.

August — *Park Ranger Henry Anderson has been hunting out the summer haunts of park wolves and has succeeded in finding what he believes to be their main summer range. This is in a section of the park that is practically inaccessible due to bog holes, rim rock, down timber and jack pines. The area is the part of the Mirror Plateau lying near the head of Timothy, Raven, Pelican and Broad Creeks. Ranger Anderson found numerous signs in this region and due to its inaccessibility and the fact that there is a large amount of game making its summer range near this point, there is no reason why the wolves should not find this area ideal summer home. Anderson will spend the remainder of the month in this locality in an attempt to exterminate as many of these predatory animals as possible.*

October — Two large wolves, one gray and one black, were killed by Henry Anderson near confluence of Pelican and Raven Creeks (these are the two mounted specimens in the park museum).

Supt. Monthly Report

1923, April — Wolf den near Tower Falls cleared out; old female killed and five pups brought out alive to Mammoth for exhibition.

December — Wolf signs have been seen near Soda Butte and on Pelican Creek.

Supt. Annual Report (1923)	1923	Eight wolves killed.
Supt. Monthly Report	1924, January	Wolf seen near Bridger Lake on January 15. . . . *Wolf signs have been very rare this season.*
	February	One wolf seen on Elephant Back near Lake; wolf sign near Mud Geyser.
	March	*Wolf signs have been very scarce throughout the entire season and we have no report of any wolf kills in the park.*
	April	*Signs of wolf exceedingly scarce. . . .*
	May	*First wolf sign reported during past year observed near Soda Butte . . . also at about the same time at Pelican Creek.*
	September	*There were no reported instances of wolf activity in the park last winter apart from an occasional lone track. None were actually seen in the park. The situation this fall gives promise of a recurrence of the wolf as we have two reports of recent date indicating their presence in the Park. Park Ranger Hall reports having seen three near Heart Lake and a wolf pack numbering twelve have been seen at Elk Park by two members of a road crew on duty near that point. This last report has not been definitely confirmed and may be exaggerated.*
	November	A number of wolf signs were observed in October but only one track has been reported for November.
	December	Two wolf signs seen on December 16 on south slope of Saddle Mountain.
Supt. Monthly Report	1925, October	Three wolf signs were observed on the east shore of Yellowstone Lake on the 20th.
Supt. Monthly Report	1926, January	*One wolf sign recently seen on Cabin Creek.*

	October	*There is believed to be a very limited number of wolves in the Park.*
	December	*Sign of one, perhaps two wolves along lower trail between Hellroaring and Tower Falls.*
Bailey (1930)	1926	Tracks on Two Ocean Pass and one wolf seen on Trident Plateau by Sierra Club party.

APPENDIX III

Summary of Wolf Reports, 1927–36, Yellowstone National Park.

Source	Date	Report
Supt. Monthly Report	1927, February	*Wolf signs have been rarely seen in the Park this winter and we have every reason to consider that there are only a very few in the entire park area.*
	October	*It is doubtful if there are more than a very few wolves in the entire park area.*
	November	*Ranger Ogston reports signs of two wolves in the vicinity of the Slough Creek mailbox.*
Supt. Monthly Report	1928, February	*Wolf signs have been rarely observed.*
	October	*There have been no wolf sign reported this season.*
Supt. Monthly Report	1929	*Wood crews at Yellowstone Lake reported seeing two gray wolves.*
Supt. Monthly Report	1930, January	*A wolf has been reported working in the Tower Falls and Hellroaring districts. The tracks have been seen many times, and two elk calves have been found that were from all evidence, killed by this wolf.*
Arnold (1937)	1934, Winter	Four wolves seen up Tower Creek.
Supt. Monthly Report	1936, April	*Five wolves were seen and reported in the vicinity of Old Faithful. Several freshly killed elk carcasses found in this vicinity suggest that the animals seen were actually wolves instead of coyotes.*

48

CHAPTER 2
THE DOCUMENTARY RECORD OF WOLVES AND RELATED WILDLIFE SPECIES IN THE YELLOWSTONE NATIONAL PARK AREA PRIOR TO 1882

PAUL SCHULLERY AND LEE WHITTLESEY

As Weaver showed in the previous chapter, by the early 1900's many people assumed that wolves and their prey were scarce in the Yellowstone National Park area prior to the establishment of the park and probably until the 1890's. This belief still prevails in many circles today, but until the following report was published in 1992 no historians had actually examined the early record of wildlife to determine if the belief was valid. As the following report suggests, there is extensive and persuasive evidence that wildlife was, in fact, abundant in the years before and just after the park was established in 1872. It can be assumed, of course, that wildlife abundance over the 12,000 or so years since the last ice age varied significantly depending upon a variety of environmental factors, including human activities; Yellowstone's ecological setting has never been stagnant, and paleoecologists suggest that it has undergone dramatic changes in the past several thousand years.

The report deals as much with prey species as it does with prey. Like recent studies that attempted to model the effects of wolves on ungulates (see Chapters 21–29), historical studies must deal with the whole animal community. It is widely agreed that if the prey were present, the predators were too.

This excerpt is from a longer paper that appeared in a 1992 National Park Service report to Congress on wolf restoration in Yellowstone National Park. In the full report, the excerpt is preceded by an item-by-item analysis of 168 accounts of the park area prior to 1882. This report greatly expanded on the historical summary provided by Weaver in the previous chapter, employing several times as many early accounts to analyze the presence of wolves and other wildlife. The discussion and conclusions from the full report are included, followed by the references cited in the excerpt.

SOURCE: P. Schullery and L. Whittlesey. 1992. The documentary record of wolves and related wildlife species in the Yellowstone National Park area prior to 1882, in J.D. Varley and W.G. Brewster, eds., *Wolves for Yellowstone? A report to the United States Congress.* Volume IV, research and analysis. Yellowstone National Park: National Park Service, pp. 1–139 to 1–160.

It is worth noting that the authors of this report have continued their research, and have added many additional accounts to the 168 reviewed for this analysis. These new accounts serve only to confirm the conclusions reached here.

INTERPRETING THE HISTORICAL RECORD

We are struck by the nearly unanimous view of those who expressed any opinion at all that large animals were abundant. Even those who saw few animals believed many were nearby, either because they saw other evidence or were told so by others or just assumed it to be so for other reasons. Descriptions of the area as a "hunter's paradise," and in other glowing terms, were common. These reports of game abundance or scarcity are analyzed below, under the heading of "Game Abundance."

We are also struck by the extent to which early park visitors routinely "blazed away" at park wildlife. If the many accounts presented here are at all representative of the average park visitor, we must be impressed with the resilience of park wildlife populations. Not only were the ungulates being killed in large numbers by skin hunters, and killed regularly by the region's miners and other settlers, but they were subjected to an indiscriminate but apparently substantial amount of recreational hunting.

The traditional view of the game having been "pushed back into the mountains" continues to intrigue us. Though the evidence here, which is persuasive that in the earliest historical period large animals were present and often abundant in the park, renders the question moot, we think it worth consideration, if only because it is so pervasive and will no doubt endure as part of the body of public "common knowledge" for a long time.

We find important things lacking in the theory that the park's wildlife were forced into the park area by settlements. First, the mechanism by which such a thing would occur is unclear. The theory seems to imply that when settlement occurred, animals occupying the settled area abandoned their native range and moved, more or less wholesale, to an entirely new one that had, apparently, been unoccupied or only lightly occupied prior to that point. This suggests that usable vacant habitat existed for some indefinite period prior to the migration, and brings up the question we have noted earlier, of why that habitat was not occupied all along.

Viewing the theory as sympathetically as possible, we might propose that the vacant habitat was of much poorer quality, and therefore only of marginal interest to the animals until they were compelled to abandon better habitats. But recent studies of Yellowstone's Northern Range (for example, Merrill et al. 1988, Frank 1990) do not support the idea that the park is poor habitat. Long–term and short–term climatic changes no doubt made it quite variable both as summer and as winter range, but the historical accounts give us no reason to doubt that it was used as winter range then, as it is now, by large animals as conditions permitted.

What we find least acceptable about the theory, however, is the supposed cause of the migrations. Where were the settlements that forced the animals into the park? The historical accounts presented here suggest that large numbers of ungulates inhabited the park area through the earliest historical period. Settlement in the Greater Yellowstone Ecosystem was slight until the 1880's. Fort Ellis, and later Bozeman, existed on the northwest corner of the Greater Yellowstone Ecosystem from prior to the time of the park's creation, but as a small outpost. Livingston, Montana, and Jackson, Wyoming, did not exist before about 1883, and Cody, Wyoming, was founded in 1895; West Yellowstone was not established until 1907.

If we must attribute the presence of the park's large animals to settlements, we must go hundreds of miles in order to find settlements and land uses of a magnitude sufficient to displace the animals. The search quickly approaches absurdity: If the elk that Osborne Russell reported as "swarming" at Yellowstone Lake were forced there, it must have been by the urban sprawl of St. Louis.

As far as animals being forced one way or another by settlement or human activities, the opposite pressures existed in Yellowstone. As numerous accounts reveal, human inhabitants of and travelers in the region, such as early tourists, the Bottlers, the miners in the Cooke City area, did their game killing in the heart of the supposed "safe" habitat, taking large numbers of animals from the Lamar Valley—the very place the theory proposes that the animals were supposed to be driven for refuge.

It is important to point out, however, that there remains the issue of whether later settlement, that is settlement of the Yellowstone region after 1882, somehow affected animal densities in the park, especially after 1886, when the U.S. Cavalry arrived to protect the park itself from poaching, thus turning it into a more genuine refuge.

HISTORICAL EVIDENCE FOR WINTERING ELK

As pointed out early in this report, Hadly's (1990) paleontological evidence is suggestive that elk used habitats in the Lamar Valley prehistorically much as they do now. Historical accounts also suggest that the present park area was used as winter range by substantial numbers of animals—thousands—in the 1880's (*Avant Courier* 1883c, Hofer 1887, Harris 1887). These accounts made rough estimates of numbers of wintering elk. In the period covered in the present report, however, we have fewer quantified reports but much general information.

Houston (1982:206) considered Blackmore's observation of an "abundance" of cast elk antlers on the Blacktail Plateau as evidence of wintering elk. Doane reported "thousands" of elk antlers in 1874 near Mount Washburn, and reported that "there are many such places in the park. . . ." (Doane 1970:473). The relative rarity of such large accumulations of antlers in the park today is a sad indication of the extent to which humans have subtly altered the landscape. The modern markets for antlers have made such accumulations impossible because of the intensity of illegal "horn hunting."

Perhaps the most important evidence of wintering elk may be the details of the slaughter as provided by Strong, Grinnell, Norris, Ludlow, and Baronett, who made it clear the animals were being killed in the winter when they were defenseless in the deep snow. Though these accounts leave no doubt that thousands of elk were being killed in the park, and were sometimes killed in winter conditions, they do not usually contain the detail in dates, numbers, or location that the later reports (after 1883) do. For example, Norris, discussing his 1875 visit, said that the Bottlers took more than 2,000 elk skins from the "forks of the Yellowstone" (the mouth of the Lamar River), but he said they did so "in the spring of 1875" (Norris n.d.), so we cannot absolutely know if this was proof of wintering elk or elk on their spring migrations into higher parts of the park.

Park gamekeeper Harry Yount gave us some of the first useful winter observations, reporting that some animals did winter in the park despite an apparently severe winter in 1880–1881. Yount said that "about 400" elk wintered on the Lamar River and Soda Butte Creek. Houston (1982:11) commented on Yount's report, saying that "only 400 animals remaining in this upper portion of the range during a severe winter is not unusual." Houston (1982:210) interpreted Yount's reports of winter conditions that year as follows: "Apparently a very severe winter as

Yount's own weather records show snow falling on 66 of 90 days from December 1880 to February 1881."

Sorting out the hide-hunting period is going to require an appreciation for the work. If we conservatively estimate the weight of an adult elk hide at 20 pounds, Bottler's 2,000 hides would have weighed 20 tons. If these were taken prior to snowmelt, then sleds of some sort might have been involved, or the skins might have been rafted down the Lamar River to the Yellowstone, and thence down to the Bottler ranch. Later, wagons could have been used for at least part of the trip. Perhaps the hides were stored and guarded until the weather made movement easier.

In short, the accounts of the park prior to 1882 demonstrate that elk and other animals wintered in the park, but only rarely provide meaningful information on their numbers. Houston (1982:23–25) reviewed interpretations of wintering elk numbers from this earlier period into recent times, suggesting, in contrast to earlier investigators (Cahalane 1941, Craighead et al. 1972), that prehistoric elk populations down the Yellowstone River Valley to the north of the park may have actually constituted a "biological barrier" to the migratory movements of elk that wintered in the park. Houston also acknowledged the ". . . possibility that densities [of wintering elk in the park today] are somewhat different now (either higher or lower) for other reasons, e.g. climatic changes, plant succession, [or] levels of predation" (Houston 1982:24).

We can only concur that the many variables that affect animal distribution surely were in effect throughout the early historical period.

OBSERVABILITY OF WILDLIFE

Observability of wildlife is another central issue in this analysis. The accounts demonstrate not only that success in seeing wildlife varied greatly from party to party within the same year or week, but also that reporting of observed wildlife varied greatly among members of the same party. It is only through an examination and comparison of as many accounts as can be acquired that the actual story of wildlife observations is fleshed out, and even then the material very quickly runs up against all the limitations that have been discussed, including observer reliability, the informality and incompleteness of the sources, and the imponderable vicissitudes of animal behavior.

Of nearly equal interest is the behavior of the wildlife once seen. Past investigators have attempted to use one or another account in which animals did not flee from travelers as proof that travelers should have been able to see wildlife routinely. But the historical accounts reveal that wildlife then, as now, are often unpredictable. One man might spook a huge herd of elk by himself, while another party might ride past another herd without displacing it at all.

WOLVES

Wolves are the foremost focus of this paper, and so we will summarize the historical record of them in greater detail than that of the other species reviewed here. Though many of the references to wolves being present were not specific as to a particular location in the park, others provide reports of sightings, howls, or other evidence of wolves in named locations (Fig. 1).

The historical record provides several sightings of wolves in the Greater Yellowstone Area, including in the present park area. William Clark stated that he saw wolves in the Gallatin Valley (Thwaites 1905, 5:260); that sighting was probably outside most definitions of the Greater Yellowstone Ecosystem (Glick et al. 1991). As well, Russell (1955:35) reported that at Ray's Lake, in the Snake River Valley southwest of the present park area, he "was awakened by the howling of wolves who had formed a complete circle within thirty paces of me and my horse at the flashing of my pistol however they soon dispersed." These sightings provide some background for the additional evidence from the Greater Yellowstone Ecosystem itself.

The first reported sighting in the present park area in the historical record is from Henderson (1894:57), who said that on August 3, 1870, somewhere in the upper Lamar Valley, probably near the mouth of Cache Creek or Miller Creek, his camp was "attacked by wolves," leaving us to wonder exactly what form the attack took. We assume that this meant he or his party actually saw the wolves near camp.

Norton (1873:8) said that in the Madison River Canyon, his party saw "two dour-looking timber wolves, who scampered affrightedly away at our approach."

Grinnell (1876:90) reported that during his 1875 visit he saw a wolf in the park, but he did not give a location. As we discussed earlier, we consider this an exceptionally reliable sighting, coming from a trained professional naturalist, but we are unable to determine from the context of the reports he left if this was a living wolf or some proof of a wolf, such as a skin.

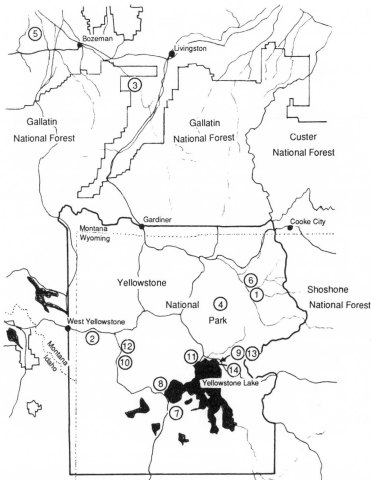

1. *sighting, group of wolves, 1870 (Henderson 1894:57)*
2. *sighting, pair of wolves, 1872 (Norton 1873:8)*
3. *sighting, single wolf, 1881 (Leckler 1884h)*
4. *howl, 1836 (Russell 1955:46)*
5. *howl, 1863 (Stuart 1876:159)*
6. *howl, 1869 (Haines 1965:27)*
7. *howl, 1870 (Everts 1871:3)*
8. *howl, 1871 (Clawson 1872a, Raymond 1873:274)*
9. *howl, 1873 (Comstock 1875:92)*
10. *howl, 1875 (Norris n.d.)*
11. *howl, 1876 (Doane 1970:480)*
12. *howl, 1879 (Geikie 1882a:228; Smith 1901:183)*
13. *bedding site, 1873 (Comstock 1875:92)*
14. *track, 1872 (Norton 1873:37)*

FIGURE 1. *Locations of wolf sightings, howls, and tracks of known location, 1836–1881. Note: This figure only includes reports for which a specific location was given by the observer. Other reports, of sightings with no specified location, of collected skins, and general statements about the presence or distribution of wolves, are reviewed in the text.*

Leckler (1884*h*) reported seeing an "immense wolf" near the head of Trail Creek, north of the park, in 1881.

Superintendent Norris, in several accounts, asserted that wolves were common in the park until the mid-1870's. He left a report of at least one specimen in his possession, saying that in the early winter of 1880, while gathering a supply of meat for his assistants, he and they were able to collect "fine hides of the bear, wolf, and wolverine" (Norris 1881*a*:6). We cannot determine if this means one hide of a wolf, or more than one. Most important of Norris's mentions of wolves is his official report of their destruction:

> The large, ferocious gray or buffalo wolf, the sneaking, snarling coyote, and a species apparently between the two, of a dark-brown or black color, were once exceedingly numerous in all portions of the Park, but the value of their hides and their easy slaughter with strychnine–poisoned carcasses of animals have nearly led to their extermination (Norris 1881*a*:42)

Excluding the Clark and Russell sightings, we have a minimum of 5 sightings of wolves in these accounts. That this is a minimum must be emphasized; the context of Norris's remarks suggests that he saw wolves more than once, possibly on numerous occasions. We are counting only his specific mention of at least one wolf hide as a sighting, but obviously his experience, whether it was with hides, poisoned carcasses, living wolves, or some combination of those led him to assume wolves were common.

Even without the numerous other historical accounts we are presenting here, we regard the Norris reports, alone, as reasonable proof that wolves inhabited and were relatively common in the park area at the time of its establishment. Though as we have pointed out Norris was not a formally trained naturalist, he was a very enthusiastic observer of nature, and we have no reason to doubt that he was seeing wolves, both alive and poisoned.

A second category of historical accounts of wolves includes howls and other noises heard and attributed to wolves. Some of the descriptions of wolf howls are almost as compelling as evidence as are the actual sightings. We counted twelve reports of at least ten different episodes of wolf howling.

Russell, on the night of August 19, 1836, on the Mirror Plateau, reported that "all is silent except for the occasional howling of the solitary wolf on the neighboring mountain whose senses are attracted by the flavors of roasted meat but fearing to approach nearer he sits on a rock and bewails his calamities in piteous moans which are re-echoed among the Mountains" (Russell 1955:46).

Stuart, on April 19, 1863, in the Gallatin Valley near the present site of Bozeman, reported that he "was serenaded by a full band of wolves last night" (Stuart 1876:159).

Folsom, on September 16, 1869, while camped near the mouth of Calfee Creek, reported that "the wolf scents us from afar and the mournful cadence of his howl adds to our sense of solitude" (Haines 1965:27).

Everts, during his 37 days of wandering alone the present park area in the fall of 1870, mentioned that he heard the "dismal howl of the gray wolf," probably south of Yellowstone Lake (Everts 1871:3). Later, after he had moved north to some unknown location between the lake a the Tower Fall area, he reported that "the prolonged howl of the wolf" was one of the things that made him "insensible to all other forms of suffering" (Everts 1871:8).

Clawson, late in the summer of 1871, reported that one night, apparently near West Thumb, "a band of hungry wolves sat upon a point some distance away and howled and yelled a most heart-rending war song, that seemed to terrify even our dog, who was a wolf-hunter by profession" (Clawson 1872a).

Clawson's account was generally corroborated by Raymond, a traveler in the same party, who said that "the prairie wolf, or coyote, and his larger cousin, the mountain wolf, howl plaintively o'nights" (Raymond 1873:274).

Comstock heard the howling of a wolf near Steamboat Point (on Yellowstone Lake on August 6, 1873, and then saw sign of it the next day: "Being much fatigued, I turned in early, but, when fairly in a doze I was aroused by the frightened movements of my mule picketed near by, and I presently heard the doleful howl of a large wolf, which was slowly approaching along the trail. In anticipation of a trifling adventure, I lay down again with my carbine close at hand. It was late in the morning when I woke, and all was quiet; but a little investigation showed that the animal had been lying in the grass at the edge of the bluff, just above my head" (Comstock 1875:92).

In 1875, Philetus Norris, on his second visit to the Yellowstone area but prior to his superintendency, reported the "prolonged howl of the mountain wolf" at the Lower Geyser Basin (Norris n.d.).

On the night of October 26, 1876, Doane reported "a pack of wolves howling far down the lake shore" of Yellowstone Lake, near present Bridge Bay (Doane 1970:480).

In 1879, probably along or near the Firehole River, Geikie reported "the mingled bark and howl of the wolves" at night (Geikie 1882a:228). Drummond left a diary of the same trip, in which he seemed to corroborate Geikie by mentioning "the wolf barking" while the party was near the Firehole River on September 10 (Smith 1901:183).

We recognize that it may be difficult for unschooled listeners to know a wolf howl from a coyote howl. We also recognize that prior to 1900, there was some overlap in the naming of the two animals; coyotes were at least occasionally known as prairie wolves. We have here, however, some very credible observers. Grinnell was a professional naturalist, Doane was a seasoned and respected western traveler whose other writings do not lead us to doubt his reliability, and Geikie and Comstock were both professional scientists. The others also seem trustworthy. We see no reason to doubt that some, if not all, of these writers were reporting the howls of actual wolves.

Besides Comstock's report of the bedding site of a wolf, Norton (1873:37) reported tracks of a wolf on Stevenson Island.

We also counted 17 general statements about the presence of wolves in the Yellowstone area. These assertions that wolves were present started as early as Gunnison (1852). We consider this combination of sightings, reports of howls, and general statements to be compelling proof that wolves were widely distributed through the park and surrounding areas prior to 1882.

The slaughter of wolves in the 1870's requires additional comment at this point. The destruction of wolves during that period may be the most significant single event to date in the history of wolf–human interactions in Yellowstone Park. Norris said that "their easy slaughter with strychnine–poisoned carcasses of animals have nearly led to their extermination" (Norris 1881a:42). The slaughter of Yellowstone wildlife was in fact no more or less intense than in many other areas of the west at the time, and wolves were being destroyed, especially by poison, in numbers that now seem nearly fabulous. Curnow (1969:31) reported that in Montana a "conservative estimate" of the number of wolves killed between 1870 and 1877 would be 100,000 per year. This number, however, suggests a density of wolves in Montana that is literally incredible; perhaps the number included coyotes and other predators. In any event, recent estimates of the number of wolves that would inhabit the park area once fully restored are around 150 (Koth et al. 1990), and if even comparable levels existed in 1870, all historical evidence suggests that Norris was right to presume their "easy slaughter." Curnow, reporting on wolfing techniques in Montana, said that "Up to one hundred wolves were found dead at one bait" (Curnow 1969:28). Unless one has been exposed to historical accounts of the wolf–poisoning campaign of the 1870's and later, it is difficult to imagine the extent to which the idea of wolf destruction seemed to obsess people; killing wolves was seen as a civic duty, done proudly.

Weaver (1978:7) reported that few sightings were made of wolves between 1881 and 1908; though much more remains to be done with historical sources from this period, we suspect that these relatively few sightings may reflect a dramatic decrease in the number of wolves present due to the poisoning campaign of the 1870's. Weaver also reported that the population, at least in northern Yellowstone, apparently began to increase after that, and that in the 1914–1926 period, ". . . a minimum of 136 wolves—including about 80 pups (59%)—were removed from dens, trapped, shot, and probably poisoned in the park" (Weaver 1978:7–8). After this period, the wolf was essentially, though not totally, gone from the park area.

If in fact the park was and is capable of supporting more than 136 wolves at any given time (and we recognize this as educated conjecture), then it seems most likely to us that the notorious wolf–killing era of 1914 to 1926, which shocks the sensibilities of many modern people, was not much more than a mopping-up operation of a job almost finished by 1880. Additional study, as well as the restoration of wolves to Yellowstone and the subsequent study of their fortunes, would shed more light on these early times.

GAME ABUNDANCE

Before reviewing the evidence for the presence of various other large mammals, we will comment on the statements of early park–area visitors regarding the abundance or scarcity of such mammals. As mentioned early in this paper, it is widely assumed that if these mammals were abundant, their predators would also be present.

We counted 77 general statements about "game" in which it was not possible to determine what species were intended. Of these, 21 were specific references some particular feature or area, such as a comment on a "game trail" being followed. The others were broader statements about game being abundant or scarce.

As pointed out earlier, some parties believed game to be abundant even if they did not see it; they saw tracks or other evidence, or they were told of its abundance by others. What we sought to determine in the present exercise was this: how many parties did believe game was scarce? The answer was, very few. Of the remaining 56 general statements about game abundance, 5 reflected the belief that game was rare in the park and 51 supported the belief that game was abundant. The writers of the 5 did not give reasons for their belief; that is, they did not say that game was scarce because it had always been scarce, or because of overhunting, or for some other reason.

We consider this an especially important exercise. It shows the extent to which the early travelers and authorities who should have known the park best differed with the viewpoint that arose around the turn of the century, a viewpoint that held that game was scarce in the mountainous regions of the west. The many early writers who described the park area as a "hunter's paradise" and in other equally glowing terms might have been surprised at how quickly their firsthand observations would be forgotten or dismissed.

This review of general statements about game also serves as a useful introduction to a review of the accounts of the other species of large mammals.

In the following review we have adopted a simple tabulation system, by which we were able to identify the types of reports. There are, for most species, seven categories of reports.

1. Sighting of an individual animal. In this category we included any sighting or killing of an individual animal. If two or more members of the same party saw the same animal, we counted it only as one sighting. In all cases, we sought to use the most conservative number; if we suspected, but were not sure, that two different accounts were discussing the same animal, we counted the two reports as one sighting.

2. Sighting of a small group. In this category we included all reports of 10 or less of an animal. This category became a convenient catch-all for the common reports that made such vague statements as, "We saw 3 moose during the day," or "during our march yesterday we shot 5 antelope." It is not possible in these contexts to determine if the animals were seen or shot singly or all at once, and so to simplify the tabulation (and, again, because it is the most conservative course in totalling number of sightings), we treated these small groups as single sightings.

3. Sighting of a herd. Many writers used terms such as "band," "group," "herd," and other words without mercy on historians. It was often difficult to know how large a group they meant. Through careful

60

review of the context, including other reports by the same writers in which they were more specific, we attempted to sort out small groups from large. Most of the time, it was obvious that they meant more, or less, than 10. As in other categories, we sought not to count duplicate sightings of the same herd as more than one sighting.

4. Sounds. Several animals besides wolves made noises readily identifiable by these early travelers. Elk bugles and mountain lion screams may have been the most noteworthy.

5. Reports of meat, skin, bones, antlers, or other parts. Sometimes in these historical accounts, the first mention of an animal occurred after its death, as when a writer reported that a member of the party brought in a load of elk meat, or that camp dinner consisted of venison. These are legitimate reports of animal presence. In some cases, as in the reports of great numbers of cast antlers on the Northern Range, they are especially significant evidence, at least as useful as sightings of the live animals. In the above review of wolf reports, we considered a report of an animal's skin as a sighting of at least as high a reliability as a sighting of the live animal. Below, because of the larger number of reports involved, we have broken skin reports into their own category with meat, bones, and antlers.

6. Reports of tracks, trails, scat, or other signs of animals. Tracks and trails were frequently mentioned in the early accounts, and though we sometimes must question the skills of the writers at identifying different kinds of tracks, these are important evidence. For example, when Leckler (1884e) described the area near Mount Washburn in 1881 as "completely covered with deer and elk tracks, in many places cut up like a barnyard," the extent of the tracks is in itself significant, regardless of which species or set of species made them. However, these very broad statements of track abundance are treated as one report, again to take the most conservative approach. It may be an indication of the changes in public tastes and tolerances that observations of feces (and its numerous euphemisms) go more or less unmentioned by these early travelers; in this instance, publishing styles and social codes tended to deny us access to an entire class of wildlife information that we would now find quite useful.

7. General statements of the presence of a species. These statements include such things as listings of animals believed to be in the park, where it is not possible to know for sure if the writer saw them. They also include some of the most important reports of animals that were seen. For example, when Raynolds reported that in the Madison River Valley, "antelopes have been visible in large numbers upon all sides"

61

(Raynolds 1868:100), or when Drummond reported that along the Madison River in 1879, there was "abundant game, antelope, everywhere for twelve miles" (Smith 1901:186), there is no category that will fully portray that abundance of antelope. If such statements described the great number of animals as a herd, specifically, or referred to "herds," then one or two sightings of herds were added to the tabulation. If the statement was less specific, as are these by Raynolds and Drummond, it was tabulated as a general statement of presence, again tending to understate the impression given by the writer. If an official report of the park, such as a superintendent's report or a government survey report, made repeated general statements of animal abundance in the same document, only one of those was counted as a general statement. If, on the other hand, such a report mentioned animals present in one part of the park, and then elsewhere in the report mentioned their presence in another part of the park, those two mentions would be tabulated separately.

In short, these categories and their tabulations as given below must be seen as absolute minimum representations. They are not presented here to suggest precisely how often early visitors saw animals, but only to allow some simple generalizations.

MOUNTAIN LION

The accounts suggest that either the mountain lion was once much more common in Yellowstone than it is today, or it was once much more willing to reveal its presence, especially by vocalization. Some parties heard lions screaming night after night, Everts (in 1870) was treed by a lion, Norris (in 1875) and Bottler (in 1871) had skins, and Strong (in 1875) said lions were "frequently killed." They were reported, interestingly enough, in several regularly visited portions of the park.

Lions are less inclined to carrion feeding, and so may have been less susceptible to the poisoning campaign. Murie (1940:15), however, reported that 121 were killed by government trappers and hunters in the park between 1904 and 1925, at which point they were regarded to have been more or less eliminated for many years. They are now (1992) known to be widely distributed on the Northern Range (Meagher 1986, Murphy and Felzien 1990).

We counted 3 sightings of lions, 9 reports of sounds, 2 reports of skins, 3 of tracks, and 17 general statements that indicated their presence.

COYOTE

Reports of coyote observations were striking in their rarity. We found 1 sighting, 1 report of barking, and 8 general statements about presence.

There may be any number of explanations for this, and probably several are partly true. For some observers, the coyote was perhaps just on the line between the large animals worth mentioning and the small ones not worth mentioning. If coyotes were common, like ground squirrels or rabbits, perhaps some observers would take little note of them. For other observers, the confusion between the wolf and the coyote (known in some circles as the prairie wolf) may have caused them to call coyotes wolves.

But perhaps most intriguing, and certainly quite plausible, is the possibility that coyotes were far less abundant then than now. In areas inhabited by robust wolf populations, coyote numbers are generally much lower than when wolves are absent (Fuller and Keith 1981, Carbyn 1982, Paquet 1991). The presence of wolves in the Yellowstone area may, in that respect, have dramatically affected the abundance of another predator—the coyote.

BEARS

Bears were seen regularly by early visitors, and many were reported killed, both in the park and in the surrounding country. Schullery (1990, 1992) suggested that, whatever losses bears suffered due to hunting or poisoning during the 1870's, they were still reasonably abundant by the early 1890's, but beyond that it is difficult to draw any conclusions. Bears are not generally gregarious, and often quite secretive (Schullery 1992). More observers mentioned grizzly bear by species than black bear, but most just said "bear," leaving it unclear if one or the other species was actually more common. Determining relative abundance of the two species is further complicated by differences in behavior and habitat use, and the black bear's known tendency to avoid grizzly bears when the two species coinhabit a region.

Grizzly bears were reported as individuals 14 times, as small groups (almost always sows with cubs) 7 times, from tracks or other traces (including 1 den) 3 times, and in general statements of presence 9 times, for a total of 33.

Black bears were reported as individuals 5 times, in small groups 3 times, from tracks 1 time, and in general statements 7 times, for a total of 16.

Unspecified bears were seen as individuals 24 times, in small groups 20 times, in meat, skin, or other parts 5 times, from tracks or other sign 16 times, and in general statements of presence 47 times, for a total of 112.

Bears of both or unknown species were therefore reported on 161 occasions, overwhelming evidence of their widespread presence in the Yellowstone Park area.

WOLVERINE

Considering the infrequency of modern sightings, wolverines were seen surprisingly often. We counted 8 individual sightings, 1 report of a hide, and 7 general statements about their presence. Wolverines might have been very hard hit by the strychnine poisonings of the 1870's.

FOX

Norris's statement that foxes of four colors were "numerous" is buttressed by 4 sightings of individuals, 1 sighting of a pair, and 6 general statements of fox presence.

It is known that foxes thrive more in the presence of wolves than in the presence of coyotes (R. Crabtree pers. commun. 1991).

LYNX AND BOBCAT

One lynx sighting was reported, along with two general statements that lynx occurred in the area. Grinnell (in 1875) did add that lynx were "sometimes killed in the Yellowstone Park," and also provided the only bobcat sighting.

OTHER SMALL CARNIVORES

Eight sightings or killings of skunk were reported, as well as 1 report of scent and two general statements that skunk were present. The most interesting observation concerning skunks was Norris's statement (1880) that he killed "hundreds" of them at Mammoth Hot Springs in order to be able to sleep peacefully.

Comstock (in 1873) provided us with our only four sightings of raccoon from the period. They, like the skunk, would be hard hit by a strychnine poisoning campaign.

Two sightings of mink were reported, along with one report of tracks and five general statements of their presence. Doane said they were "abundant" south of Yellowstone Lake (in 1870), and Norris (in 1880) said they were "not numerous" in the park.

Two sightings of individual otters were reported, along with 8 general statements, some of which suggested that otters were very numerous in some parts of the park.

Marten, fisher, and badger were rarely mentioned.

ELK

The historical record has neither the resolution nor the depth to establish with any precision the number of elk inhabiting the park area prior to 1882. The historical record does, however, make it clear that elk were common throughout the park, and were observed at various times in large numbers in virtually every part of the park where large numbers now occur. The one exception is the geyser basins along the Firehole River, where elk were sometimes seen or shot but never reported in the herds observed elsewhere. We suspect that part of the reason for this may be that the geyser basins, being the foremost park attraction, and being so open, were among the first areas to be hunted heavily. Unlike the Northern Range, which most of these travelers crossed with relatively few stops, the valley of the Firehole River was a destination, and thus was visited more intensively by those interested in the park's main attractions.

The evidence of the earliest observers—for examples, Russell's comment (in 1837) that the country around Yellowstone Lake was "swarming with elk," or his obviously justifiable confidence (in 1839) at Yellowstone Lake that even with 2 arrow wounds he could easily find and kill 2 or 3 elk, or Henderson, Gourley, and Blackmore's comments about large numbers of elk in the northeastern area in and near the park—were supported by many later observers. The large numbers killed during the 1870's—such as Bottler's admitted kills—indicate that the northern range was inhabited by thousands of elk at that time. Early in 1883, two years beyond our study period, the Bozeman newspaper reported 5,000 elk between Mammoth Hot Springs and Cooke City (*Avant Courier* 1883c), as well as an abundance of other wildlife (*Avant Courier* 1883a). After that, as mentioned earlier, the park was routinely thought to contain many thousands of elk.

There were 43 sightings of individual elk, 53 of small groups, 35 of herds, 9 of sounds, 25 of meat, hides, bones, or antlers, 31 or tracks, trails, or other sign, and 84 general statements of presence, for a total of 280 reports.

We consider the volume, extent, and detail of this material sufficient to allow us to say with confidence that elk were abundant throughout the Greater Yellowstone Ecosystem prior to 1882.

BISON

Various observers reported bison in most regions of the park inhabited by them today. The observations cause us to suspect that bison numbers might have been lower than today, but we are not entirely confident about this, partly because of the skin-hunting of the 1870's. In 1880, for example, Norris believed there were about 600 in the park, in three herds; if there were that many then, there may have been more prior to the hunts and a decade of visitation. In 1881, Yount reported bison still in Slough Creek, Hellroaring, and the Amethyst Mountain area, as well as smaller groups on Alum Creek and west of the park.

There were 6 reports of individuals, 8 of small groups, 17 of herds, 8 of meat, skin, or bones, 9 of tracks, trails, or other sign, and 26 general statements of presence.

MOOSE

Moose were commonly observed and reported in southern Yellowstone Park. Gray (in 1872) found them in the northwest corner of the park, and Clawson (in 1871) and Bradley (in 1872) mentioned them west of the park. Norris reported that "scores if not hundreds" were killed in the spring of 1875, and they seem to have become rarely seen by the late 1870's.

We are intrigued by the accounts of Henderson (in 1870) and Norris (in 1880) that suggest that moose were at least occasional inhabitants of northern Yellowstone Park.

There were 4 reports of individuals, 2 of small groups, 2 of sounds, 2 of tracks or other sign, and 23 general statements of presence.

PRONGHORN

Pronghorn were apparently very abundant in most suitable habitats in the Greater Yellowstone Ecosystem, and were mentioned as appearing, often by the hundreds, in the Madison Valley west of the Park, down the

Yellowstone River through Paradise Valley, and in the Lamar Valley. Norris (in 1880) also said they appeared on the Blacktail Plateau, Sulphur Mountain, and Mary's Lake areas. Houston (1982) reported that their early historical numbers (1860's and 1870's) may have been as high as 1,000 or more in the park.

Norris (in 1880) and Grinnell (in 1875) agreed that pronghorn were slaughtered by the thousands, though Yount (in 1880) thought them still common in "most of the open regions" of the park. We counted 18 reports of individuals, 24 of small groups, 24 of herds, 7 of meat, 1 of tracks, and 45 general statements of presence.

Pronghorn might present us with a visual bias in the historical record, being more often an open–country animal (though some observers did express surprise at finding Yellowstone pronghorn in forests) and therefore more easily seen.

MULE DEER

Deer also seem to have been very abundant. Russell (in 1839) offered the tantalizing observation that there were "vast numbers" of them in the geyser basins, and many other observers seemed to see them routinely, some seeing them (or reporting them) more often than they reported elk. Grinnell (in 1875), Strong (in 1875), and Norris (in 1877) all reported that thousands were slaughtered during the 1870's.

Barmore (1980) has suggested wintering mule deer numbers were ". . . grossly similar from the early 1900's and, perhaps, since primeval times to the present." It appears to us that, if anything, they were more numerous in 1870 than now, but were at least as common. If, by "vast numbers," Russell meant that thousands of mule deer were living in the geyser basins, we must doubt him just on the basis of available habitat in that area. Herds of mule deer were rarely reported by other observers. Russell's comment is too incomplete to do much more with it than consider the ecological realities of the situation.

There were 38 individual sightings, 29 reports of small groups, 3 of herds, 1 of sounds, 10 of meat, hides, or bone, 18 of tracks or other sign, and 70 general statements of presence.

BIGHORN SHEEP

The accounts provide limited suggestive evidence that bighorn sheep were more numerous, and possibly present in more locations, during the

1830–1881 period than they are now. Though many were reported killed during the 1870's, they were also reported as still abundant at the end of that period by Norris (in 1880) and Yount (in 1881). Because of their susceptibility to domestic stock diseases, changes in numbers of bighorn sheep in the historical period may be more difficult to interpret than those of other species.

There was 1 report of an individual animal, 9 of small groups, 15 of herds, 8 of meat, hides, or bone, 9 of tracks or other sign, and 34 general statements of presence.

WHITE-TAILED DEER

White–tailed deer seem not to have been common in the park area during the period we studied. Some observers saw or killed a few. Strong (in 1875) implied that Doane told him "herds" of white–tailed deer lived in the park in 1870.

Murie (1940), Barmore (1980), and Houston (1982) all agreed that the park seems to ". . . represent the extreme upper limit of marginal winter range" white-tailed deer (Houston 1982:182). If that is correct, it has been more or less continually the case as far back as the historical record reaches.

There was 1 report of a small group of white-tailed deer, and 10 general statements of presence.

BEAVER

Beaver were considered very abundant by travelers who mentioned them, though actual sightings are far rarer than are mentions of dams, lodges, and other workings.

Meek (in Victor 1870) said that the Yellowstone country "abounded" in beaver in 1830, but their numbers declined due to trapping. Russell hunted for them at various locations during his travels in the present park area, apparently finding enough of them to continue trapping, but giving us little information about his actual success. He did leave us the tantalizing observation that in 1835, the local Sheepeater Indians had killed nearly all of the beaver in some portion of the Lamar River drainage.

Some of the reports give an idea of beaver distribution. Russell spoke of trapping them at several locations around the park area, but did not say how many he and his companions caught; we assume from their extended efforts that they were successful in finding at least some beaver. Hamilton reported beaver caught in "large quantities" on Pelican Creek in 1839, and Doane reported that they were "abundant" south of Yellowstone Lake in 1870, the same year Everts saw them swimming "unscared" at Heart Lake. Peale (in 1871) and Raymond (in 1871) found numerous dams south of Yellowstone Lake and at Burnt Hole. Stanley (in 1873) reported beaver evidence "everywhere" in the park, especially on the tributaries of Yellowstone Lake. By 1873, according to Comstock, they were "still common in portions" of the park but were in trouble from trapping. Seguin found dams and lodges at Swan Lake Flat in 1879, as did Drummond in 1879 at Henry's Lake, Strahorn in 1880 at Yellowstone Lake, and Doane again in 1876 at Heart Lake.

Note that in the above summary, none of the accounts said exactly how many beaver they actually saw. Because of that we had to list most of these reports under the heading of general statements of presence. We counted no sightings of individual beavers or of small groups, 1 sound (tail slapping), 4 reports of meat or hides, 6 reports of tracks or other sign (workings and dams), and 21 general statements of presence.

Norris proudly reported that he had saved the park from inundation by allowing extensive trapping, saying that trappers were taking "hundreds, if not thousands" from the park every year.

This record gives us reason to wonder about both EuroAmerican and Native American influences on Yellowstone beaver in at least two periods between 1830 and 1880, and thus to wonder about the fortunes of the beaver thereafter. If during the trapping era beaver were substantially reduced (or, as Russell suggested for the Lamar Valley, essentially eliminated), then the beaver numbers of the 1870's may have been a reflection more of that earlier event—that is, a response to that event—than representative of prehistoric numbers. If Norris was right that beaver numbers were greatly reduced in the 1870's, then the history of beavers in the park area since then must be evaluated with extreme caution.

For example, the poacher Ed Howell, apprehended in 1894, maintained that clandestine trapping was still routinely conducted at that date. In an interview published in *Forest and Stream*, Howell reportedly said this:

There are trappers in the Park all the time during the fur season. I occasionally saw men fishing, and one of them I knew was trapping and used the fish line as a blind. The soldiers did not see through his device, for it takes a mountaineer to see all the signs (*Forest and Stream* 1894).

If trappers not only reduced beaver in the 1870's but kept their numbers down until nearly the turn of the century, then the reported irruption of beaver after 1900 becomes an even more interesting event.

The historical record of beaver after this period is confused. Skinner (1927) estimated there were 10,000 in Yellowstone Park, but two years later Sawyer estimated about 800 (Seton 1929). Warren (1926) studied the beaver of the region around Yancey's Hole at a time when the population was thought to be causing a "problem of overstocking" and was also thought to be in the process of destroying the aspen on that portion of the northern range.

Recent investigators (Glick et al. 1991) have used the 1920's as a benchmark by which to emphasize current low levels of beaver numbers in Yellowstone National Park, when, as Warren reported, the 1920's appear to have been a time of exceptionally high beaver numbers. It is difficult for us, without more historical information and the assistance of ecological specialists, to evaluate these apparent swings in beaver abundance in Yellowstone, but it is clear that not enough attention has been paid to human–caused reductions of beavers, perhaps in the early 1800's and certainly in the 1870's, the consequences of which must have been substantial. Considering the beaver's ability to influence riparian landscapes, these reductions should be of interest to ecologists attempting to understand the changes in those landscapes on the Northern Range since the 1870's.

MOUNTAIN GOAT

We counted one reported sighting of a goat, near the northeast corner of the present park area in 1864 (Vaughn 1900:35), by a party of men who had not seen a goat before. This sighting, though of considerable interest, is not conclusive because of the possible confusion of a goat with a bighorn sheep. We also counted one general statement of mountain goat presence in the park, Calfee's (1896:2) problematic statement that he could find a mountain goat within five miles of Mud Volcano. If mountain goats occupied the park area during the early historical period, they were apparently quite rare.

CONCLUSIONS

We offer two sets of conclusions. The first concern the historiography of this material, that is what the historical accounts have taught us about their nature as evidence.

70

1. As a general rule, the more accounts that are evaluated from a particular party's experience in the park, the more the story of their experiences with park wildlife is fleshed out. One observer in a group frequently noted animals not noted, or even observed, by another member of the same group. On rare occasions, members of the same group disagreed dramatically about wildlife observations, but most of the time they corroborated and complemented each other's accounts.

2. There were sometimes large differences in the success of different parties in the same year at observing wildlife.

3. Large, noisy parties were able to frighten wildlife and decrease their chances of observing it; members of those parties often saw more wildlife when traveling alone.

4. The behavior of animals when first observed by, and observing, early travel parties was widely variable. Sometimes animals fled, sometimes they didn't.

5. Most writers of accounts of the park prior to 1882, with a few notable exceptions among sportsmen, were far more likely to discuss the park's most famous features (geysers, waterfalls, canyons, and the lake) than they were to report on animal observations. Multiple accounts from single parties suggest that animal observations were often incidental. This leads us to a general conclusion that reports of wildlife observations—whether of tracks, actual animals, or other evidence—in these early accounts will tend to understate the number of animals observed.

6. The historical record as used by previous investigators, and limited to no more than two dozen accounts, is perilously slight for the purposes of more than anything but the most general of comments about animal presence and abundance.

7. Even the much larger historical record we employed in the present study lacks the depth or resolution to allow accurate estimates of animal numbers. The record is not sufficiently detailed, for example, to allow us to say with any confidence that elk numbers on the Northern Range during any given year in that period equalled, exceeded, or were less than, at present.

8. The historical record will, however, allow for meaningful general impressions of the relative abundance of various species of animals over the course of the period 1830 to 1881, and in the case of some species, may permit arguable hypotheses regarding their comparative abundance then and now.

Here, then, are our conclusions about the abundance and distribution of wolves and other species in the period 1830 to 1881.

1. Wolves were present and distributed throughout the present Greater Yellowstone Ecosystem.

2. Other predators and scavengers, including mountain lions, bears (both species), wolverine, coyote, fox, and smaller mammals were present. In the case of mountain lions, their numbers or willingness to encounter humans (or some combination of the two) made them more evident to travelers than they are today. Wolverine and fox may have been more abundant, and coyotes less abundant, then than now.

3. Almost all (more than 90%) observers who commented on the abundance of wildlife in the park area expressed the belief that it was very abundant. This included almost all of the observers who did not actually see many animals. For a combination of reasons, including the observation of tracks and other signs, communication with other travelers and residents of the area, and some received knowledge or standing presumptions, even those who did not personally see animals in numbers assumed them to be present.

4. Elk were widely distributed throughout the park area, and were observed, often in groups and occasionally in large herds, in every portion of the park where such observations would be expected today. Bighorn sheep may have been more abundant then than now, especially in the earlier part of the period. Mule deer were common. Bison were present in several parts of the park, and still survived in the hundreds in 1880. Moose were common in the southern part of the park, and were even rarely reported near or on the Northern Range. White-tailed deer were never common, and mountain goats apparently did not occur in the park.

5. The historical record suggests that the park was winter range prior to 1882, and at times this winter range was occupied by large numbers of animals. After 1882 the historical record is clearer, and even more convincing that thousands of animals wintered in the park. Then, as now, severity of winter conditions had a great effect upon the number of animals present.

6. The combination of skin-hunting, recreational hunting, subsistence hunting by residents, carcass-poisoning, and commercial trapping dramatically affected the wildlife regime in Yellowstone in the 1870's. The apparent effects included a great reduction, perhaps even the near-extermination, of wolves, and a great reduction in beaver. Other effects that might be inferred but which are not supported as clearly by the

72

historical record include reduction of smaller carnivores, especially wolverine and fox. The effects of these human activities on the native ungulates are less clear, but probably included short-term reduction in numbers, and changes in habits, movements, or distribution to adjust to increasing numbers of visitors along popular human travel routes.

The historical accounts, then, will not provide satisfaction for those who want precise answers to such questions as, "How many wolves and elk were in the park in 1800?" They do, however, provide an important piece of the puzzle when used fully and carefully. We hope to refine these interpretations with future research, especially in the period between 1882 and 1916.

We offer a last impression, not about the park but about the Greater Yellowstone Ecosystem. As we reviewed the accounts of early travelers to this region, we were often struck by their reports of wildlife abundance: large herds of pronghorn to the west and south of the present park area and down the Yellowstone River Valley; vast bison herds along the Yellowstone River on the north edge of the Ecosystem and smaller herds in many other locations in and near the park; large herds of elk along the Yellowstone River, along the Rosebud and the Clark's Fork, in the Shoshone to the east of the park area, and elsewhere around and in the park.

Frank (1990), in an evaluation of herbivory on Yellowstone Park's Northern Range, said that, "It is surprising that this study represents only the second ecosystem possessing a large complement of its native large herbivore fauna where primary production and consumption have been measured. The novelty of such data is likely a reflection of the woeful worldwide rarity of these ecosystems." To that we would add an equally troubling thought, that by their very rarity these ecosystems tend to look unusual even to educated observers; the perturbations and even destruction that humans have visited on such ecosystems generally occurred before the ecological sciences were out of their infancy.

There is a sad irony here, one that the park has often suffered under as America has attempted to care for it. Today, there is considerable public conviction that Yellowstone is in some sense overpopulated with large animals. No doubt there is still much to learn about these animals and their range, and there is ample evidence that EuroAmericans have tampered with both in significant ways. We still have a lot to learn, and don't yet fully understand just what effects we have had here. But the irony remains that, if those early travelers returned today and traveled across the Greater Yellowstone Ecosystem, they would probably tell us that as far as the animals go, the park is the only place that still looks right.

LITERATURE CITED

Avant Courier [Bozeman]. 1883a. Game features of the Yellowstone Park. Bozeman, Mont., Jan. 11.

―――. 1883c. Killing game in the park. Feb. 15.

Barmore, W. J. 1980. Population characteristics, distribution and habitat relationships of six ungulates in northern Yellowstone Park. Final report. Yellowstone files.

Bradley, F. H. 1873. Report of Frank H. Bradley, geologist of the Snake River Division. Pages 190–274 *in* F.V. Hayden, *Sixth annual report of the U.S. Geological Survey of Montana and portions of adjacent territories . . . for the year 1872.* USGPO, Washington.

Cahalane, V. H. 1941. Wildlife surpluses in the national parks. *Trans. North Am. Wildl. Conf.* 6:355–361.

Calfee, H. B. 1896. Calfee's adventures—he and his companion's blood curdling trip to the park over a quarter century ago. Ms. made from newspaper clips, Yellowstone National Park Research Library, Yellowstone Park, Wyoming.

Carbyn, L. N. 1982. Coyote population fluctuations and spacial distribution in relation to wolf territories in Riding Mountain National Park, Manitoba. *Can. Field-Nat.* 96:176–183.

Clawson, C. C. 1871. Notes on the way to Wonderland, or a ride to the infernal regions. Deer Lodge. *New North West.* Sept. 9, 16, 23, 30 (1871a); Oct. 14 (1871b); Nov. 4, 11 (1871c), 18 (1871d), 25; Dec. 2, 16 (1871e).

―――. 1872. The region of the wonderful lake—Yellowstone. Deer Lodge. *New North West.* Dec. 2, 16, 1871; Jan. 13, 27 (1872a); Feb. 10 (1872b), 24; May 18 (1872c), June 1, 1872.

Comstock, T. 1875. Geological report. Pages 85–95 in W.A. Jones, *Report upon the reconnaissance of northwestern Wyoming including Yellowstone National Park, made in the summer of 1873,* USGPO, Washington.

Craighead, J. J., G. Atwell, and B. W. O'Gara. 1972. Elk migrations in and near Yellowstone National Park. *Wildlife Monograph* No. 29. 48pp.

Curnow, E. 1969. The history of the eradication of the wolf in Montana. Master's Thesis, Univ. of Montana. 99pp.

Doane, G. C. 1970. *Battle drums and geysers.* Ed. by O. Bonney and L. Bonney. Swallow Press, Inc., Chicago. 622pp.

Everts, T. C. 1871. Thirty-seven days of peril. *Scribner's Monthly* 3:1–17, Nov.

Forest and Stream. 1894. Park poachers and their ways. May 26, 42:444.

Frank, D. A. 1990. Interactive ecology of plants, large mammalian herbivores, and drought in Yellowstone National Park. Masters Thesis, Univ. of Washington. 124pp.

Fuller, T., and L. B. Keith. 1981. Non-overlapping ranges of coyotes and wolves in northeastern Alberta. *J. Mammal.* 62:403–405.

Geikie, A. 1882a. *Geological Sketches at Home and Abroad.* Macmillan and Company, London.

Glick, D., M. Carr, and B. Harting. 1991. *An environmental profile of the Greater Yellowstone Ecosystem.* Greater Yellowstone Coalition, Bozeman, Mont. 132pp.

Gray, T. B. The Road to Wonderland. (Bozeman) Avant Courier, August 22, 1872.

Grinnell, G. B. 1875. Personal notebook #295. Southwest Museum, Los Angeles, California.

———. 1876. Zoological report. Pages 68-89 in W. Ludlow, *Report of a reconnaissance from Carroll, Montana Territory, on the Upper Missouri to the Yellowstone National Park and return, made in the summer of 1875.* USGPO, Washington.

Gunnison, J. W. 1852. *The Mormons, or Latter-Day Saints.* Philadelphia, Lippincott, Grambo, and Company.

Hadly, E. 1990. Late Holocene mammalian fauna of Lamar Cave and its implications for ecosystem dynamics in Yellowstone National Park, Wyoming. M.S. thesis, Northern Arizona University. 128pp.

Haines, A. L., ed. 1965. *The Valley of the Upper Yellowstone.* University of Oklahoma Press, Norman. 79pp.

Harris, M. 1887. *Annual report of the superintendent, Yellowstone National Park.* USGPO, Washington, D.C. 28pp.

Henderson, A. B. 1894. Journal of the Yellowstone Expedition of 1866 under Captain Jeff Standifer . . . Also the diaries kept by Henderson during his prospecting journeys in the Snake, Wind River and Yellowstone Country during the years 1866–72. Ms. no. 452, Beinecke Library, Yale Univ., Coe Collection, New Haven Conn. Typescript at Yellowstone National Park Research Library, Mammoth, Wyo. 68pp.

Hofer, E. 1887. Winter in wonderland. *Forest and Stream* 28(1):222–223, (2):246–247, (3):270–271, (4)294–295, (5):318–319; editions of April 7, 14, 21, 28, and May 5.

Houston, D. B. 1982. *The northern Yellowstone elk, ecology and management.* Macmillan, New York. 474pp.

Koth, B., D. Lime, and J. Vlaming. 1990. Effects of restoring wolves on Yellowstone area big game and grizzly bears: opinions of fifteen North American experts. Pages 4–51 to 4–81 *in Wolves for Yellowstone? A report to the United States Congress, Volume 2, Research and Analysis.* National Park Service, Yellowstone National Park, Wyo.

Leckler, H. B. 1884. A camping trip to the Yellowstone National Park. *American Field* 2:41–42, 71–72, 93–94, 117, 141–142 (1884a), 166, 190–191, 214 (1884b), 236–237 (1884c), 261–262 (1884d), 286, 310–311 (1884e), 335–336 (1884f), 359–360 (1884g), 382–383 (1884h), 407–408, 430–431, 455–456 (1884i); editions of Jan. 12, 19, 26; Feb. 2, 9, 16, 23; March 1, 8, 15, 22, 29; April 5, 12, 19, 26; May 3, 10.

Meagher, M. M. 1986. Cougar and wolverine in Yellowstone National Park. Resource management office information paper, Yellowstone National Park. 3pp.

Merrill, E. H., M. S. Boyce, R. W. Marrs, and M. K. Bramble-Brodahl. 1988. Grassland phytomass, climatic variation and ungulate population dynamics in Yellowstone National Park. Final report, Univ. of Wyoming. 74pp.

Murie, A. 1940. *Ecology of the coyote in the Yellowstone.* Fauna of the National Parks No. 4. USGPO, Washington, D.C. 206pp.

Murphy, K. M., and G. S Felzien. 1990. The ecology of the mountain lion (*Felis concolor missoulensis*) in the Northern Yellowstone Ecosystem. Wildlife Research Institute cumulative progress report No. 3. 32pp.

Norris, P. W. n.d. Meanderings of a mountaineer, or, The journals and musings (or storys) of a rambler over prairie (or mountain) and plain. Ms. prepared from newspaper clippings (1870-75) and handwritten addition, annotated about 1885. Huntington Library, San Marino, Calif.

———. 1878. *Report upon the Yellowstone National Park to the Secretary of the Interior by P. W. Norris, Superintendent, for the year 1877.* USGPO, Washington. 9pp.

———. 1880. *Report upon the Yellowstone National Park to the Secretary of the Interior by P. W. Norris, Superintendent, for the year 1879.* USGPO, Washington. 31pp.

———. 1881a. *Annual report of the Superintendent of the Yellowstone National Park to the Secretary of the Interior for the year 1880.* USGPO, Washington.

Norton, H. J. 1873. *Wonderland illustrated; Or, Horseback rides through the Yellowstone National Park.* Harry J. Norton, Virginia City, Mont. 132pp.

Paquet, P. C. 1991. Winter spacial relationships of wolves and coyotes in Riding Mountain National Park, Manitoba. *J. Mammal.* 72:397–401.

Peale, A. C. 1871 Diary. Typescript from book #1971. USGS Field records, Denver Colo. Copy at Yellowstone National Park Research Library.

Raynolds, W. F. 1868. *The report of Brevet Brigadier General W. F. Raynolds on the exploration of the Yellowstone and the country drained by that river.* 40th Cong., 1st Sess., Sen. Ex. Doc. 77. USGPO, Washington. 174pp.

Raymond, R. W. 1872a. Sketches of western travel. I. By an exploring party. Deer Lodge. *New North West,* May 25, p. 4.

———. 1873. The heart of the continent: the hot springs and geysers. *Harper's Weekly* 17:272-274, Apr. 5.

Russell, A. 1955. A. L. Haines, ed. *Osborne Russell's journal of a trapper.* Univ. of Nebraska Press, Lincoln.

Schullery, P. 1988. *The bear hunter's century.* New York, Dodd, Mead & Company. 252pp.

———. 1990. Early Yellowstone bears: solving the historical puzzles. *Yellowstone Grizzly Journal* winter:5–7.

Seton, E. T. 1929. *Lives of game animals.* Vol. 4, Pt. 2. Garden City, Doubleday, Doran & Company.

Skinner, M. P. 1927. The predatory and fur bearing animals of the Yellowstone National Park. *Roosevelt Wildl. Bull.* 4:163–281.

Smith, G. A. 1901. *The life of Henry Drummond.* McClure, Phillips, and Company, N.Y. 503pp.

Stanley, E. J. 1878. *Rambles in Wonderland; Or, Up the Yellowstone.* D. Appleton and Company, N.Y. 218pp.

Strahorn, R. E. 1881. *The enchanted land or an October Ramble among the geysers, hot springs, lakes, falls, and Cañons of Yellowstone National Park.* New West Publishing Company, Omaha.

Strong, W. E. 1968. R. A. Bartlett, ed. *A trip to the Yellowstone National Park in July, August, and September, 1875.* Univ. of Oklahoma Press, Norman. 164pp.

Stuart, J. 1876. The Yellowstone Expedition of 1863. Contributions to the Historical Society of Montana 1:149–233.

Thwaites, R. G. 1905. *Original journals of the Lewis and Clark expedition.* Vol. 5. Dodd, Mead & Company, N.Y. 395pp.

Vaughn, R. 1900. *Then and now; Or, Thirty-six years in the Rockies.* Tribune Printing Company, Minneapolis. 461pp.

Victor, F. F. 1870. *River of the west.* R. W. Bliss and Company, Hartford, Conn. 602pp.

Warren, E. R. 1926. A study of the beaver in the Yancey region of Yellowstone National Park. *Roosevelt Wildlife Annals* 1(1–2):12–191.

Weaver, J. 1978. *The wolves of Yellowstone.* U.S. Dept. of Interior, National Park Service, Natural Resources Report Number 14. 37pp.

Yount, H. C. 1881a. Report of the gamekeeper. Page 50 in P. W. Norris, *Annual report of the superintendent of the Yellowstone National Park.* USGPO, Washington.

———. 1881b. Report of the gamekeeper. Pages 62–63 in P. W. Norris, *Fifth annual report of the superintendent of Yellowstone National Park.* USGPO, Washington.

CHAPTER 3
GRAY WOLF, *CANIS MEXICANUS
NUBILIS* SAY

EDMUND HELLER

Edmund Heller was a prominent and widely published naturalist who produced this brief essay in 1925 as part of his larger report titled "The Big Game Animals of Yellowstone National Park." Among his other credentials was the co–authorship, with Theodore Roosevelt, of an important natural history book on African wildlife. Perhaps it was because of his African experiences that he took a broader and longer view (as well as a more romantic view) of the place of wolves in Yellowstone than did some of his contemporaries.

Does not the wolf also deserve a place in the Yellowstone Park? He is the noble or ignoble hero of much of our literature. Who would not give a year of his life to see a wild wolf or a whole pack of wolves trailing down an elk or deer? The carnivorous animals that kill their prey are always our choice in story and in the hunting field. If they were not killers that show pluck and courage we should not admire them. But since we admire the wolf and are thrilled by his exploits why not tolerate him, at least in our wilderness parks. Great elk herds are not conducive to a balanced piece of nature without the wolf to add fire and alertness to their lives. Protected like cattle the elk become like cattle. Herds of hoofed game, without the presence of a few carnivorous beasts whom they fear, lose much of their character and interest. Should we not be glad to pay for wolf's mere presence and his "demoniac" howl with one or two elk a month for food?

There are but few wolves now remaining in the Yellowstone; they are almost exterminated in a land where at least their voice should be heard. I was saddened last year in Yellowstone Park not to hear a wolf howl. Northern Michigan and Wisconsin outdo the Yellowstone as a wilderness in which the howl of the wolf is still a woodland melody. In that land of forest and swamps he howls nightly. He lives far from the ranch of the stockman, and no lumberman or forest owner fears him or wishes

SOURCE: E. Heller. 1925. The big game animals of Yellowstone National Park. *Roosevelt Wildlife Bulletin* 2(4):430.

to accomplish his extermination. I hope some day to see a pack of wolves in full cry after their hoofed quarry and see with my own eyes how they pull down their game. I do not advocate the support of many wolves in our parks, but a few would help secure a condition of balance amid our wild life and maintain the alertness of the game animals.

CHAPTER 4
GRAY OR TIMBER WOLF. *CANIS NUBILIS* SAY.

By MILTON SKINNER, 1927

Milton Skinner spent many years in and around Yellowstone Park, sometimes working as a naturalist there and producing many articles and at least four book–length works about the park and its wildlife. As John Weaver pointed out in Chapter 1, Skinner provides erroneous information on occasion, and this selection is no exception. In other publications, Skinner's shallow knowledge of the historical record of Yellowstone wildlife is apparent; thus he has the mistaken impression that wolves were originally rare in the park. But for all its shortcomings, Skinner's account of wolves, reprinted here from his monograph The Predatory and Fur-Bearing Animals of the Yellowstone National Park, *contains much of interest, especially in his equivocal view of the place of wolves in wilderness. On the one hand, he considered them very harmful to other wildlife; on the other hand, he admitted that they "play their part" in the evolution and well–being of other species. In that way, Skinner represents a sort of transitional position between the old view that wolves were entirely evil and a more recent view that wolves are neither demon nor saint; they just do what they do.*

A large proportion of the wolves in Yellowstone National Park, possibly as much as 40 percent, are black, and the remainder are gray. Originally the wolf was a rare animal here, but it is likely that a few wandered in from time to time. They began to increase about 1914, soon numbered about sixty, and maintained themselves until severe hunting by the Park Rangers has again reduced their numbers to the point of extermination.

Wolves range throughout the more open parts of the Park, usually following the elk herds to and fro in their spring and autumn migrations. Localities where I have seen them, range from 6,000 feet up to timber line at 9,500 feet, and while most of them were in open valleys, some wolves were in the forest. My records are mostly for the northern and eastern sections of the Park, possibly because there is not enough food in the

SOURCE: M. Skinner. 1927. The predatory and fur-bearing animals of Yellowstone National Park. *Roosevelt Wildlife Bulletin* 4(2):185–186.

Two gray wolves killed by Ranger Henry Anderson near Pelican Creek in 1922 as part of the National Park Service's predator control program. These two were mounted by the Jonas Brothers, Denver, and are now on exhibit at the Horace Albright Visitor Center at Mammoth Hot Springs. NPS photo.

southern and western sections where the game animals do not go in so large numbers.

In summer, they catch small prey, such as mice, woodchucks, rabbits and squirrels, and attract very little attention. In winter they kill elk and deer, and even antelope and mountain sheep, and cause considerable damage; but even so, it is likely they kill mostly the old, the diseased, and the unfit. Probably as many as two or three elk were killed every day during the winter, a few years ago, but this was counterbalanced somewhat by the good the wolves did in devouring dead animals and carrion.

While the wolves in the Yellowstone National Park are bolder than they are outside, they are still wilder and more wary than other Park animals.

Wolves' dens are apt to be in natural caves or cavities among the rocks and glacial debris. They breed every year, one litter a year of three to six pups. Other authorities give a higher figure elsewhere. Three lots of pups that I knew of were born about March 1, but did not leave the dens for some time after that date. A pair of wolves keep together throughout all seasons and probably mate for life. The rate of increase without artificial control and where food is plentiful is about 60 percent of all wolves present.

Probably there is no danger to people in the Yellowstone because of these wolves. Possibly a man might be in danger in winter if he encountered a pack of wolves made aggressive by poor hunting. It is possibly just as well to keep them in awe of man by more or less steady hunting. These wolves are too seldom seen to be of any value to visitors although all are interested to know they are present.

The wolf is of positive value as a scavenger and as a killer of weak and diseased wild stock. There is little doubt but that they played their part in developing speed and cunning among many forms of animals and in preventing epidemics.

CHAPTER 5
GRAY WOLF: BUFFALO WOLF,
CANIS LYCAON NUBILIS SAY

VERNON BAILEY

Vernon Bailey was chief field naturalist of the United States Biological Survey when this passage was published in 1930 in his book Animal Life of Yellowstone Park. *Though portions of this material also appear in chapter 1, it seemed useful to include the work here in its entirety, both because of its interesting anecdotal material and because it reveals the extent to which wolves and wolf–prey relationships were still misunderstood. In his closing paragraph, Bailey wildly overestimated the rate at which wolves kill large mammals and, even more surprising, seemed to have entirely lost touch with the simple reality that wolves and their prey evolved together and had in fact shared the same ranges in North America for thousands of years.*

The large gray wolves at times have become abundant in the park and wrought great havoc among the game animals, but at present they are being hunted so persistently over much of the outside range as well as in the park that they have become extremely scarce. During the summers of 1914 and 1915, they were especially destructive in the park and were following the elk herds to the high pastures of Mirror Plateau, returning with them in winter to the valleys along the Lamar and Yellowstone rivers. In the summer of 1915, Mr. Frazier, at the Buffalo Ranch [*the current Lamar Ranger Station*], told me that wolves had been very troublesome during the preceding winter and had killed many elk. He said that from the ranch he would often hear an elk bawling in the night and the next morning see ravens circling over a half–eaten carcass. During June of that year, Mr. Frazier killed two half-grown wolf pups and caught two more, which were kept chained up at the ranch. During July and August, 1915, I found where a family of wolves had killed and eaten a young elk in Slough Creek valley and found wolf tracks along Slough Creek and Lamar valleys up to the mouth of Mist Creek, also along Pelican Creek, and later a few tracks on Fox Creek at the southern edge of the park.

SOURCE: V. Bailey. 1930. *Animal life of Yellowstone National Park.* Springfield, IL: Charles C. Thomas, pp. 134–137.

Tracks were especially numerous along Pelican and Raven creeks, where at least ten or a dozen wolves hunted in one pack.

In November, 1915, Donald Stevenson counted nine separate tracks, where a band of wolves had crossed a sandbar on Pelican Creek, but at that time they were leaving that section of the park and following the elk herds to lower levels, In January, 1916, they were found in the Lamar and Yellowstone valleys, where Stevenson and Black secured four of the old wolves and later a family of seven pups. With persistent hunting and trapping during the spring this band of wolves was broken up, and apparently most of those not procured were driven out of the park. Evidently a few remain, however, and, as they breed rapidly, constant care must be exercised to prevent their becoming established in numbers to do serious damage to the game. In 1926, I saw a few tracks on Two Ocean Pass and the members of the Sierra Club party saw one wolf on the side of Trident Plateau.

BREEDING HABITS

The fact is now well established that wolves pair permanently or until one of the pair meets with some accident. The male guards the den, hunts for the mother wolf and young, and later leads the family and pack.

The large families of young are generally born in the latter part of March or early in April, the number ranging from seven to nine, but litters of eleven and thirteen have been recorded. When first born the young are almost black, but in a few weeks they begin to fade to a dull yellowish gray. The dens are usually situated in caves or hollows among rocks or sometimes in large burrows on steep hillsides. One found by Stevenson and Black, on the rough slope near Hellroaring Creek on March 26, was watched for some days in an effort to shoot the old wolves, which finally became suspicious and carried the pups away to another location farther up the side of the mountain.

The den was described as composed of four or five large burrows dug into the open hillside, and had evidently been used for several years, as a score or more of old elk skulls were lying about, and one fresh elk head that had recently been brought in was found. On April 14 this family of wolves was located about a mile from the first den in a natural cave among some loose rocks. Back about eight feet from the entrance of the cave seven wolf pups, estimated to be three weeks old, were secured. A freshly killed young elk was found about half a mile from the den and

In August 1922, rangers captured a litter of wolf puppies on Blacktail Deer Plateau after shooting their mother. The litter was kept and shown at park headquarters at Mammoth Hot Springs for a week. The photo, which shows William Bickett and his younger brother Wally enjoying the puppies, was donated to the park photo archives by Mr. Bickett in 1994. NPS photo.

Chief Ranger Sam Woodring enjoying the captured wolf puppies, which were destroyed by order of Yellowstone Superintendent Horace Albright in keeping with park policy. NPS photo.

there were pieces of elk meat in the den with the pups. The old wolves were very shy and kept well out of sight when the den was being watched, but were frequently heard howling and answering each other from different points, and the old male was several times seen guarding the den from a point high above. The male is considerably larger than the female, weighing well over a hundred pounds.

DESTRUCTION OF GAME

Wolves are powerful animals, and their habit of hunting in pairs, families, or packs enables them to pull down and kill any game animals, even to the size of full–grown buffalo or elk. Where game is abundant, as in the park region, they kill mainly those animals easiest to obtain, which are generally the young and cows. They prefer freshly killed meat and usually kill one or more animals every night for food. On Pelican Creek, in 1915, along the trails which they were constantly using, their droppings were made up entirely of elk hair, and a scarcity of elk calves was very noticeable among the herds in that section. Ravens were especially numerous there at that time, as in sections where game is being regularly killed. One game animal killed every twenty–four hours is probably not too much to allow for each adult wolf where game is abundant. It is therefore evident that wolves and game cannot be successfully maintained on the same range.

CHAPTER 6
YELLOWSTONE WOLVES

MARGUERITE ARNOLD

Marguerite Arnold, a long–time resident of Yellowstone, reported in 1937 on the last known wolf pack activity in Yellowstone National Park, apparently in 1934. Among the things that make this account so interesting is her (and her ranger husband's) obvious enthusiasm for the wolves as exciting and beautiful animals, which were by 1937 protected by policy in the park. Notice also her remark about the destructiveness of the coyotes. Within a few years, a pioneering study of Yellowstone coyotes by Adolph Murie would largely vindicate them from the charge of killing "too many" elk and deer. The pendulum that had swung so far to one extreme earlier in the century, when predators were considered uniformly bad, had begun to swing back.

For more than ten years the big timber wolf and the mountain lion have been more or less a myth in Yellowstone Park. True, each year someone sees, hears, or observes the tracks of what was *undoubtedly* a wolf or a lion. Some of these reports are, without question, authentic, although one is inclined to question the lad who, sleeping out not more than half a mile from Park headquarters, "heard a mountain lion scream in the night." That there used to be many more wolves is shown by old wildlife reports, some of which state "they are much too common", "they destroy many elk" and so on. Vernon Bailey, in his *Animal Life of Yellowstone National Park*, says, "During the summers of 1914–1915 they were especially destructive in the park and were following the elk herds to their high pastures of Mirror Plateau, returning with them in winter to the valleys along the Lamar and Yellowstone Rivers." It is well known that wolves and mountain lions are the most destructive of predators, yet they have become so scarce in this section of the country that for a number of years both have been protected in our greatest National Park, and during the past two years the coyote has joined the ranks of the protected.

In former years, during the winter months, Yellowstone rangers spent a lot of their time hunting the wily coyote, which, if allowed to multiply

SOURCE: M. Arnold. 1937. Yellowstone wolves. *Nature Magazine* 30(2):111–112.

87

National Park Service naturalist and artist Edmund J. Sawyer illustrated Marguerite Arnold's article with three drawings of the wolves she described. This one shows one of the wolves she described as "so close that I could see the black line that runs from the corner of the eye back across the face."

unmolested, takes a heavy toll of deer and antelope. Often a winter-killed elk lured coyotes to repeat-ed feasts, and rangers with their rifles took advantage of this fact. My husband returned late one evening from a patrol on skis to the head of Tower Creek, and I sensed immediately, before he said anything, that something unusual had happened. Ben made a practice of telling the baby and me all about the taking of each "dog" as he brought him home. Most of the stories were thrilling too. This particular night I rushed to the door to see the quarry he had brought, but found nothing. Finally he said, "Guess what?—and then a long pause during which I became more curious and impatient. "I just saw four wolves!" "Oh, not wolves," I said, foolishly, knowing very well there was no mistake this time. We had observed what we were satisfied were wolf tracks, but had said little or nothing about them because we

knew of the "un-doubtedly" re-ports. We knew wolves to be more or less mi-gratory in habit

Sawyer's interpretation of Arnold's description of "two huge black fellows loping easily along the trail."

88

and thought the tracks had been made by one or a pair of them traveling through the district.

So Ben told me how, on the way up, he had found the carcass of an old winter-killed cow elk that coyotes were beginning to work on. On the way back, just before looking over the top of a little knoll that hid him from the carcass, he had heard the sound of crunching bones, so he was especially careful, knowing the "dogs" were there eating. As he peered cautiously over the top he said he refused to believe his eyes. His first thought was that bears had come out of hibernation, although it was mid-winter, but there, tearing and gulping at the tempting food, were four great, dark, hulking wolves. In the background three coyotes stayed at respectful distances, hungrily watching the feast. The wolves appeared three times larger than the slim, gray coyotes, and nearly black by comparison. As Ben crouched the gun lay forgotten at his side in the snow. The wolves literally lunged into the carcass, pulled back with a huge bite, "wolfed" it down and were right back for more. Finally a slight shift in the wind or the uncanny danger sense of the coyotes prevailed, and one by one they slipped away into the fast-gathering dusk. Soon the wolves, gorged, left also, trotting off unhurriedly along the trail.

The next day was one of the red letter days of my life in Yellowstone. It has always been my highest ambition to observe and study all the animals here in their natural setting. Lying prone in the marsh grass all of one afternoon I watched a family of six otters at play, and I have pried closely into the intimate family life of bear, buffalo, elk, deer, antelope and many others. When lions and wolves were plentiful I was too young to be anything but frightened by the prospect of getting near one. All unexpected, here was my golden opportunity. So, when the next dusk started to gather, I pulled on my snowshoes and started out, leaving my generous husband at home with the wee one, so mother could have her adventure. Climbing the long steep hill, I about decided it was to be fruitless effort—that it was most unlikely that the wolves would return to the same spot. But I used every precaution in stalking the spot, nevertheless. For the last two hundred yards the trail was nearly straight up, and, between the exertion and the excitement, I was certain any animal within half a mile would be frightened away by the pounding of my heart and my gasps for breath. But I kept on, and finally, near the very summit, I lay flat for a few seconds to regain some of my composure. While I waited there, not more than seventy-five yards now from the elk, I could distinctly hear a crunching of bones—my trip had not been

The four coyotes stood back and watched as the two wolves "commenced tearing out meat and bones, gouging, springing in, pulling back, gulping down huge bites."

entirely in vain!

It is a treat for a housewife to be able to observe just one lone coyote at his meal, and now I knew I would see at least that. Finally my curiosity got the better of me and before I was much rested I raised my eyes slowly, slowly, up behind a small sagebrush and over the crest of the hill. There I saw not one, but four coyotes at their evening feast of elk. I felt a slight disappointment at first that none of the wolves were there, but was soon absorbed in the antics of the "little wolves." After that evening I can readily understand why it is so difficult to sneak up on a coyote. They gnaw on a bone for a while or dig around inside the carcass and then up goes a head to test the wind and at the same time to make a visual and sound survey. Fortunately the wind stayed in my favor and, with just my eyes over the top of the hill and a grove or dark firs back of me, they failed to see me at all. Once or twice one looked right at me and I "froze" to escape the notice I felt was imminent. By this time it was really growing dark, and I was just about to attempt an exit, when something caught my eye down one of the animal trails. It couldn't be! It was! There was no doubt at all even though I had never in my life seen such an animal before, no, not even in a zoo. Not just one of them, but two huge black fellows loping easily along the trail, noses down as though following a scent. They had a peculiar jack–knife gait like that of a greyhound, utterly different from the gliding, noiseless gait of the coyote. On they came, straight toward me and the carcass, and my heart did something 'way up in my throat. They didn't look up at all but loped straight into the choicest part of the elk and commenced tearing out meat and bones, gouging, springing in, pulling back, gulping down huge bites. The coyotes did not leave the scene but discreetly withdrew from striking distance and sat, or walked slowly about, intently watching their big cousins. They appeared to be of an entirely different family from the great dark wolves—so much smaller, more slender and much lighter in color. The heavy shoulders and forequarters of the wolves were especially impressive. I remember blinking and straining my eyes to see every single detail in the fast–thickening dusk, and just after that the climax of the whole episode occurred. One of the wolves decided to look about and see that all was well and started off at an angle that brought him to the edge of the hill not more than forty feet from where I was hiding. He was so close that I could see the black line that runs from the corner of the eye back across the face. As he stood, broadside, I could see perfectly how proportionately more powerful he was than any coyote. I certainly held my breath then, for he turned and looked straight at me! I was in plain view, but I remained perfectly motionless as he looked at me with an uncomprehending stare for part of a minute—it seemed ten! Finally he turned silently and, without a sound, disappeared into the night. The others were, even then, not warned, for their activities continued undisturbed. But I could no longer contain myself—childishly I "had to see what they would do if they saw me." I stood up. Simply that and as quietly as I could, but the remaining wolf and the four coyotes scattered without a sound in as many directions. I don't know how I got back to the cabin, I was so excited and so brimming over with my story. I guess I was a little bit frightened too, as I realized what great hulking beasts those wolves were!

It will be many a day ere an adventure comes to me that will eclipse this twilight meeting with the big wolves.

CHAPTER 7
THE LAST WOLF, 1943

INTERVIEW WITH LEO COTTENOIR

The following interview appeared in Yellowstone Science, *the quarterly publication of the Yellowstone Center for Resources, Yellowstone Park, Wyoming. It describes the last known killing of a wolf in the Greater Yellowstone Ecosystem before the 1990s, when a gray wolf that migrated into the area from northern Montana was killed near the south boundary of the park by a hunter.*

Leo Cottenoir was working as a sheepherder on the Wind River Reservation in 1943 at the time of the incident. Mr. Cottenoir's tribal affiliation is with the Cowlitz tribe in southwestern Washington, but when he was young he married a member of the Shoshone tribe and thus resides on the Wind River Reservation. This interview was conducted on September 28, 1992, by Dick Baldes, Wind River Reservation project leader, and David Skates, assistant project leader, U.S. Fish and Wildlife Service.

Dick Baldes: How did you happen to kill this wolf?

Leo Cottenoir: If any lambs were out late in the evening, we left them out with a lantern or flagging so that coyotes wouldn't bother them. We were cutting out lambs this morning, and we heard this coyote yipping, and the herder said, "You'd better get on your horse and ride up there and see if they're bothering those ewes and lambs." So I rode my horse about half a mile up Muddy Creek.

They were all right, but then I heard some coyotes yipping further up country, so I got on my horse and rode up on a ridge, and looked down on an old reservoir the Soil Conservation Service had put in years before, and it looked like an old coyote and two pups down there. I thought they might have got a lamb down, and were feeding on it, so I rode back down the hill and into the draw.

As I got close to the reservoir, the coyotes took off through the rocks, and I took a shot at them (I had my rifle) and missed them, and this wolf came out of the rocks. It was a wolf and two full-grown coyotes, instead of a full-grown coyote and two pups.

SOURCE: D. Baldes, L. Cottenoir, and D. Skates. 1993. The last wolf, 1943 (interview with L. Cottenoir). *Yellowstone Science* 1(4):10–12.

David Skates: Did you know that it was a wolf at the time?

LC: Well, he started down and I knew it had to be a wolf because it was so much bigger than the rocks. It was going through my mind about the wolf stories I'd heard, and I shot at him. He was coming toward me. I shot and missed him twice on the hillside, and I shot [again]. I knew I'd hit hit him, because you know when you've hit an animal with a rifle [because of the sound of the impact]. He went around a little knoll where I couldn't see him, so I reloaded the rifle, and [saw that] he was lying there on the hillside. I watched him a while, and he didn't move, so I went up there and he was dead.

I'd shot him through the lungs—I'd torn his heart and lungs up. He got away probably 50 or 60 yards after he was hit. So I went to put him on my horse, but the horse wasn't going to stand still, because he smelled that wolf and that was something strange. I got the saddle blanket back on, and took him back to camp. The old sheep herder seen him, and he said, "My gosh, where did you get the lobo?" Of course, he'd seen wolves when he was younger. He was a man, oh, about in his sixties—in his late sixties.

DS: This wolf was killed in May?

LC: In the twenties. The 23rd or 24th of May. There was an article in the [Wyoming State] *Journal* about it in the fifties, it was 1953, I guess, because it had been 10 years before that I brought this wolf in.

DS: So it was May of 1943. Did you realize at the time that this was probably the last wolf killed in Wyoming?

LC: I never had any idea. I thought if there was this one, there would be more of them.

I don't have any idea where he could have come from. I know he did come from Owl Creek, over the mountains. My father-in-law had seen his tracks when he came over.

DS: At the time, did you think it was a wolf with those two coyotes, or did you think it was a coyote?

LC: No, [at first] I thought it was a full grown coyote and two pups. Probably a half mile from where I'd seen them, they circled down in the draw there. But, boy, he sure looked big when he did come out of there. It went through my mind, I'd read stories about wolves attacking people, or something like that. I completely missed him twice [laughter]. When he turned sideways, I got him.

Leo Cottenoir with head of wolf he killed in 1943. Photograph taken in 1992 by Dick Baldes, U.S. Fish and Wildlife Service.

DS: When was the last one killed prior to that time?

LC: Nobody seemed to know. It had to be, like I said, the last one [killed] by Croskey [a rancher in the Owl Creek Mountains] was 1914 or along in there.

DS: So this was the first wolf killed since 20 or 30 years prior? There hadn't been anything killed that had been documented?

LC: Well, the fact was, the bounty had been taken off them 20 or 25 years before, because there weren't any more killed. That's why there weren't any killed, except for coyotes. I ran into a den of coyotes, a den of six pups, and brought them into the sheriff's office there, they had a bounty on them, and he gave me five dollars apiece for those pups.

DS: How big would you say this animal, this wolf was?

LC: Seventy, eighty pounds—seemed like it, anyhow. Because the horse didn't want to stand still. He was big, two, three times as big as a coyote. You can see he's much bigger, two or three times bigger than a coyote, much bigger, and they have such long legs, and big feet, too.

DS: And the reason you didn't get a full mount is that the hair was slipping pretty badly?

94

LC: Yes, Engle [a local taxidermist] said he'd like to have mounted the whole thing. I'm surprised, as well as the head's hair is staying on, that he couldn't have mounted the whole thing at the time. The way this has stayed, looked like the whole thing would have stayed right, too.

DS: Looks good.

LC: I believe his [the man who killed the previous wolf] name was Croskey, he used to have a store over there by Paul Hines store is now, probably about 1912, 1914 or around there. The wolves were bothering the cattle so the stockman put a bounty on an odd-colored one and then they would kill any color of wolf they seen just so they could collect the bounty, and of course it had to be this certain off-color one that the bounty was on, but that's how they got rid of the wolves.

DS: Yeah, they got a whole bunch of wolves for the price of a few.

LC: Yeah, but I guess they did business; the stockmen were leery. Up around Yellowstone they are worried about [wolves] killing calves, but no more than they would kill, I don't think a single wolf [would kill many]; it would have to be a pack like those dog-like animals in Africa, hyenas. They hunt in packs.

DS: Did you hear the fellows prior to your generation talk about wolves being hard on cattle or was it primarily sheep?

LC: Well, I think it was probably cattle, especially calves. Just like most predatory animals will either get the weak or the young because they're easy to get.

I still think they ought to have wolves in there. They are a native animal, native to the country and something that has always been there. Fact of the matter, man is the greatest predator there is anyhow, regardless of the predatory animals. Cause he will kill, he's always after something to kill. If it was deer or antelope or rabbits or prairie dogs, he's always shooting at something. If they had their way everything would be extinct, there wouldn't be anymore animals.

DB: Leo, when you first walked up on the wolf and you probably knew that it was something really rare, did that bother you a bit, knowing that, thinking back, that it probably was the last one?

LC: Well, no. But it was kind of sad to think that he was the only one that I'd ever seen and I killed him. Of course, at the time I was thinking there was nothing else I could do. But at the time he was endangering my sheep herd. If I hadn't killed him, he would have been just like the coyotes.

Coyotes were a problem, still are a problem. I've killed several of those. You'd use to get up early in the morning. Coyotes would come in about daylight and they would never kill a small or weak one; no, the fattest one was the one they'd get. And the first thing they did was cut it up and eat the stomach out of a lamb and get the milk out of it.

DS: I've heard of that.

LC: And sometimes they would get to chasing an old ewe, and they wouldn't kill it right away, but chew the bag just to get the milk. They are a cruel animal. They say they never get a weak or poor one but always a choice lamb every time. In some ways it's sad to have killed the only one [wolf] that was around, but in other ways I'm glad it was me that got to get him because somebody would have got him, I'm sure.

DS: Do you think there were any other wolves in the area?

LC: That I don't know. I was wondering. He was a mature male and You'd think there would be other wolves, females or pups or something else because he had to come from a long ways to get there and I never have heard of anyone over on the Owl Creek side that saw a wolf either.

DS: During the time after or before you killed this wolf, did you ever hear any howling at night?

LC: I never did, no. But they say this Ralph White, the rancher over on Five Mile Creek, or what we used to call Tea Pot, but it's the Five Mile conservation district, he said he thought he heard them howling at night over there, but nobody ever saw one.

DS: Was this after?

LC: This was after I killed it.

CHAPTER 8
REVIEW OF *THE WOLVES*
OF NORTH AMERICA

ALDO LEOPOLD

*In 1944, Aldo Leopold, regarded as the father of modern wildlife management in
North America, wrote this impassioned plea for wolf preservation as part of a book
review of* The Wolves of North America, *by Stanley Young and Edward
Goldman. The Young and Goldman book was a reference work, full of anecdotes of
the wolf's natural history and demise. Leopold, as one of the most creative thinkers
in wildlife ecology, saw beyond such admittedly engaging recitation and repeatedly
criticized the authors for not displaying "any consciousness of the primary ecological
enigmas posed by their own work. For example: Why did the heavy wolf population
of presettlement days fail to wipe out its own mammalian food supply?" Leopold
concluded by asking the question that he believed Young and Goldman should have
asked: "Are we really better off without wolves in the wilder parts of our forests and
ranges?"*

*It is important to keep Leopold in the context of his times; he was not opposed to
wolf control and thought it probably necessary in most places. His knowledge of the
Yellowstone situation was imperfect; as we have already seen, there were wolves in
Yellowstone long after 1916. Also, he held the common view of the time, that
Yellowstone's wolves were a distinct and presumably extinct type, a view over-
turned by research reviewed later in this volume. Still, his statements about the need
for preserving some wolves in places like Yellowstone have a modern ring.*

Viewed as conservation, *The Wolves of North America* is, to me, in-
tensely disappointing. The next to the last sentence in the book asserts:
"There still remain, even in the United States, some areas of considerable
size in which we feel that both the red and the gray [wolves] may be
allowed to continue their existence with little molestation." Yes, so also
thinks every right–minded ecologist, but has the United States Fish and
Wildlife Service no responsibility for implementing this thought before it
completes its job of extirpation? Where are these areas? Probably every
reasonable ecologist will agree that some of them should lie in the larger

SOURCE: A. Leopold. 1944. Review of *The wolves of North America. Journal of
Forestry* 42(12):928–929.

national parks and wilderness areas; for instance, the Yellowstone and its adjacent national forests. The Yellowstone wolves were extirpated in 1916, and the area has been wolfless ever since. Why, in the necessary process of extirpating wolves from the livestock ranges of Wyoming and Montana, were not some of the uninjured animals used to restock the Yellowstone? How can it be done now, when the only available stocks are the desert wolf of Arizona, and the subarctic form of the Canadian Rockies?

CHAPTER 9
HISTORY OF WOLF MONITORING IN IDAHO

The Final Environmental Impact Statement: The Reintroduction of Gray Wolves to Yellowstone National Park and Central Idaho, *published by the U.S. Fish and Wildlife Service in 1994, contained among its appendices several summaries of recent wolf–related activities by management agencies. Chapters 9 through 13 are drawn from that document. They complement the earlier accounts and suggest the growing attention paid to wolves by managers in the three–state area around Yellowstone.*

Sightings of wolves have been reported occasionally in Idaho since they were believed to have been eradicated in the early 1930's. Despite this history of infrequent sightings and the recently increased level of monitoring reports of wolf sightings, there is only marginal evidence to suggest that wolves are more abundant in Idaho today than they were 10–20 years ago.

Before the 1980's, sightings and reports of wolves primarily occurred incidental to other outdoor activities. Few, if any, surveys had been conducted. However, in 1978 a hunter shot a wolf near Warm Lake in the Boise National Forest, and in 1981 an Idaho Department of Fish and Game wildlife biologist photographed a wolf in the Clearwater National Forest during a big game survey flight.

Kaminski and Hansen (1984) researched historical information on the presence of wolves, searched agency files, and interviewed personnel for records and reports of wolf occurrence. In 1983 and 1984 they conducted the first extensive field survey for wolves in central Idaho. They found evidence of 1–4 single wolves during their field surveys, but found no evidence of pack activity.

In 1985 Hansen (1986) analyzed random wolf reports, sent questionnaires to hunters, trappers, and outfitters, and conducted field surveys during winter in northern Idaho. He found no conclusive sign of wolves in any of the areas he searched. Concentrations of wolf reports were not

SOURCE: U.S. Fish and Wildlife Service. 1994. *Final environmental impact statement: The reintroduction of gray wolves to Yellowstone National Park and central Idaho.* Helena: U.S. Fish and Wildlife Service, pp. 6–84 to 6–86.

apparent, but more sightings occurred along the Montana-Idaho border than elsewhere.

Siddall (1989) analyzed random and solicited reports of wolves received between September 1988 and April 1989. Of 248 reports Siddall analyzed, 78 were rated (Weaver 1978) as probable, 137 were rated as possible, and 33 were discounted. Analysis of the reports suggested a concentration of reports from the Boise and Payette National Forests in the Bear Valley, Warm Lake, and Landmark areas in central Idaho, and areas in and near the Clearwater National Forest in northern Idaho. Other apparent concentrations occurred on the Nez Perce National Forest near Dixie and near the North Fork Salmon River.

Johnston and Erickson (1990) analyzed random and solicited wolf reports received between June 1989 and February 1990. Of 170 reports they analyzed, 78 were rated (Weaver 1978) probable and 92 were rated possible. Concentrations of reports were evident from between the Lochsa and North Fork Clearwater River drainages, east and south of Dworshak Reservoir, in the South Fork Clearwater River drainage, the Upper South Fork Salmon River and Middle Fork Salmon River, and northwest of Stanley in the Cape Horn area.

In July 1991 an Idaho Department of Fish and Game employee videotaped 2 wolves in the Bear Valley area in the Boise National Forest. One month later, however, a wolf was found poisoned in that area. Presence of wolves has not been confirmed in the Bear Valley area since then.

Rachael (1993) analyzed 207 wolf reports received by the U.S. Fish and Wildlife Service, the Idaho Department of Fish and Game, and all National Forests in Idaho between January 1991 and June 1993. Concentrations of reports occurred in 3 areas: the Bear Valley area of the Boise National Forest (where 1 of 2 wolves known to occur there was found poisoned in July 1991), the Red River Ranger District of the Nez Perce National Forest, and the area west of Lolo Pass and north of the Lochsa River in the Clearwater National Forest. More than 93% of all sightings were of single animals.

A wolf that was radio–collared in Glacier National Park in September 1990 was located in the Kelly Creek drainage of the Clearwater National Forest in Idaho in January 1992, just west of the Idaho–Montana border. That wolf was located in the Kelly Creek area during regular telemetry flights until autumn 1993. Multiple attempts to receive a signal from this animal's radio collar since then have failed, and the transmitter has exceeded its expected life; however the animal was observed by Fish and Game Department personnel in a helicopter in early February 1994.

Personnel from the Idaho State Office of the USFWS spent several weeks with Forest Service personnel during winter of 1991 and 1992 and summer of 1992 conducting surveys in the Boise National Forest, the Nez Perce National Forest, and elsewhere in Idaho. Presence of only 2 wolves was confirmed (both in the Bear Valley area where 1 was later found poisoned).

A USFWS temporary biologist and volunteer began conducting surveys for wolves and investigating timely reports of wolves throughout the state in June 1993. Positive evidence of a wolf(ves) was found on the Nez Perce National Forest, but its current presence could not be confirmed. Presence of wolves was not documented from other parts of the state in 1993.

Two temporary biologists for the Nez Perce National Forest conducted surveys for wolves and goshawks in the Red River Ranger District during summer 1993, and Forest Biologist Steve Blair has been coordinating immediate responses to credible, timely wolf reports on the forest. Forest Service personnel were able to obtain positive evidence (scats and tracks) of wolves in summer 1993. However, a USFWS wolf survey crew from Washington that conducted extensive efforts to locate wolves in the Nez Perce National Forest during a 1-month period during summer 1993 found no positive evidence of wolves.

Several other National Forests have been cooperating in the effort to survey for wolves. In summer 1993 a part-time survey crew for the Panhandle National Forests investigated a series of reports near Wallace, Idaho, but failed to obtain positive evidence. Challis National Forest personnel have conducted wolf survey programs since 1990 and contributed to identifying wolves in the Bear Valley area in 1991. Payette National Forest personnel have participated in a wolf survey program in west–central Idaho since 1990. In addition to monitoring the radio-collared wolf in the Kelly Creek drainage of the Clearwater National Forest, Forest Biologist Dan Davis, has been coordinating rapid responses to credible, timely reports of wolf observations.

Two special interest groups have also contributed to the effort of surveying for wolves in Idaho. Wolf Haven has conducted several howling surveys in cooperation with land management agency biologists in Idaho since 1991, but these surveys have not led to the confirmation of the existence of wolves. The Wolf Recovery Foundation, a private organization from Boise, has also sponsored numerous wolf howling surveys throughout Idaho. These surveys have not been successful in confirming the presence of wolves. The foundation also sponsored a 1-800 number for the public to report wolf sightings.

The USFWS has continually requested that the public and state and federal agency biologists report sightings of wolves or wolf sign in a timely manner. The USFWS plans to continue to survey for wolves in 1994 in close cooperation with land management agency biologists.

Single wolves have probably inhabited or travelled through Idaho in recent years. However, despite numerous wolf surveys conducted throughout the state, and hundreds of thousands of sportsmen and recreationalists who spend over 8,000,000 visitor–days in central Idaho annually, and the hundreds of hours Idaho Department of Fish and Game wildlife biologists spend conducting survey flights of big game populations on winter ranges each year, few wolves have been confirmed to exist in Idaho. Although a few single animals probably occur in the state and the population of wolves in western Montana is increasing, wolf recovery in Idaho and elsewhere is dependent upon successful pair formation and reproduction. No evidence of breeding activity or packs of wolves has been reported in the state.

LITERATURE CITED

Hansen, J. 1986. Wolves of northern Idaho and northeastern Washington. Montana Cooperative Wildlife Research Unit unpublished report. 88pp.

Johnston, J., and J. Erickson. 1990. Public survey of central Idaho wolf occurrence: June 1989–February 1990. Central Idaho Wolf Recovery. 9pp. + appendices.

Kaminski, T., and J. Hansen. 1984. Wolves of central Idaho. Montana Cooperative Wildlife Research Unit unpublished report. 111pp.

Rachael, J. S. 1993. Recent reports of occurrence of wolves in Idaho. Prepared for U.S.D.A. Forest Service, Missoula, Mont. Order No. 43-0343-3-0207. 16pp.

Siddall, P. 1989. Public survey of central Idaho wolf occurrence. Boise National Forest unpublished report. 20pp.

Weaver, J. L. 1978. *The wolves of Yellowstone*. U.S.D.I. National Park Service, Nat. Res. Rep. No. 14. Washington, D.C. 38pp.

CHAPTER 10
GRAY WOLF MONITORING IN MONTANA

As with the previous chapter and the next three chapters, this account is excerpted from the Final environmental impact statement: The reintroduction of gray wolves to Yellowstone National Park and central Idaho, *published in 1994.*

Eradication of the gray wolf was initiated in Montana in 1883 with the advent of a bounty system and was completed by a federal agency by the 1930's. At the same time the wolf was being eradicated from the southern portions of Alberta and British Columbia. In the late 1960's the British Columbia provincial government allowed wolf populations to increase in the southeastern portion of the province by reducing wolf hunting and trapping. The Alberta province reduced its predator control program in the 1960's. Reduction of predator control programs and reduced hunter harvest allowed for wolf populations to increase and recolonize southward toward Montana and Glacier National Park (Singer 1975). Since the 1960's sightings and documentation of wolves in northwestern Montana has steadily increased. The wolf was listed as a predator in Montana until 1973 when it was protected by state law and the federal Endangered Species Act of 1973.

Although wolves were rarely seen in Montana in the early 1900's, reports of sightings persisted through the first half of the twentieth century with a significant increase around the 1960's. Singer (1975) collected 77 wolf sightings for the period of 1910–1975, 24 of which were made from 1960 to 1975 in and around Glacier National Park. Kaley (1976) updated Singer's report and obtained 53 additional sightings around Glacier National Park in 1976. Most reports were of single animals (63%) or pairs (22%), with 2 packs of 6 wolves being reported in 1968 and 1973 (Brewster and Fritts 1992). Singer reported that 14 wolves were shot, and 15 trapped between 1910 and 1974 in the North Fork of the Flathead

SOURCE: U.S. Fish and Wildlife Service. 1994. *Final environmental impact statement: The reintroduction of gray wolves to Yellowstone National Park and central Idaho.* Helena: U.S. Fish and Wildlife Service, pp. 6–87 to 6–90.

River drainage. Residents observed what they believed to be wolf pups in 1948, 1967, 1971, and 1973 although a den was never found.

The Wolf Ecology Project was established in 1972 by Dr. Robert Ream from the University of Montana. Under Dr. Ream's guidance the Project collected wolf observations and searched for wolves in Montana. Day (1981) and Ream and Mattson (1982) recorded and analyzed wolf observation reports including accounts of sightings, howling, tracks, dens, scats, kills, dead wolves, and scent posts from western Montana, Idaho, and northwestern Wyoming during 1972 through 1979. A total of 400 reports were collected (Brewster and Fritts 1992). Day (1981) collected 372 wolf reports, of which 93 were questionable and not used. His "very good" category consisted of 5 wolves that were killed in 1964, 1968, 1972, 1974, and 1977. These animals were probably dispersers from Canada. A wolf was also killed in southwestern Montana in 1941 (Flath 1979). A majority of the reports (261) were from 1967 to 1977 (Day 1981). Single animals comprised 71% of the observation reports. Day used clumpings of sightings to determine wolf distribution and possible establishment, similar to the monitoring system that was adopted by the U.S. Fish and Wildlife Service in 1989. The reports indicated two clumpings: one was in northern Montana centered around Glacier National Park and the Bob Marshall Wilderness area; the other was in the Beaverhead National Forest in southwestern Montana and the adjacent Salmon and Targhee National Forests in Idaho (Day 1981). Subsequent searches did not locate or confirm any pack or breeding pair.

Flath (1979) collected wolf reports from southwestern Montana from 1968 to 1978 and described an increase in wolf observations in 1968 that steadily declined from 1974 to 1978. Most of the reports (90%) were of singles or pairs with no evidence of resident wolf pack activity. One possible den was reported in 1974.

From July 1970 to 1978, the Wolf Ecology Project (Ream and Mattson 1978) collected 78 wolf reports within the Rocky Mountain Front or within 10 km of its boundaries; 42 were rated very good, 30 good, and 6 fair. Reports were of 38 sightings, 39 of wolf sign, and 1 dead wolf. Findings indicated that there was no resident population, only single wolves moving through the area.

Ream and Mattson (1982) found that reports west of the Continental Divide were centered along the North and Middle Forks of the Flathead River and in the Kootenai area in extreme northwestern Montana. East of the Continental Divide, reports occurred along the Rocky Mountain front along the Glacier National Park/Bob Marshall Wilderness complex (Brewster and Fritts 1992).

The Wolf Ecology Project and the U.S. Fish and Wildlife Service collected, recorded, and investigated wolf observations from 1970 to 1988. The information was recorded and stored in a computer data base. In 1989, the U. S. Fish and Wildlife Service implemented a 3-phase monitoring system to determine the establishment and distribution of wolves in Montana and Wyoming. An observation card was developed based on the information sheet that had been used by the Wolf Ecology Project and distributed to all land management agencies to record wolf observations or sign. Training was also provided to agency personnel about wolf biology and ecology and how to look for and record sign and observations. As the information was obtained it was placed into the computer data base and analyzed for clumping of sightings. Clusters of multiple animals or of different color combination of animals suggest the presence of breeding pairs or pack activity. Numbers of reports have gone from 158 in 1989 to 180 in 1993, with a high of 370 in 1992 (U.S. Fish and Wildl. Serv. 1992).

Surveys are normally conducted when a cluster of sightings are received from an area. In 1991, approximately 7,400 miles or roads and trails were surveyed by U.S. Fish and Wildlife biologists (900 miles by snowmobile, 1,200 miles by trail bike). U.S. Forest Service biologists surveyed 2,825 miles of trails and roads in 70 different drainages along the Rocky Mountain Front. In 1992, U.S. Fish and Wildlife biologists surveyed 14,000 miles of roads and trails (1,700 miles by snowmobile, and 1,000 miles by trail bike). In 1992, U.S. Forest Service biologists surveyed 1,007 miles of trails in 55 different drainages along the Front. A lone male wolf was discovered during the 1991 surveys and is being monitored on an occasional basis by tracks and other sign. Wolf activity of single and multiple animals was documented in 6 drainages in 1991 and of only single animals in 1992 (U.S. Fish and Wildlife Serv. 1992). Surveys were continued in 1993 with approximately the same level of intensity as in 1991 and 1992, however, the information from those surveys has not been compiled.

In 1992, 12 students from San Francisco State University conducted surveys for 14 days in an area west of Kalispell. In 1993, 12 students surveyed the Upper Yaak area and 16 students surveyed the area around Lost Trail Pass for 14 days each. A possible howl was heard in each area but no wolf activity was found. Personnel from Wolf Haven International and U.S. Fish and Wildlife Service biologists provided training for the survey participants.

The first denning of wolves in Montana in over 50 years was documented in Glacier National Park in 1986 (Ream et al. 1986). Since that time wolves have been increasing in number and distribution in northwestern Montana (U.S. Fish and Wildl. Ser. 1992). In the winter of 1993–94, there were 5 breeding pairs or packs living completely within northwestern Montana, 1 pack with a territory partially in Montana and Canada, and 2 packs in Canada adjacent to the Montana border. Approximately 65–70 wolves inhabit Montana and at least 5 litters (24 pups) were born in 1993. Several members of all packs have been radio-collared to determine pack dynamics and to document progress towards recovery goals.

In summary, reports of wolves have been made in Montana since the species was essentially eradicated in the 1930's. No doubt many of the reports involved coyotes, domestic dogs or other animals. Many others probably involved single (probably dispersing) wolves from Canada. The increase in sightings after 1968 seems to have been associated with the reduction of wolf control and harvesting in Canada. Wolf sightings continue to increase as the species becomes established in Montana and disperse to other areas of the northwest. The historical pattern clearly indicates that as the wolf's range expands southward, reports of wolves may proceed establishment of breeding pairs or packs by many decades.

LITERATURE CITED

Brewster, W. G., and S. H. Fritts. 1992. Taxonomy, genetics and status of the gray wolf (*Canis lupus*) in western North America: A review. Pages 3–33 to 3–93 in J. D. Varley and W. G. Brewster, eds. *Wolves for Yellowstone, Volume IV Research and Analysis*. National Park Service, Yellowstone National Park, Wyo. 750pp.

Day, G. L. 1981. The status and distribution of wolves in the northern Rocky Mountains of the United States. M.S. Thesis, Univ. of Montana, Missoula. 129pp.

Flath, D. L. 1979. The nature and extent of reported wolf activity in Montana. Paper presented at Montana Wildl. Soc. Meeting. Missoula, Mont. 17pp.

Kaley, M. R. 1976. Summary of wolf observations since spring 1975. Unpublished Report. Montana Coop. Wildl. Res. Unit, Missoula. 197pp.

Ream, R. R., and U.I. Mattson. 1982. Wolf status in the northern Rockies. Pages 362-381 in F. H. Harrington, and P. C. Paquet, eds. *Wolves of the world: Perspectives of behavior, ecology, and conservation*. Noyes Publ., Park Ridge, N.J.

Ream, R. R., and U. I. Mattson. 1978. Current status of the gray wolf (*Canis lupus*) in the Rocky Mountain Front. Unpublished Report. Univ. of Montana, Missoula. 18pp.

Singer, F. J. 1975. The history and status of wolves in northern Glacier National Park, Montana. Glacier Nat. Park Sci. Paper No. 1, West Glacier, Mont. 55pp.

U.S. Fish and Wildlife Service. 1992. 1991–1992 annual report of the Montana interagency wolf working group. Unpublished Report. U.S. Fish and Wildl. Ser., Helena, Mont. 24pp.

CHAPTER 11
GRAY WOLF MONITORING IN WYOMING

Most of Yellowstone National Park is in Wyoming and, as the following report indicates, some of the most interesting wolf reports, including an actual dead wolf (which had apparently traveled to the area from northwestern Montana), have come from national forest lands to the east and south of the park. This summary of Wyoming wolf monitoring suggests again the difficulty of demonstrating wolf presence conclusively.

EARLY WOLF MONITORING SURVEYS

A survey for wolves was initiated in 1974 to determine the status of wolves in northwestern Wyoming (Vining 1975). The results of that survey were ". . . inconclusive as to the existence of a 'wolf' in Wyoming." Evidence collected (primarily scats) suggested the presence of a "large canine" in the Shoshone National Forest east of Yellowstone National Park (YNP). Vining's survey could not estimate the number of "large canines" nor estimate distribution in northwest Wyoming. Vining described his survey as superficial and recommended continued efforts to determine the status of wolves in Wyoming. Weaver (1978), in survey work in and near YNP, detected 2 instances in 1975 and 1977 of what may have been a lone wolf in the Shoshone National Forest 1 km–22 km east of YNP. Wolf packs or wolf reproduction were not detected in either the Vining (1975) or Weaver (1978) survey efforts during the 1970's.

The Wyoming Game and Fish Department (WYGF) summarized 9 reports of wolves from 1978 to 1985 (Yellowstone National Park, unpub. data). Reports were sporadic (never a cluster of similar reports within the same year), were of single animals, and did not show concentrated activity or indicate the presence of wolf pack activity in northwestern Wyoming.

SOURCE: U.S. Fish and Wildlife Service. 1994. *Final environmental impact statement: The reintroduction of gray wolves to Yellowstone National Park and central Idaho.* Helena: U.S. Fish and Wildlife Service, pp. 6–90 to 6–91.

RECENT WOLF MONITORING PROGRAM ACTIVITY

In 1989, the FWS instituted a more aggressive wolf reporting system and established a network of state and federal agency contacts to record reports of wolf sightings. The FWS also encouraged the public to report wolf sightings to appropriate authorities. All reports of wolves were recorded on a wolf observation card and entered in a computer database. Training sessions conducted in 1989 and 1991 and provided instruction and techniques on locating, verifying, and documenting wolf presence in an area. Employees from several federal agencies and WYGF attended these sessions.

In 1990, personnel from the FWS, USDA Forest Service, Bureau of Land Management, and WYGF participated in a meeting to upgrade the wolf reporting system in Wyoming and review possible reports of wolves in 1989 and 1990. Review of sightings and associated surveys did not indicate any wolf pack activity.

In 1991, the FWS received reports of wolves in the Dubois area, southeast of YNP. Fish and Wildlife Service conducted interviews with people and surveys of the area in March 1991 but did not find wolf presence. National Park Service and WYGF personnel conducted additional field surveys in the Du Noir area in August 1991 but wolf presence was not detected. Fish and Wildlife Service, USDA Forest Service, and WYGF personnel conducted an additional survey later in August 1991 in the Dubois area and did not find convincing or conclusive evidence of wolves or wolf presence in the area. An additional winter survey was conducted in the Dubois area in December 1991 by the FWS and WYGF, and no evidence of wolves or wolf packs was found. In summary, the wolf monitoring system in Wyoming showed a concentration of wolf reports in the Dubois, Wyoming area southeast of YNP. Based on the concentration of reports, several surveys were conducted in 1991 and no convincing evidence of wolf presence was found. Additionally, no evidence of breeding activity, reproduction or wolf pack activity was found. In the fall 1991, the FWS in cooperation with the WYGF, began a new effort to gain information from hunters. Posters on wolf presence and identification and wolf sighting report cards were made available at state game check stations.

In 1992 and 1993, the FWS continued to collect reports of wolf sightings in Wyoming. Following an incident in late September 1992 when a wolf was killed south of Yellowstone National Park, FWS, National Park Service, and WYGF personnel searched a 100 mi^2 area where

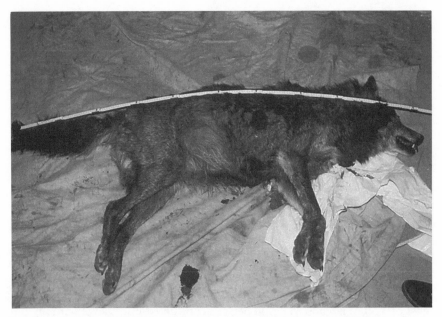

On September 30, 1992, a moose hunter in the Fox Park area of the Teton Wilderness, just south of Yellowstone National Park, shot the black 92-pound wolf shown in this and the facing photo, reportedly mistaking it for a coyote. DNA tests eventually established that the animal was apparently a recent migrant from northwestern Montana. Extensive surveys of the area revealed no evidence of additional wolf activity. NPS photos by John Mack.

the animal was killed and found no evidence of the presence of other wolves or wolf activity.

In an effort to further increase awareness of wolves and encourage people to report when they see wolves or wolf sign, FWS personnel gave 14 presentations and training sessions on wolves and wolf identification during April and May 1993. Presentations and training sessions were held throughout the Yellowstone area in Wyoming and Idaho and personnel from USDA Forest Service, BLM, WYGF and the general public attended. Based on a small cluster of reports of wolf activity in the Thorofare area southeast of Yellowstone, FWS and USDA Forest Service personnel conducted a field survey of the area in early July 1993. No evidence of wolves or wolf sign was found.

Fish and Wildlife Service personnel conducted wolf surveys in January 1994 in several areas east and south of YNP. Surveys detected only 1 instance of possible wolf sign (tracks) in the Berry Creek area south of

YNP. The tracks suggested presence of a lone wolf. Large tracks were again reported in the Pacific Creek area south of YNP and could be the Berry Creek animal. Both reports suggest perhaps 1 lone wolf may be inhabiting areas south of YNP. To date no surveys or confirmed reports suggest breeding or reproduction of wolves, or wolf pack activity in northwestern Wyoming. Additional surveys may be conducted in the future based on clusters of credible wolf reports. Additional presentations and training session to increase awareness and information about wolves will continue in the future.

CHAPTER 12
GRAY WOLF MONITORING IN
YELLOWSTONE NATIONAL PARK

This chapter is especially helpful in summarizing known wolf sightings in Yellowstone since 1978, when John Weaver's report (Chapter 1) was published.

Wolf sightings have been infrequently reported throughout Yellowstone and the surrounding area from the late 1920's (when the last known wolves were killed in Yellowstone) to the present. Weaver (1978) provides a summary of wolf extermination in Yellowstone and possible occasional occurrence in and near Yellowstone from the late 1800's to April 1977. Weaver believed 2 packs of wolves may have been present during the mid-1930's but they did not persist. For the next 30 years wolf reports (singles and pairs) were sporadic. An increase of reports occurred from 1967 to 1977 and was probably due to implementation of a system recording wolf sightings. During the 1970's, sporadic reports suggested mostly single animals in the northeast and northwest portions of the park. Tracks and howls suggested a lone, large canid may have been in an area 1–22 km east of the park in the Shoshone National Forest in spring 1977 (Weaver 1978). Weaver (1978) did not find any evidence of persistent wolf pack activity during the 1970's. Meagher (1986) summarized a total of 106 possible wolf reports from 1977 to 1986. Of the 106, 95 (90%) were judged to be coyote or impossible to categorize. The remaining 11 reports were determined to represent 9 possible occurrences of wolves in the Yellowstone National Park area. If the 9 occurrences were wolves, all were considered transients and the data did not suggest resident (pack) activity up to 1986 (Meagher 1986).

Since Meagher's (1986) report, wolf sightings have continued to be reported and with interest in wolf reintroduction into Yellowstone and the gray wolf EIS, reports of wolves have greatly increased to 177 reports

SOURCE: U.S. Fish and Wildlife Service. 1994. *Final Environmental Impact Statement: The reintroduction of gray wolves to Yellowstone National Park and central Idaho.* Helena: U.S. Fish and Wildlife Service, pp. 6–91 to 6–94.

in and around Yellowstone (160 in Yellowstone) for 1993. Of the 1993 total only 2 reports appear suggestive of single wolves.

In recent years, additional activities have been initiated to increase both the public and park employee awareness of wolves and encourage them to report possible sightings of wolves in Yellowstone. Yellowstone's reporting system for rare animals (including wolves) has also been updated, revised, and computerized to facilitate the analysis and summarization of rare animal sightings. Currently, anyone believing they saw a wolf is asked some basic questions regarding animal location, description, track measurements (if any), and the habitat in which it was seen. All wolf reports in research files from 1987 to 1993 were entered into a computer database to facilitate analysis. Basic information in the database included the month, day, year, and time of sighting, number of wolves, if photos were taken, track length and width if appropriate, location, and description of habitat. The answers to these questions are recorded on a Rare Animal Sighting form. Many times, based on the quality of the report, type of description, and location, reports are investigated to collect additional data (look for tracks, scats, measure vegetation etc.) in an effort to better determine the species of animal seen. If the visitor or employee took photos or videos, the Park asks if copies can be made and those copies are included with the report. Many times photos can positively identify the animal. All data from a report is then recorded in a computer database. Currently, anyone may report a wolf sighting in the park by contacting any of the park Visitor Centers, ranger stations, park rangers, or contacting the Bear Management Office (where reports are summarized and entered into a computer database). All reports are taken regardless of the quality and entered into the database.

SUMMARY OF REPORTS FROM 1986 THROUGH 1993

Reports of possible wolves in the Yellowstone area have been few from 1986 to 1990, averaging 8/year. Reports of wolves in Yellowstone greatly increased between 1991 and 1993, probably due to the increased interest in and publicity about wolves and wolf recovery in the Yellowstone area.

In 1992, several reports were received (tracks, sightings, photos) suggesting at least 2 individual wolves were present in the Yellowstone area. One apparently wild wolf was filmed feeding on a bison carcass in Yellowstone's Hayden Valley. Another different individual was killed September 30, 1992, south of Yellowstone National Park and search ef-

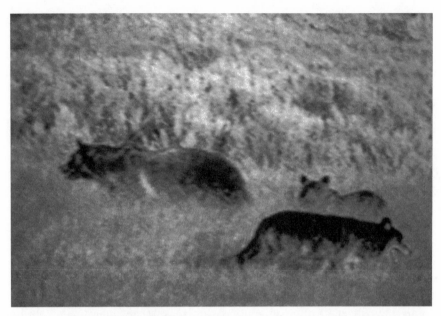

On August 7 and 8, 1992, professional film producer Ray Paunovich of Bozeman, Montana, sighted and filmed a large wolf-like animal in Hayden Valley in central Yellowstone National Park. These images were made form a video of that film footage, and thus are not of highest quality, but do show the animal's general size and shape. In this picture, the "wolf" is passing in front of a sow grizzly bear and young bear. The young bear (probably a yearling) has turned its head to watch the "wolf" pass, although the adult bear and the wolf studiously avoided eye contact. Courtesy of Busch Productions, Inc.

forts the following week by National Park Service, Wyoming Game and Fish, and U.S. Fish and Wildlife Service personnel revealed no other wolves present in about a 100 mi^2 area. In 1993, only 2 reports appeared suggestive of wolves. One report was of wolf tracks in the Otter Creek area and 1 was a sighting of a wolf–like animal feeding on a bison carcass. To date, no wolf reports have indicated any concentrated wolf activity in Yellowstone and no reports have revealed the presence of pack activity or successful breeding in Yellowstone National Park.

CONCLUSIONS

Reports of wolves submitted to Yellowstone National Park have greatly increased from 1987 to 1992. Most reports were classified as unknown because too little information was present to verify or determine

The "wolf" shown near a grizzly bear, who is on a bison carcass (a raven is flying on the right). Courtesy of Busch Productions, Inc.

what a person may have seen. Many reports were determined to be Yellowstone's large coyotes and many reports have photos supporting such conclusions. Physical evidence, photos, and large tracks suggest 2 separate wolves may have been in or near Yellowstone in 1992. Reports in 1993 suggest 1 or 2 wolves may have been in Yellowstone National Park in 1993. None of the reports, suggestive of wolves, indicate concentrated activity of multiple animals indicative of pack formation, breeding, or reproduction.

OTHER ACTIVITIES

Every year during all seasons, biologists spend hundreds of hours surveying ungulate herds or locating radio-collared wildlife from aircraft in Yellowstone and no one has reported seeing wolves or wolf-like animals in the park from 1986 to 1993. In early 1993, a survey was conducted over part of Yellowstone's northern range to search for wolves or wolf sign; nothing was found. In late spring, a Forest Service employee reported hearing wolves howling south of the park. Soon after a survey flight was conducted in the area to look for wolves or possible rendezvous sites. Nothing was found. Additionally, U.S. Fish and Wildlife Service and Forest Service personnel visited this backcountry location

The leg length of the animal is more obvious photographed in shorter grass. This animal did not appear to be the same one that was shot the following month in Fox Park, south of Yellowstone National Park (see previous chapter). Courtesy of Busch Productions, Inc.

searching for wolf sign for several days and found none. No wolf howling was heard. No further reports of multiple wolves were received from the area.

Numerous information and training sessions have been held for park and concessions employees from 1992 to 1994. In February 1992, a informative presentation was given to park rangers resource management coordinators, and other park staff discussing wolf identification and sign (tracks, scats, etc.), wolf recovery in northwestern Montana, the upcoming wolf EIS process, and where to report possible wolf sightings. In July 1993, National Park Service and U.S. Fish and Wildlife Service personnel gave 5 workshops to park and concessionaire employees regarding wolf ecology, wolf identification, wolf recovery efforts in northwestern Montana, and where to report possible sightings of wolves. Also in July 1993, information was provided to all ranger subdistricts and visitor centers in the park describing the revised Rare Animal Observation system, how to fill out possible wolf reports, and where to send the reports. The new computerized system was introduced and instructions were included on how to fill out the form. In Yellowstone Today, the park newspaper given to all visitors at the park gates when they enter, an informative article described the history and status of wolves in Yellowstone and characteristics of wolf identification, and encouraged visitors to send all reports of wolves to the Bear Management Office or contact the appropriate authorities.

In January 1994, another series of meetings was held primarily for ranger and resource management personnel to inform them of the Rare Animal Observation system, how to report wolf observations, how to identify tracks, take measurements, make casts and where to report sightings of wolves and other rare animals. Continued monitoring for wolves, collection and analysis of reports, and periodic informative articles will continue.

LITERATURE CITED

Meagher, M. 1986. Summary of possible wolf observations 1977–1986. NPS information paper. 2pp.

Weaver, J. 1978. The Wolves of Yellowstone. U.S. Department of the Interior, National Park Service, Natural Resources Report No. 14. 37 pp.

CHAPTER 13
SUMMARY OF WOLF STATUS AND
RECOVERY IN NORTHERN
ROCKY MOUNTAINS

The history of the wolf in the United States combines industrial-scale slaughter of almost all wolves with extraordinary persistence and durability of a few others. The three states around Yellowstone, having eliminated most wolves more than 70 years ago, have been the scene of occasional reports of individual animals ever since. This chronology tracks this process of destruction and survival, with special emphasis on the halting reestablishment of packs in northern Montana and the equally slow legislative and administrative process of actively encouraging wolf recovery.

1700 Wolves were abundant throughout all of North America, north of Mexico City, except extreme desert regions.

1850 Extermination of ungulates and large predators, including bison and wolves, began in the West.

1900 Big game and predators were decimated by unregulated harvest and settlement.

1910 Wolves were virtually eliminated in eastern U.S., greatly reduced in West.

1915 U.S. Biological Survey initiated wolf control in West.

1925 Viable wolf populations were reported eliminated from West.

1944 The last documented wild wolf was killed in the greater Yellowstone area.

1950 Reports of wolves in Wyoming, Montana, and Idaho continued. Lone wolves were killed in Montana and Idaho every decade until the present time.

1966 British Columbia began recovery and wolf populations increased southward. Reports of wolves continued in U.S. and increased slowly. Wolf reintroduction into Yellowstone National Park was recommended by several biologists.

1971 The first interagency meeting for management of the northern

SOURCE: U.S. Fish and Wildlife Service. 1994. *Final environmental impact statement: The reintroduction of gray wolves to Yellowstone National Park and central Idaho.* Helena: U.S. Fish and Wildlife Service, pp. 6–24 to 6–26.

Rocky Mountain Wolf was held in Yellowstone National Park. Reports indicated there may have been 10–15 wolves in Yellowstone area and 5–10 in Glacier National Park.

1972 Wolf research by Wolf Ecology Project, University of Montana, began by evaluating wolf reports and sightings. They found no evidence of wolf packs in Montana.

1973 The ESA was enacted; wolves became protected in the U.S.

1973 Wolves became protected by Montana State law.

1974 An Interdisciplinary Wolf Recovery Team was appointed and led by a Montana Fish and Game representative. Introduction was considered in selected areas.

1977 Wolves became protected by Idaho State law.

1978 A lone wolf was photographed and another killed in central Idaho.

1978 The Wolves of Yellowstone report indicated no wolf packs in the Yellowstone area; viable populations ended by 1925.

1979 A lone wolf was monitored adjacent to Glacier National Park.

1980 A lone wolf depredated on livestock near Big Sandy, Montana, and was killed by FWS. This was the first documented depredation in over 50 years.

1980 The "Northern Rocky Mountain Wolf Recovery Plan" was completed by the FWS.

1986 The first wolf den in the western U.S. in over fifty years was documented in Glacier National Park.

1987 The revised "Northern Rocky Mountain Wolf Recovery Plan" was reviewed by the public and approved by the FWS.

1987 National Park Service director Mott suggested beginning EIS for reintroduction to Yellowstone. Park Service began wolf information program.

1987 A wolf pack near Browning, Montana, depredated on livestock and was removed by the FWS. Representative Owens (Utah) introduced a bill to require the NPS to reintroduce wolves to Yellowstone National Park (H.R. 3378 Sept. 30, 1987). It was not passed.

1988 The Interim Wolf Control Plan was approved by FWS. The Wolf Recovery Program in Montana was staffed and funded.

1988 Congress directed National Park Service and FWS to conduct *Wolves for Yellowstone?* studies and mandated appointment of Wolf Recovery Coordinator.

1989 Depredating wolves from Marion, Montana, were relocated, leading to the establishment of the Ninemile wolf pack near Missoula,

Montana. Representative Owens (Utah) introduced bill to Congress requiring initiation of EIS for wolf reintroduction to Yellowstone (H.R. 2786 June, 1989). It was not passed.

1990 Senator McClure (Idaho) introduced a bill "to provide for the reestablishment of the gray wolf in Yellowstone National Park and central Idaho Wilderness" (5.2674 May, 1990). It did not pass.

1990 The NPS and FWS completed the first *Wolves for Yellowstone?* report, Vol. I and II.

1990 Congress established the Wolf Management Committee. No Congressional or agency action was taken on the Committee's May 1991 recommendation.

1991 Congress funded the FWS to support the Animal Damage Control Wolf Management Specialist position in the West.

1991 A black wolf was illegally poisoned on a livestock allotment in a central Idaho Wilderness area.

1991 Two separate radio-collared wolves moved into Idaho. One stayed, the other went back to Canada.

1992 Congress directed the FWS, in consultation with the Park Service and the Forest Service, to prepare a DEIS on wolf recovery in Yellowstone National Park and central Idaho.

1992 The NPS and the FWS completed the second *Wolves for Yellowstone?* report, Volumes III and IV.

1992 An estimated 40 wolves in 4 packs occupied northwestern Montana. All packs except the Ninemile Pack, which resulted from relocation of a problem wolf in 1989, and Murphy Lake Pack were still in the Glacier National Park area. Lone wolves continued to be reported throughout Montana, Idaho, and Wyoming but no wolf reproduction was documented in Idaho or Wyoming.

1992 A possible wild wolf was photographed in Yellowstone. A wolf was shot just south of Yellowstone. No other wolves were located despite increased monitoring.

1992 Congress directed the FWS to complete final EIS by January 1994 and that it expected the proposed alternative to conform to existing law.

1993 An estimated 45 wolves in 5 packs occupy northwestern Montana. Monitoring efforts increased in Idaho and Wyoming but no wolf packs were located.

1994 An estimated 7 breeding pair (65–70 wolves) are being monitored in northwestern Montana. No breeding pairs located in Idaho or Wyoming or in the proposed experimental population areas.

Part II

Recent Wolf Research
and Natural History

Few animals have produced more diverse opinion and a larger body of common knowledge than the wolf. All regions that either now have or once had wolves maintain and cultivate a folk tradition about those animals, and those traditions are usually a mixture of savvy observation, occasional research findings, and emotion-laden lore. The Northern Rockies are no exception to such traditions; newcomers, several generations of Euroamericans, and hundreds of generations of Native Americans all have invested the wolf with a remarkable variety of traits and qualities.

A region's cultural view of an animal is at least as important as whatever science may try to teach us about that animal, and usually the traditional values and attitudes associated with the animal will get the most attention and endure the longest in the public mind. It has often been noted that the struggle to restore wolves to Yellowstone was not an ecological issue; it was a social one. People who knew how wolves behaved and were qualified to make some general predictions of how they would fit in Yellowstone did not believe that the wolf would cause massive disruption of either the ecological setting or the human community. These people could marshall impressive statistics to prove their point.

But in a region where wolves had been eliminated for three or more generations, and where most people had learned their wolf lore from ancestors who themselves had probably seen few wolves, flat and unromantic scientific statistics were no competition for what was already "known" to be true about the animals. Science, with all its shortcomings and unemotional theory, would always prove inadequate in convincing

121

people that local common knowledge was wrong, whether that common knowledge favored or opposed wolves.

It might seem a little odd, then, that one of the most significant milestones in the process by which wolf recovery advanced was scientific. The gray wolf was classified as an endangered species in 1973, and the first Northern Rocky Mountain Wolf Recovery Plan was published by the U.S. Fish and Wildlife Service in 1980 (a revised and much improved edition appeared in 1987; part of it is quoted in Chapter 51). But the mere placement of legal machinery to accomplish recovery was no guarantee it would happen. The next significant step must have seemed to many people who favored wolves as proof that wolves were still a long way from arriving, just as it must have seemed to many people who opposed wolves as a waste of money and time because they already knew all they needed to know about wolves.

That step was taken in 1988, when the Senate-House Interior Appropriations Conference Committee appropriated $200,000 for the National Park Service and the U.S. Fish and Wildlife Service to conduct studies related to wolf restoration. The Conference Report (100th Congress, 2nd Session, H.R. Report 100–862, to accompany H.R. 4867) outlined the goals of the studies:

> The managers agree that the return of the wolf to Yellowstone NP is desirable. There are a number of concerns about the reintroduction and $200,000 has been included to study questions which have been raised. The managers believe the studies should address, but not be limited to the following:
>
> 1. The issue of whether wolves would or would not be controlled either within or without the Park;
> 2. How a reintroduced population of wolves may affect the prey base in Yellowstone NP and big game hunting in areas surrounding the park;
> 3. Would a reintroduced population of wolves harm or benefit grizzly bears in the vicinity of the park;
> 4. Clarification and delineation of wolf management zone boundaries for reintroduction; and
> 5. An experienced wolf coordinator with the FWS will oversee the program in full cooperation with the NPS.

Many people involved in the debate over the restoration of wolves to Yellowstone viewed this action by Congress skeptically; it had all the earmarks of a decision deftly avoided through further studying. But as it turned out, whatever Congress or any constituency had in mind, the research initiated in that year resulted in a significant advance in the wolf recovery dialogue. In 1990, and again in 1992, the two agencies, working in cooperation with universities and cooperative researchers, published massive reports entitled *Wolves for Yellowstone? A Report to the United States Congress*, Volumes I–IV, containing more than 1,400 pages of data and analysis. Volumes II (1990) and IV (1992) were the full reports, while Volumes I (1990) and III (1992) were "executive summaries" that provided concise overviews of the findings.

These reports had far-reaching effects on the analysis of wolf-related issues and were of great use to managers, but their full texts had a fairly limited audience. They were made available to the public through distribution to many government offices, all public libraries in greater Yellowstone, and more than 100 special interest groups, and they were not expensive, but it's obvious that only a tiny percentage of the public read them. On the other hand, some of their most important (or at least most startling) findings were reported widely in newspapers, and either the full reports or the executive summaries were apparently read by many decisionmakers. Thus, the reports did advance the process of understanding that led eventually to the environmental impact statement and the arrival of the first wolves.

Very few *existing* wildlife populations, much less wildlife populations that are only being proposed for existence, have been subjected to such an extensive scientific examination, one that crossed numerous disciplines and drew on the expertise of national authorities. Perhaps the most significant role these studies would play was in the preparation of the environmental impact statement for wolf recovery. By addressing the important public questions so thoroughly, the reports to Congress laid a solid foundation for that next step. Cumbersome legal procedures frustrate many of us, but looking back on this one it is obvious that without *Wolves for Yellowstone?* both advocates and opponents of wolves would still be debating the "whether-or-not," and would still be struggling with their own sets of beliefs and confusions about wolves. The wolves now roaming the Yellowstone area remind us of how much we have yet to learn about them, but we've come a long way in only a few years.

It has always seemed a waste to me, that more people are not exposed to these costly and important research findings, so I have included almost all of the executive summaries in Part Two. I have rearranged them from their order in those two volumes, to integrate common topics from both reports. I have omitted only the analysis of early historical accounts of wolves in Yellowstone, because of its numerous firsthand accounts were excerpted as Chapter 2 of this book. The institutional affiliations of the authors are those at the time they completed their studies.

SECTION ONE
NATURAL HISTORY AND IDENTIFICATION

We begin with some general background on the natural history, ecology, and identifying characteristics of wolves. Chapter 14 is drawn from a wide variety of scientific sources, and is based on studies of wolves in many places. It takes a necessarily broader view than John Weaver did in Chapter 1; he constructed as much as could be known about the natural history of Yellowstone wolves from the historical literature.

CHAPTER 14
WOLF BIOLOGY AND ECOLOGY

BIOLOGY

Taxonomy

Wolves have existed throughout North America and have occupied nearly all habitats in the Northern Hemisphere except for true deserts. Early taxonomists divided the North American gray wolf into 24 subspecies based on skull characteristics, body size, and color; often utilizing few specimens. The subspecies of wolf that was described for the central Rocky Mountains, *Canis lupus irremotus*, was similar to other subspecies in the western United States and southwestern Canada.

Contemporary research using multivariate statistical analysis and molecular genetics, along with larger sample sizes suggests that 24 subspecies are unwarranted and that 5 North American subspecies are more reasonable. These subspecies overlap extensively with each other since they represent averages and trends in morphology that occur within a given geographical area. Genetically, there is very little distinction among gray wolf populations, at least in part due to the mobility of the species. Currently, all populations of wolves in the lower 48 states, regardless of subspecies classification, are listed as endangered except for the gray wolf in Minnesota which is listed as threatened.

Physical Characteristics

The wolf is the largest wild member of the dog family Canidae. Coat color ranges from white to shades of gray to black. In Minnesota, most wolves are gray or shades of brown. However in Montana, black wolves are as common as gray wolves. Adult males average 90–110 pounds with an extreme range of 43–175 pounds, while adult females average 80–90

SOURCE: U.S. Fish and Wildlife Service. 1994. *Final environmental impact statement: The reintroduction of gray wolves to Yellowstone National Park and central Idaho.* Helena: U.S. Fish and Wildlife Service, pp. 6–27 to 6–31.

This year-old female wolf in a Yellowstone acclimation pen (late winter 1995) already shows the long-legged character that makes adult wolves such excellent long-distance travelers. NPS photo by Jim Peaco.

pounds with an extreme range of 39–125 pounds. Males are usually 5–6.5 feet long from nose to tail tip, and females range from 4.5–6 feet in length. Most wolves stand 26–32 inches tall at the shoulder.

With long legs and a deep narrow chest, the wolf is well suited for far-ranging travel. Wolves have large feet which aid in wintertime travel over crusted snow and allow them an advantage for preying on various ungulates, which can sink much deeper into the snow. Front feet are slightly larger than rear feet. Wolf tracks average about 4 inches wide and 5 inches long including the claw marks. Wolf and large domestic dog (great Dane, St. Bernard, and Irish wolfhound) tracks are similar in size, and often impossible to differentiate from each other in the field.

Adult wolf tracks are surprisingly large and almost impossible to confuse with coyote tracks. Photo taken in late March in Yellowstone by Douglas Smith, NPS.

Two important means of communication for wolves are howling and scent-marking. Within a wolf pack, howling serves in the identification, location, and assembly of separated pack members. It may also be particularly useful in facilitating the movements of pups and adults from one rendezvous site to the next. Howling may serve a social function when pack members rally around the alpha individuals and greet each other. It is also a means of advertising the presence of the pack within its territory, and the pack's willingness to defend resources such as pups, a kill, and the territory from other wolves. This avoids direct conflicts between packs.

Scent-marking is the application of an animal's odor to its environment. It is used by wolves to communicate information regarding territory, position in the dominance hierarchy, location of food, and even the behavioral or physiological condition of the animal. Scent-marking usually involves urinating or defecating. Scent marks are commonly made at route junctions and especially along the edges of pack territories. These scent marks inform lone wolves or packs when they are entering another pack's territory.

All six members of the Crystal Creek group of wolves in Yellowstone acclimation pen, late January 1995. The alpha male can be identified, third from left, by his raised tail. NPS photo by Jim Peaco.

Pack organization

The basic social unit in wolf populations is the pack. A pack consists of 2 to 30 wolves (average about 10) which have strong social bonds to each other. Packs are formed when 2 wolves of the opposite sex develop a pair bond, breed, and produce a litter of pups. Central to the pack are the dominant (alpha) male and (alpha) female. The remaining pack members are usually related to the alpha pair and constantly express their subordinate status through postures and expressions when interacting with the dominant pair. Young members approaching sexual maturity may challenge the dominant animals, which can result in changes in each wolf's social position in the pack.

Wolves become sexually mature at 2 years of age. Breeding within the pack usually occurs only between the top-ranking alpha male and female. Although courtship behavior occurs in varying degrees throughout the year, the actual breeding season occurs from late January through April, depending on the latitude. Wolves in higher latitudes generally breed later. Wolves in Yellowstone National Park (45 degrees latitude) breed any time from late January to late February and possibly early March. During the breeding season in late winter, the pack may move extensively within its territory.

Pregnant wolves complete digging of dens as early as 3 weeks before the birth of the pups. Most wolf dens are burrows in the ground, usually in sandy soil. Wolves may also den in hollow logs, rock caves, or abandoned beaver lodges. Some dens are used traditionally by a wolf pack from year to year. Also, certain specific areas (on the order of 5 mi^2, 13 km^2) may contain several den sites which are used in different years by the pack. Some wolf packs can be sensitive to human disturbance during this season and may abandon the den if disturbed. This poses a particular risk to very young pups that cannot regulate their own body temperature.

Wolf pups, in general, are born in late March to May after a 63-day gestation period. In Yellowstone, wolf pups were born any time from late March though April. Litter sizes of wolves usually range from 4 to 7. In Yellowstone National Park, the average litter size taken from dens in the early 1900's was 7.8 pups and varied from 5 to 13. Average litter size in northwestern Montana now averages just over 5 pups per litter.

With the denning area established in the spring, pack movements center around the den. However, adult pack members often travel throughout their territory for food. The maternal female is usually at the rendezvous site more than other adults, but she may also travel throughout the territory as pups grow and are weaned. All pack members may help feed the female and pups. Pack members also provide play and protection for the growing pups. The pups are weaned at 5 to 6 weeks of age.

A wolf pack will usually move from the den site (or occasionally from a second den site) to the first rendezvous site when the pups are 6–10 weeks of age which is in late-May through early July. The first rendezvous site is usually within 1–6 miles (2–10 km) of the natal den and often consists of meadows and adjacent timber with surface water nearby. A succession of rendezvous sites are used by the pack until the pups are mature enough to travel with the adults, usually by September or early October. Each successive rendezvous site is usually 1–4 miles (2–6 km) from the previous site. Occupancy times vary from 10–67 days. As with dens, rendezvous sites may receive traditional use by wolf packs year after year. Wolves appear less sensitive to human disturbance at later rendezvous sites than they do at the first one.

At three weeks of age, wolf pups like this one being held by Yellowstone Wildlife Veterinarian Mark Johnson, are still easily handled. Three weeks later the pups will probably be weaned and much more mobile. NPS photo by Douglas Smith.

By about October, pups are mature enough to travel with the adults, and the pack moves throughout the territory. As the pack travels throughout its established territory, the alpha wolves usually lead the pack and choose the direction and specific routes of travel. Wolves often travel on established routes including trails, roads, and frozen waterways, occasionally cutting across from one such route to another. Daily travel distances for wolf packs are typically in the range of 1–9 miles (2–15 km), while distances between successive kills vary from 8–34 miles (13–55 km). Wolf packs in Yellowstone National Park included both summer and winter ranges of ungulates within their territories.

In most wolf populations, packs occupy exclusive territories. Territories may range in size from 80 mi^2 (210 km^2), as in Minnesota, to over 660 mi^2 (1,700 km^2) as in Alberta. Territories in northwestern Montana average about 300–400 mi^2 (780–1,040 km^2). Lone wolves may range over areas in excess of 1,000 mi^2 (2,590 km^2). As pack members are traveling, they deposit urine and scat markers which identify their territories. Foreign wolves entering established territories may be killed.

Mortality

Wolves die from a variety of causes: malnutrition, disease, debilitating injuries, interpack strife, and human exploitation or control. In areas with little or no human exploitation, the primary causes of mortality are disease and poor nutrition in pups or yearlings and death of adults from other wolves. Mortality rates in unexploited populations can average about 45% for yearlings and 10% for adults. In Minnesota during 1969–1972, September appeared to be a critical month for malnourished wolf pups to survive. Minnesota wolf pups with body weights less than 65% of standard weight had a poor chance of survival, whereas pups of at least 80% of standard weight had a high survival rate. Body weights appeared related to available food supply. Mortality rates of wolf pups in exploited populations can reach 80%.

Fall and winter may be critical periods for wolf survival. Beginning in the fall, wolf mortality rates are most influenced by the degree of exploitation or control by humans. Overwinter (October–March) mortality rates within packs ranged from 0%–33% for a minimally exploited population to 14%–88% for a heavily exploited population. Established wolf populations apparently can withstand human–caused mortality rates of 28%–35% without declining. Protected wolf populations can increase at rates of 28%–35%.

Dispersal

The nature and extent of dispersal in wolves appears related to wolf density and prey availability. In low-density populations, these animals may disperse just out of their natal pack's territory into an unoccupied area, find another lone wolf of the opposite sex, and form a new pack. In high-density populations, such animals may stay in the pack, if possible, and wait for changes in the rank order and opportunities to mate. If forced out, these loners may trail a pack or live in the buffer zones between territories to avoid packs. In some situations, young adult wolves may disperse hundreds of miles. However, mortality is often high among dispersing animals and therefore, the chances of finding a mate and successfully establishing a new pack are low. Wolves may disperse at ages ranging from 9–28 months or more. Dispersal in late winter by yearlings is common.

Wolves in Yellowstone must share the prey base with several other predators, including grizzly bears, who are known to displace wolves from carcasses. NPS photo by Mike Sample.

ECOLOGY

Niche

In North America, the wolf is a predator primarily of large ungulates. All biological and social aspects of the wolf make it adapted for this role. No other carnivore in the western United States replaces the ecological role of the wolf. Although the coyote (*Canis latrans*) occasionally preys upon young, old, and vulnerable ungulates, its main diet consists primarily of small animals. The coyote does not prey year-round on large ungulates. Other wild animals that regularly prey on large mammals in North America include mountain lions (*Felis concolor*) and black (*Ursus americanus*) and grizzly bears (*Ursus arctos*). Although the mountain lion regularly preys on large ungulates, its methods of hunting (primarily "ambush") and social organization (solitary) contrast sharply with the socially cooperative methods of the wolf. Black and grizzly bears, usually solitary by nature, stalk and kill moose, elk, and deer and take mostly calves but occasionally take vulnerable adult ungulates as well.

133

Food Habits

In general, wolves depend upon ungulates for food year round. In northern Montana, elk, moose, and deer (mule and white-tailed deer) are the principal prey species. Smaller mammals can be an important alternative to ungulates in the snowfree months. These small mammals include beaver, marmots, ground squirrels, snowshoe hare, pocket gophers, and voles. In various areas of North America, during years of abundant beaver populations, beaver have comprised 25%–75% of the spring-fall diet of wolves, so in those areas or situations, they may prey less on young ungulates. Nonetheless, when these figures for beaver are converted to a biomass basis, ungulates still constitute the bulk of the summer diet and certainly of the annual diet. In areas where beaver are not so abundant, ungulates usually account for more than 90% of the biomass consumed by wolves.

Prey Consumption Rates

On an average, wolves eat 9 lbs of meat per wolf per day during winter. Although the wolf is capable of eating large quantities of food in a short time, such quantities are not always available. Thus, wild wolves may have to go for several days at a time without eating. Wolves probably could fast for periods of 2 weeks or more while searching for vulnerable prey. When food is available, wolves can replenish themselves to prepare for another period of fasting. The wolf, with its large stomach capacity, seems well adapted for this cycle of feasting and extended fasting.

The frequency of kills by a wolf pack varies tremendously, depending on many factors including: (1) pack size, (2) diversity, density, and vulnerability of prey, (3) snow conditions, and (4) degree of utilization of the carcasses. Because the wolf's prey varies in size from small mammals to beaver to bison, the kill rate of each species varies according to the amount of food each provides.

In Minnesota, where wolves eat white-tailed deer almost exclusively, estimated kill rates range from 15–19 deer per wolf per year. In areas where elk are the dominant prey, these kill rates are generally lower. In Riding Mountain National Park, 1 wolf averaged 14 ungulates killed per year which included deer, elk, and moose. Based on prey abundance in Yellowstone, the primary prey is expected to be elk and mule deer. It has been estimated that wolves will kill an average of 12 ungulates/wolf/year.

Among the large ungulates, Yellowstone wolves will prey most heavily on elk. This aerial photo from early spring 1995 shows five of Yellowstone's wolves at a kill site. NPS photo by Douglas Smith.

Influence of Wolf Predation on Ungulate Populations

Wolf predation on larger ungulate populations usually results in smaller fluctuations in ungulate numbers over the years. Smaller die-offs from winter-kill may occur because wolves are preying on weakened animals before they die.

Wolf predation is one component of total annual mortality in many ungulate populations. Wolves usually do not deplete their prey populations, but may keep some prey species at low levels if ungulate populations are already low and other limiting factors exist. Computer models have predicted that wolves in the Yellowstone area may reduce ungulate numbers by 5%–30% and decrease fluctuations in the population, but would not have devastating effects on the prey populations.

Influence on Other Predators

Wolf impacts on other predators can vary. Coyotes may be less abundant in Yellowstone with wolves present, and red fox (*Vulpes vulpes*) may benefit from wolf presence. Bears and wolves usurp carcasses from each other, and wolves occasionally prey upon bears and vice versa, but published information suggests neither species would be significantly affected. Brown bears and gray wolves coexist throughout much of North America and Eurasia. Sympatric populations of wolves and grizzly bears do not appear to significantly impact survival or reproduction of the other. Some indirect competition for spring carrion, winter-

135

weakened ungulates, and newborn calves may occur between wolves and grizzlies in Yellowstone. However, based on data from other geographic areas, grizzlies appear quite able to coexist with wolves; because grizzlies are omnivorous and not totally dependent upon ungulates, it is likely grizzlies will easily adapt to the presence of wolves.

CHAPTER 15
CHARACTERISTICS OF COYOTES AND WOLVES

Species: Coyote (*Canis latrans*)
Appearance: delicate
Height: 16–20 in. (0.4–0.5 m)
Length: 3.4–4.25 ft
   (1.1–1.3 m)
Weight: 20–35 lb (9–16 kg)
Color: varies from gray to
   tan to rust
Ears: long and pointed
Muzzle: long and narrow
Legs: thin and delicate

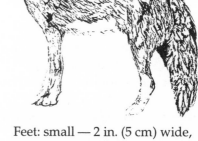

Feet: small — 2 in. (5 cm) wide,
   2.5 in. (6 cm) long
Tail: hangs straight down or
   out

Species: Wolf (*Canis lupus*)
Appearance: massive
Height: 26–34 in. (0.6–0.9 m)
Length: 5–6 ft (1.5–2.0 m)
Weight: 70–120 lb (32–54 kg)
Color: varies from white to black to silver-gray
Ears: rounded and relatively short
Muzzle: large, broad, and blocky
Legs: thick and long
Feet: very large — 3.5–4 in. (9–10 cm) wide, 4–5 in. (10–13 cm) long
Tail: hangs straight down or out

width 3-3/4"

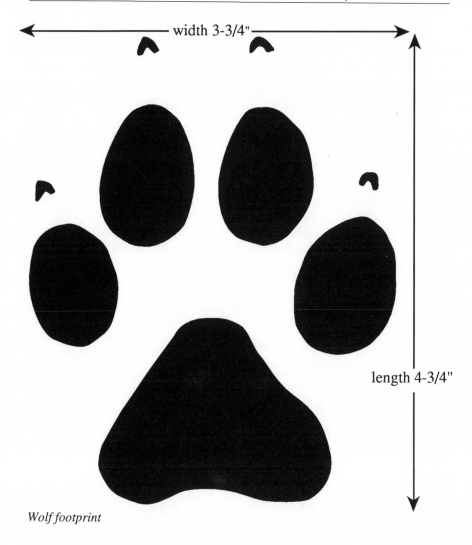

length 4-3/4"

Wolf footprint

All drawings in this chapter are by Renee Evanoff, Yellowstone Center for Resources.

PART TWO

SECTION TWO
PREHISTORIC AND HISTORICAL RESEARCH

As explained in Chapter 2, there is a continuing uncertainty in both public and scientific circles over whether wolves were native, or very common, in the Yellowstone area prehistorically. Although the evidence provided in Chapter 2 suggests that wolves and their prey were numerous in the early to mid-1800s, there are other approaches to analyzing earlier periods. The authors of Chapters 16 and 17 agree that the wolf was native to Yellowstone prior to 1800, although they are unable to determine how abundant wolves or their prey were.

CHAPTER 16
A REVIEW OF ARCHEOLOGICAL AND
PALEONTOLOGICAL EVIDENCE FOR THE
PREHISTORIC PRESENCE OF WOLF AND RELATED
PREY SPECIES IN THE NORTHERN AND CENTRAL
ROCKIES PHYSIOGRAPHIC PROVINCES

KENNETH P. CANNON,
NATIONAL PARK SERVICE,
MIDWEST ARCHEOLOGICAL CENTER

1. A study area of the northern and central Rocky Mountain Physiographic Province was defined and 36 archeological and paleontological sites within the area were selected for review.
2. The review consisted of prehistoric and historic deposits which span
   the last 25,000 years and contained significant faunal assemblages.
3. Gray wolf remains are documented from 10 dated prehistoric deposits
   in the study area. Evidence of wolves in the region begins about 12,000
   years ago and continues into historic period. Prehistoric remains of
   wolves have also been recovered from deposits at Lamar Cave in
   Yellowstone National Park.
4. Elk are a persistent number of the regions faunal assemblage beginning about 10,000 years ago. Limited numbers in the faunal record
   may be the result of hunting and butchering practices, as opposed to
   their presence in the region.
5. Bison have also been a long–time member of the region's faunal assemblage. Bison have been recovered from Pleistocene through historic deposits. Limited numbers of bison from archeological sites in
   the mountains may be a result of the economic orientation of prehistoric groups occupying the higher altitudes.
6. Deer, bighorn sheep, and pronghorn are also present in significant
   numbers from the region's archeological and paleontological sites.
   Specific procurement patterns of these species in comparison to larger
   ungulates (bison and elk), may be factors reflecting the disparity on
   frequency between prehistoric and modern populations.

SOURCE: J. D. Varley, and W. Brewster, eds. 1992. *Wolves for Yellowstone? A
report to the United States Congress*, Volume III, executive summaries.
Yellowstone National Park: National Park Service, p. 17.

141

CHAPTER 17
ARE WOLVES NATIVE TO
YELLOWSTONE NATIONAL PARK?

JOHN W. LAUNDRÉ,
IDAHO STATE UNIVERSITY

Available literature was perused to test the hypothesis that gray wolves were not residents of the Yellowstone National Park area prior to the arrival of humans of European descent. This hypothesis is based on the contention that wolves arrived in the area along with elk after being forced from lower elevations by human pressures. The following findings and conclusions resulted from this literature review.

1. Wolves were found to have occurred at several high elevation Holocene sites in Wyoming, Montana, and Idaho. This demonstrated that wolves can live at elevations similar to those in Yellowstone National Park.
2. Wolf remains were found in a Holocene site of approximately 1,000–1,200 years B.P. in the Lamar Valley in the north central part of the park. Elk remains were also found in the same paleontological site.
3. Wolves have very likely been part of the mammalian assemblage of Yellowstone National Park from at least 1,000 years B.P. to the time of their extirpation in the 1930's.
4. Based on the evidence from Lamar Cave, the hypothesis that wolves were not present in the Yellowstone National Park area prior to the advent of humans of European descent was refuted.
5. Wolves can realistically be considered part of the native fauna that existed in Yellowstone National Park prior to the arrival of Europeans.

SOURCE: J. D. Varley, and W. Brewster, eds. 1992. *Wolves for Yellowstone? A report to the United States Congress*. Volume III, executive summaries. Yellowstone National Park: National Park Service, p. 19.

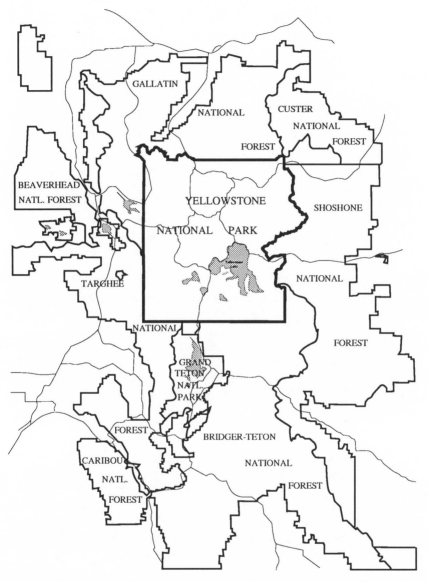

Greater Yellowstone Area, map by Renee Evanoff, Yellowstone Center for Resources

PART TWO

SECTION THREE
PREY BASES AND RELATED ISSUES

One of the central questions surrounding wolf restoration has been what effects a restored wolf population would have on the park area's other native animals, especially the ungulates—elk, deer, bison, bighorn sheep, moose, and pronghorn—but also smaller animals such as beaver. Some of these species, especially pronghorn and moose, have small or isolated populations, and an additional predator is potentially an additional stress. But sportsmen's groups and outfitters have expressed concern even about the most abundant species, such as elk and deer, which are major prey species for wolves in other areas.

The researchers addressed the prey issues from several perspectives. Chapters 18, 19, and 20 provide background on the numbers of animals of each species, while Chapters 21 through 28 offer predictions, based on computer modeling, of what the effects may be on various species and herds. Notice that predictions of this sort are typically made within a range of percentages. The most commonly heard assertion from the people involved in this sort of projection is that it may give us some good guidelines, but only the wolves will tell us for certain just what effects the wolves will have.

A few general conclusions emerge from these studies. One is that the Greater Yellowstone Ecosystem provides an exceptional prey base, one of the densest of any wildland ecosystem in the world. Another is that although the wolves may be able to reduce certain herds in size, there is no reason to expect the sort of apocalyptic havoc predicted by some opponents of wolf restoration. A third is more my own impression than anything I have read here. It is that this system of predators and prey, with its lively set of climatic and other environmental variables, is so complex that whatever effects wolves have will be hard to measure with much precision, because of the "background noise" of all the other factors that are at play.

CHAPTER 18
THE UNGULATE PREY BASE FOR
WOLVES IN YELLOWSTONE NATIONAL
PARK I: FIVE SPECIES ON THE
NORTHERN RANGE, ELK PARKWIDE

FRANCIS J. SINGER,
NATIONAL PARK SERVICE

1. Population and harvest data from the 1980's are presented for eight ungulate species that occur in Yellowstone National Park: bighorn sheep (*Ovis canadensis*), bison (*Bison bison*), elk (*Cervus elaphus*), mule deer (*Odocoileus hemionus*), moose (*Alces alces*), mountain goat (*Oreamnos americanus*) pronghorn (*Antilocapra americana*), and white-tailed deer (*Odocoileus virginianus*). Five of these ungulates, elk, mule deer, moose, white-tailed deer and pronghorn utilize Yellowstone's northern range. Data are also presented for the eight elk herds that winter, summer, or reside year-round within the park boundary including the Clarks Fork, North Fork Shoshone, Carter Mountain, Jackson, Sand Creek, Gallatin, and Madison-Firehole herds.

2. During the period 1980–1988, an average of about 17,457 (range of counts 10,226–19,000) elk wintered on Yellowstone's northern range, and about 1,900 elk wintered on three other ranges within Yellowstone National Park. Mule deer counts averaged 1,914 (1,007–2,274), pronghorn 392 (102–495), bison 433 (233–594), and bighorn sheep 195 (218–607) on the northern winter range. A minimally recovered wolf population of 10 pairs of about 100 wolves would correspond to the following mean ratios for the 1980–1988 period: 1) 1 wolf:145 ungulates on the northern winter range within the park (14,491 ungulates), 2) 1 wolf:231 ungulates for all of the northern winter range and all other park winter ranges combined (23,085 ungulates), and 3) 1 wolf:186 ungulates for all of the northern range both inside and outside Yellowstone National Park (18,555 ungulates).

3. During the period 1980–1988, the eight species of ungulates occupying Yellowstone National Park during summer exceeded 37,804 individu-

SOURCE: National Park Service. 1990. *Wolves for Yellowstone? A report to the United States Congress*. Volume I, executive summaries. Yellowstone National Park: National Park Service, pp. 5–6.

als. A mean estimated 31,136 elk from eight herds spent the summer within the park. Summering elk spent an average of 138–160 days in the park, or about 38–43% of the year. A minimally-recovered wolf population of 10 pairs or about 100 wolves would correspond to the following mean ratios for the 1980–1988 period: 1 wolf:378 ungulates during summer parkwide (37,804 ungulates). Wolf to ungulate ratios ranged from 1 wolf:96 to 1 wolf:328 ungulates in seven wolf-occupied areas elsewhere in North America. Yellowstone's summer ungulate numbers are underestimated since an unknown additional number of mule deer and moose migrate into the park each summer. Hunters also utilize the ungulate prey base, as do other predators within Yellowstone Park. These predators include grizzly bears (*Ursus arctos*), black bears (*Ursus americanus*), coyotes (*Canis latrans*), and mountain lions (*Felis concolor*). Wolf to ungulate ratios should be used for preliminary estimates only because of:

1) functional responses of wolves to changes in prey densities,
2) lags in numerical responses of wolves,
3) the role of buffer prey species, and
4) differences due to the proximity of the ungulate population to its nutrient-climate ceiling.

4. The 1988 drought reduced plant biomass and caused early plant senescence, while the 1988 fires burned portions of winter ranges in the fall. Several arctic storm fronts exacerbated winter severity. As a result, during the winter of 1988–1989, many ungulates were winterkilled and the late season harvest of elk increased. Due to both of these factors, elk population estimates for the northern winter range declined 40%; mule deer counts declined 21%, and pronghorn counts declined 25%. Recovery to at least prefire levels is necessary before gray wolves (*Canis lupus*) could be restored to Yellowstone given that the restoration process would take several years.

CHAPTER 19
THE UNGULATE PREY BASE FOR WOLVES IN YELLOWSTONE NATIONAL PARK II: ELK, MULE DEER, WHITE-TAILED DEER, MOOSE, BIGHORN SHEEP, AND MOUNTAIN GOATS IN THE AREAS ADJACENT TO THE PARK

JOHN A. MACK, FRANCIS J. SINGER,
AND MARY E. MESSAROS,
NATIONAL PARK SERVICE

ELK

Portions of eight elk (*Cervus elaphus*) herds occupy Yellowstone National Park during the summer with 25,000–31,000 elk summering in the park annually in the 1980's. Summer estimates of the eight herds total 36,000–49,000 elk; including animals that summer outside the park. Winter ranges for three herds (Carter Mountain, Jackson, and Sand Creek) are quite distant from areas gray wolves (*Canis lupus*) would likely occupy. Portions of four elk herds, totaling about 13,480–20,880 elk, winter within Yellowstone National Park. These four herds include portions of the northern herd (11,600–19,000 elk), the Gallatin herd (about 580), the Madison-Firehole (800–1,400), and the North Fork Shoshone herd (Thorofare group, about 500 elk). Annual harvests for the eight herds averaged 7,032 elk during the 1980's.

Population Trends

During the last 20 years, population estimates for eight elk herds increased dramatically by about 17,000 elk (80% increase). Population estimates for the Sand Creek and northern range herds increased about fourfold. The Jackson and Madison-Firehole herds remained relatively stable. The Gallatin herd was reduced but then increased slightly during

SOURCE: National Park Service. 1990. *Wolves for Yellowstone? A report to the United States Congress.* Volume I, executive summaries. Yellowstone National Park: National Park Service, pp. 7–18.

the last 20 years. Population estimates of elk from seven herds increased an average of 38% (range 10–67%) during the 1980's (Table 1). Only the Madison-Firehole herd declined. Currently, elk numbers for the Jackson, Carter Mountain, North Fork Shoshone, Clarks Fork, and Sand Creek herds exceed management goals.

Migrations

Seven elk herds are strongly migratory and the Madison–Firehole herd is nonmigratory. Distances between winter and summer ranges vary from 8–64 km (5–40 miles). Spring migrations to summer range for the Sand Creek herd lasted 46 days. Calving for migratory elk typically occurs enroute to summer ranges; except during springs with less snow when calving may occur on summer ranges. Calves born to elk migrating long distances may occasionally be available to wolves. Use of summer ranges in Yellowstone varied from 138 to 160 days (Table 1). Fall migrations to winter ranges averaged 19 days for the Jackson elk herd and 27 days for the Sand Creek herd. Migration patterns changed little over the past 20 years. Exceptions include (a) a higher proportion of northern range elk summer west of Yellowstone Lake (b) a former migration of about 800 elk from the Jackson herd to southwest Yellowstone National Park (Cole 1969) was reduced to 100–150 by the late 1970's (B. Smith, in prep.), (c) the proportion of Jackson elk migrating into Yellowstone National Park and the Teton Wilderness through the Togwotee Pass area has declined.

MULE DEER

North and Northwest of Yellowstone National Park

Mule deer (*Odocoileus hemionus*) populations increased dramatically north of Yellowstone National Park in Montana. Helicopter counts of mule deer on the northern range increased 78% (from 1,007 to 1,795) during the 1980's (Table 2). An increase in the harvest in the upper Gallatin suggests mule deer may have increased there also. Deer harvests averaged 726 per year, of which about 9% were white-tailed deer (*Odocoileus virginianus*). Antlerless harvests in Montana increased fivefold during the 1980's due to management efforts to reduce deer populations. A few deer from other areas in Montana may migrate into Yellowstone National Park. Two adult does marked on the Boulder River

TABLE 1. Elk population statistics for 8 elk herds located within and/or adjacent to Yellowstone National Park (YNP) during the 1980's.

Herd Unit	Estimated Population Size	Mean Harvest 1980's	Percent Population Change 1980's	Percent Herd that Summer in YNP[1]	Mean Days in YNP During Summer	Distance (kn) of Winter Range from YNP	Sex and Age Class of Harvest (%)			
							Spike Bulls	Bulls	Adult Cows	Calves
Gallatin	2,500	912	+20[2]	48	150	includes YNP	35	37	24	3
Northern	16,500–21,000	1,401	+31	90	—	includes YNP	10	23	45	22
Clarks Fork	3,000	713	+67	83	160	32	14	33	44	9
North Fork Shoshone	2,800	570	+64	78	160	8–13	21	43	32	4
Carter Mountain	3,000	658	+55	a few	—	48	25	26	39	10
Jackson	11,000	2,530	+18	28	150	48	53[3]		36	11
Sand Creek	3,800–4,900	914	+10	21	138–150	64	32	31	37[4]	—
Madison-Firehole	800–1,400	tr	decline	100	—	includes YNP	—	—	—	—
Total	43,400–49,600	7,698								
Mean			+38							

[1] Based upon movements of 386 radio collared elk.
[2] Increase occurred almost entirely in the Madison River segment of the herd.
[3] Includes spikes and bulls.
[4] Includes some calves.

Sources: Craighead et al. (1973), Houston (1982), Rudd (1982), Rudd et al. (1983), Brown (1985), Trent et al. (1985), Carlson (1987), Yorgason et al. (1987), Hurley et al. (1989), Boyce (1989), Singer (1990), B. Smith per. commun.

summered near Slough Creek campground and one doe from the Bridger Mountains summered near Madison Junction.

East of Yellowstone National Park

Mule deer population estimates east of the park increased about 77% during the 1980's to about 14,000 according to computer models (Table 2). Harvests averaged 1,599 per year during the 1980's. Some mule deer from the Clarks Fork, North Fork Shoshone, and South Fork Shoshone probably migrate into Yellowstone National Park for the summer.

South of Yellowstone National Park

About 2,000–2,600 mule deer occur in the Jackson and Targhee herd units south of Yellowstone National Park (Table 2). Population estimates have doubled during the 1980's but some of the increase may have been due to new methods of estimating herd size. Harvests averaged 685 per year during the 1980's.

West of Yellowstone National Park

Mule deer numbers for the Sand Creek herd averaged 1,599 for five trend counts during the 1980's. Few deer from the Sand Creek herd summer in Yellowstone National Park. The herd appears to be increasing.

WHITE-TAILED DEER

Occasionally white-tailed deer are seen in Yellowstone National Park during the summer, however, no winter sightings occur within the park. Healthy or expanding whitetail populations winter distant from areas wolves would likely occupy. Examples in Montana include Tom Miner Creek, Rock Creek, Yellowstone River downstream from Point of Rocks, Stillwater River, and the Boulder River. Examples in Idaho include Conant Creek and the Snake River. Therefore, wolf restoration is not predicted to affect white-tailed deer.

MOOSE

North and Northwest of Yellowstone National Park

Moose (*Alces alces*) on the northern range in Montana increased during the early 1980's with indices suggesting the population was relatively

TABLE 2. Mule deer population statistics in areas adjacent to Yellowstone National Park (YNP) during the 1980's.

Herd Unit	Estimated Population Size	Mean Harvest 1980's	Percent Population Change 1980's	Extent of Summer Migration into YNP	Distance (km) of Winter Range from YNP	Sex and Age Class of Harvest (%)		
						Adult Males	Adult Does	Fawns
North of YNP[a]								
Upper Gallatin	—	130	increasing	extensive	borders YNP	—	—	—
Northern Range	3,000	596+[b]	+78	extensive	borders YNP	—	—	—
East of YNP								
South Fork Shoshone	4,800	792	+16	probable	27	78	21	1
North Fork Shoshone	2,500	242	+108	probable	48	85	15	tr
Clarks Fork	7,000	565	+123	probable	32	80	19	1
South of YNP								
Jackson	1,200–1,600	608	+250	probable	48	66	32	2
Targhee	800–1,000	77	+82	probable	24	83	17	0
West of YNP								
Sand Creek	1,337–1,983	256	counts sporadic	limited	16–48	70	30[c]	—
Total	20,637–21,883	3,266						
Mean			+110					

[a]An unknown number of deer from the Boulder and Stillwater Rivers may migrate into YNP as evidenced by several marked individuals (Claire Simmons, Mont. Dept. Fish Wildl. and Parks, Big Timber, pers. corres.).
[b]Does not include the harvest in a small portion of Hunting District 314 which lies on the northern winter range.
[c]Includes some fawns.

Sources: Foss (1987), Kuck et al. (1989), Hurley et al. (1989), Lockman et al. (1989).

151

stable during the late 1980's (Swenson 1985a, Singer 1990). The moose population was estimated at 200 animals ten years ago (Houston 1982). A sightability–corrected estimate of population size is in progress. Average harvest north and northwest of the park was 116 moose (Table 3).

East of Yellowstone National Park

Moose populations east of the park are believed to be relatively stable except for the Thorofare area where they may have declined. An average of 44 moose were harvested annually (Table 3). The Thorofare area (bordering the southeast corner of the park) accounted for 55% of the moose harvest east of the park but permit numbers for this area were reduced during the 1980's. The Thorofare herd unit includes the best moose habitat. The North and South Forks of the Shoshone River include marginal habitat. In the Sunlight Basin herd unit losses of riparian habitat have occurred on private land.

South of Yellowstone National Park

An estimated 2,600 moose occupy the Jackson and Targhee herd units south of the park. Trend counts for the Jackson herd increased 78% during the 1980's. Some of this increase may be due to the greater efficiency of the counts. Population models suggest the Jackson and Targhee herds increased 5% and 130%, respectively, during the 1980's. Average harvest was 360 moose per year (Table 3). Moose migrate from Jackson and Targhee herd units into Yellowstone. Moose migrations from the Jackson herd into Yellowstone National Park were verified by radiotelemetry. Biologists estimate 40% of the Targhee herd summers in Yellowstone National Park.

West of Yellowstone National Park

Counts of moose west of the park in Idaho averaged 435 in the early 1980's. No counts were made between 1982 and 1987. In December 1988, during a fixed wing survey 923 moose were observed. Harvests averaged 25 and other known losses (illegal kills, road kills, etc.) averaged seven per year (Table 3). Moose occupy four winter ranges 8–56 km (5–35 miles) from Yellowstone National Park. Marking studies suggested about 1/4 of the moose from the Falls River herd (nearest the park) spent the summer in Yellowstone National Park. A few animals from the other herds may also migrate into the park.

TABLE 3. Moose population statistics in areas adjacent to Yellowstone National Park (YNP) in the 1980's.

Herd Unit	Estimated Population Size	Mean Harvest 1980's	Percent Population Change 1980's	Extent Summer Migration into YNP	Distance (km) of Winter Range from YNP	Sex of Harvest (%) Adult Males	Adult Females	Calves
North of YNP								
Northern Range[a]	200	36	stable	includes YNP	includes YNP	75	17	8
Upper Gallatin[b]	—	17	—	extensive	8–16	}		
Hebgen Lake[c]	—	63	—	extensive	includes YNP			
East of YNP								
Crandall	—	9	—	possible	—	100	—	—
Sunlight Basin	—	5	—	probable	3	100	—	—
North Fork Shoshone	—	3	—	probable	48	100	—	—
South Fork Shoshone	—	3	—	possible	48	100	—	—
Thorofare	—	24	—	includes YNP	includes YNP	100	—	—
South of YNP								
Jackson	2,300	329	greatly increased	verified[e]	—	76	21	3
Targhee	300	31	+130	probable	—	86	11	3
West of YNP								
Fall River	149[d]	25	stable	verified[f]	8	100	—	—
Big Bend	220		stable	probable	32	100	—	—
Junipers			stable	few/none	56	100	—	—
Island Park	192		stable	few/none	19	100	—	—
Total		545						

[a] Includes Montana hunt districts 316, 317, 318, 322, 328.
[b] Includes Montana hunt districts 306, 314.
[c] Includes Montana hunt districts 307, 309, 310, 361.
[d] Actual aerial counts.
[e] One radiocollared cow captured in the Buffalo Fork summered in YNP (Garvis Roby, Wyom. Dept. Game and Fish, Jackson, pers. corres.).
[f] 24% of marked moose migrated into YNP (Ritchie).

Sources: Ritchie (1978), Houston (1982), Trent et al. (1984), Alt and Foss (1987), Chu et al. (1988a), Hurley et al. (1989), Lockman et al. (1989).

BIGHORN SHEEP

North and Northwest of Yellowstone National Park

During the last 20 years, bighorn sheep (*Ovis canadensis*) populations increased in Montana north of the park. The Mount Everts–Specimen Ridge herd increase fourfold from 1965–1979. Bighorns recolonized the Cinnabar Mountain herd in 1965 and between 1967 and 1977 increased from 16 to 120 animals. All northern populations remained stable or declined slightly during the 1980's except the Mount Everts–Specimen Ridge population which had a major dieoff in 1982 due to an infectious keratoconjunctivitis epidemic. A minimum of 406 bighorn sheep are found north of the park (Table 4). Harvests declined during the 1980's and averaged 22 legal rams. Most bighorns from the Tom Miner, Cinnabar Mountain, and Mount Everts–Specimen Ridge populations migrate into Yellowstone National Park.

East of Yellowstone National Park

Bighorn sheep from the Clarks Fork, Trout Peak, Wapiti Ridge, and Younts Peak herds east of the park increased an average of 7% during the 1980's (Table 4). These four herds total about 2,900 bighorns. Annual harvests averaged 91 legal rams. All four herds range near Yellowstone National Park but only limited migrations occur into the park. Wapiti Ridge is the exception with year-round ranges found in the Thorofare-Trident area of the park.

South of Yellowstone National Park

Bighorn sheep from the Targhee and Jackson herds range south of Yellowstone National Park. Occasional bighorn sightings on Mount Sheridan (in the park) may include individuals from the Targhee herd. The Jackson herd probably ranges outside areas wolves would likely inhabit. The Targhee and Jackson herds consist of about 100 and 500 bighorns, respectively. Populations of both herds were relatively stable during the 1980's. Annual harvests averaged 17 legal rams during the 1980's (Table 4).

TABLE 4. *Bighorn population statistics in areas adjacent to Yellowstone National Park (YNP) during the 1980's.*

	Estimated Population Size	Mean Harvest 1980's	Percent Population Change 1980's	Extent Summer Migration into YNP	Distance (km) of Winter Range from YNP
North of YNP					
Spanish Peaks (301)[b]	—	4	—	none	32
Taylor–Hilgard (302)	—	3	—	none	16
Cinnabar (300)	80–130	} 8	stable	most herd	13
Mountain (300)					
Tom Miner (300)	80–100		declined	most herd	5–8
Mount Everts–Specimen Rdg. (303)	136[c]	2	declined[d]	most herd	includes YNP
Stillwater (500)	40–50	3	declined	none	48
Rosebud (501)	70–100	2	stable	possible	32
East of YNP					
Clarks Fork	500	13	stable	a few	5–8
Trout Peak	500	19	+14	a few	13
Wapiti Ridge	1,000	28	+14	includes YNP	includes YNP
Younts Peak	900	31	stable	a few	13–24
South of YNP					
Jackson	500	15	stable or slight decline	none	56
Targhee	100	2	stable	a few	24
West of YNP No nearby populations					
Totals	3,906–4,016+	130			

[a] Harvest consists of 3/4-or-larger curl rams.
[b] Montana hunting district numbers in parenthesis.
[c] Actual count of sheep from Mount Everts along the Yellowstone River to the Specimen Ridge area.
[d] Population reduced by a pinkeye epidemic in 1982 (Meagher 1982).

Sources: Houston (1982), Keating (1982, 1985a), Meagher (1982), Hurley (1985), Irby et al. (1986), Hurley et al. (1989), Lockman et al. (1989), M. Meagher pers. commun.

MOUNTAIN GOATS

Less than 100 mountain goats (*Oreamnos americana*) inhabit areas adjacent to Yellowstone where wolves might occur (Table 5). About 8–12 mountain goats actually occur within the park. Some potential for mountain goat increase exists and Laundré (1990) predicted Yellowstone National Park could possibly support 100–500 individuals.

INFORMATION NEEDS

If wolves are reintroduced into Yellowstone National Park, more information will be required for ungulate herds subjected to both wolf predation and hunter harvest. The following state-of-the-art information should be obtained for each herd unit:

1. Annual aerial trend counts.
2. Annual aerial sex and age classifications.
3. Accurate sex and age information of hunter harvest.

TABLE 5. *Nonnative mountain goat populations in areas adjacent to Yellowstone National Park (YNP) (adapted from Laundré 1990).*

Herd Unit	Estimated Population Size	Distance (km) from Yellowstone National Park
North of YNP		
Absaroka	100	0–24
Gallatin Range	a few	0–45
East of YNP		
Beartooths	150–180	19
South of YNP		
Palisades	250	80
West of YNP		
Spanish Peaks–Hebgen Lake	300	10–24
Total	800–830	

4. Corrections of trend counts for animals not seen.
5. Annually updated harvest models predicting the effects of hunter harvest and wolf predation upon hunted ungulate herds.
6. Research models predicting effects of large-scale perturbations (wolves, fires, habitat alterations and acquisitions) upon ungulate herds.

An information rating index was used to quantify the information known on ungulates in the park area (Table 6). The index takes the form:

$$I = (D/(T^*H))^*100$$

where:

I = Index in percent
D = Total number of data categories filled from all herds of a species
T = Total number of data categories
H = Total number of herds of a species

Currently, elk have the highest information rating index of 58%. Mule deer are rated at 42%, bison at 29%, bighorn sheep at 28%, and moose at only 18%. Mountain goats and white-tailed deer were not rated because they are rare and inconsequential to wolf recovery.

TABLE 6. Research and inventory during the 1980's of the ungulate herd units located within or immediately adjacent to Yellowstone National Park.

Herd Unit	Annual Aerial Count	Annual Sex/Age Classification	Cementum Annuli Aging of Harvests	Radio-telemetry Studies of Movements/Distribution	Manage. Harvest Models	Sigtability Corrected Pop. Est.	Pop. Est. by Harvest Model	Research Pop. Model(s)
Elk								
Gallatin	X	X		X	X			
Northern	X	X	'88/89	X	X	X		2 habitat; 2 wolf effects
Madison-Firehole	X	X						
Clarks Fork	X	X	X[a]	X	X		X	
North Fork Shoshone	X	X	X[a]	X	X		X	
Carter Mountain	X	X	X[a]		X		X	
Jackson	X	X		X				wolf effects
Sand Creek	X	X	1986–89	X			X	wolf effects
Bison								
Northern	X	X						wolf effects
Mary Mountain	X	X						
Pelican Valley	X	X						
Mountain Goats								
Absarokas	X	X						
Gallatin	X	X						
Palisades		X						
Moose								
Northern Range	X	X			X	In progress		
Upper Gallatin								
Hebgen Lake								
Crandall								
Sunlight Basin								
North Fork Shoshone								

South Fork Shoshone					
Thorofare	X	X		X	X
Jackson	X	X		X	X
Targhee		X		X^b	
Falls River		X	} —Not	X	
Big Bend		X	annually	X	
Junipers		X			
Island Park					
Bighorn Sheep					
Spanish Peaks	X	X		X	
Taylor–Hilgards	X	X		X	
Cinnabar Mountain	X	X			
Tom Miner	X	X			
Mount Everts-Bear Creek	X	X		X	
Stillwater		X	X		
Rosebud		X	X	X	
Clarks Fork		X	X	X	
Trout Peak		X	X		
Wapiti Ridge		X			
Younts Peak					
Jackson	X	X		X	X
Targhee	X	X		X	X
Mule Deer					
Upper Gallatin	X	Partial			
Northern Range	X	X	X	X	X
South Fork Shoshone	X	X	X	X	X
North Fork Shoshone	X	X	X	X	X
Clarks Fork/ Sunlight	X	X		X	X
Jackson	X	X			
Targhee	X	X			
Sand Creek		Prior to 1987			

a A sample of the harvest are aged.
b Movement studies by visual marking collars (Ritchie 1978).

CHAPTER 20
DISTRIBUTION OF BEAVER IN
YELLOWSTONE NATIONAL PARK, 1988–1989
SUSAN L. CONSOLO AND DONAY D. HANSON,
NATIONAL PARK SERVICE

1. Much of Yellowstone National Park is marginal beaver (*Castor canadensis*) habitat, but beaver have persisted here since the park's inception.
2. In 1988–1989, 460 km (285 miles) of riparian habitat in Yellowstone National Park was surveyed to determine current presence and distribution of beaver. Forty-three stream segments or lakes had signs of current beaver activity, and 42 reliable observations of at least 27 individual beavers were collected.
3. Beaver are expected to be a secondary prey item if wolves (*Canis lupus*) return to Yellowstone; however, they could be vulnerable to the effects of predation in portions of the park where they are sparsely distributed.
4. More information and work is needed on the following: 1) levels of beaver trapping and poaching along park boundaries; 2) comparisons of historic records of beaver with trends in climate, hydrology, and riparian vegetation; and 3) development of a long-term monitoring program for beaver presence and abundance in Yellowstone National Park.

SOURCE: National Park Service. 1990. *Wolves for Yellowstone? A report to the United States Congress*. Volume I, executive summaries. Yellowstone National Park: National Park Service, pp. 19.

CHAPTER 21
WOLF RECOVERY FOR YELLOWSTONE
NATIONAL PARK: A SIMULATION MODEL
Mark S. Boyce,
University of Wyoming

A stochastic simulation model of gray wolf (*Canis lupus*) recovery for Yellowstone National Park was developed based upon existing data on wintering ungulates in the park and extrapolations from observations of wolf predation in other areas. The following conclusions may be reached based upon the behavior of this computer model:

1. Consummation of wolf recovery will depend in part on the number of wolves released in the park. There is a moderately high probability of extinction for the initial inoculum if fewer than ten wolves are released. Approximately 30 wolves should be released if assurance of wolf recovery is desired.
2. There is no combination of management choices where wolf predation has devastating consequences to elk (*Cervus elaphus*) populations in the park. The reason is that social behavior limits wolf densities so that wolf population cannot attain total numbers high enough to depopulate the elk herd.
3. Wolf predation will cause a reduction in the number of bison (*Bison bison*), elk, moose (*Alces alces*), and mule deer (*Odocoileus hemionus*) in the park. Mean elk numbers may be expected to be 15%–25% lower if wolf recovery is accomplished. The effect of wolves on bison numbers will be less, with a reduction of only 5%–15%. Moose numbers on Yellowstone's northern range may decline if heavy hunter harvest is sustained in Montana. Mule deer may be locally susceptible to wolf predation, but the population is secure from extirpation because wintering areas exist where it is unlikely that they will suffer predation by wolves. It is assumed that wolves will have minor consequences to other vertebrates including bighorn sheep (*Ovis canadensis*) and pronghorn (*Antilocapra americana*).

Source: National Park Service. 1990. *Wolves for Yellowstone? A report to the United States Congress*. Volume I, executive summaries. Yellowstone National Park: National Park Service, pp. 21.

4. Wolf recovery in Yellowstone National Park is not contingent upon discontinuing elk hunting north of the park in Montana. However, continued hunting when combined with wolf recovery will result in smaller ungulate populations in the park. Termination of elk hunting after wolf recovery could increase the number of elk wintering in the park by 5%–15%, while reducing variation in elk numbers by 20%–30%.

5. Ungulate numbers in Yellowstone National Park undergo substantial fluctuations due to climatic variation. The variance in ungulate numbers is predicted to decrease subsequent to wolf recovery, i.e., wolves will have a stabilizing effect on ungulate population size.

6. If the recovery zone includes additional public lands surrounding Yellowstone National Park, there is a substantially higher probability that wolf recovery can be accomplished. This additional land will increase the total number of possible wolf territories in the greater Yellowstone ecosystem and thereby reduce the probability of extinction for the introduced wolf population.

7. Wolf numbers are expected to fluctuate substantially, but they should eventually reach 50–120 animals under most management scenarios. If wolves are culled at 40% or more, there is a high probability that the wolf population will be extirpated. Once established, it is expected that 15–25 wolves may leave the park each year.

8. It is impossible to precisely predict the consequences of wolf recovery in the greater Yellowstone ecosystem because vagaries of climate can have enormous consequences to any ecological process. Any realistic model of wolf recovery must be stochastic, i.e., include random variation in certain ecological variables.

9. To refine predictions of the model, research is required to obtain detailed information on plant-herbivore dynamics, on moose and deer population dynamics in the park, and on the functional response of wolf predation. Implementation of wolf recovery should be accompanied by a carefully-designed monitoring program to test predictions of this model.

CHAPTER 22
THE POTENTIAL IMPACT OF A
REINTRODUCED WOLF POPULATION
ON THE NORTHERN
YELLOWSTONE ELK HERD

EDWARD O. GARTON, ROBERT L. CRABTREE,
BRUCE B. ACKERMAN, AND GERALD WRIGHT,
UNIVERSITY OF IDAHO

There is extensive, long-term information available on the population dynamics of the northern Yellowstone elk (*Cervus elaphus*) herd. This data can be used to make fairly precise predictions of annual changes in elk population size as a result of winter severity (particularly snow hardness and depth), winter range size, the effects of fire on habitat, and hunter harvest outside the park. Information available from the literature on gray wolf (*Canis lupus*) population dynamics and feeding behavior allows one to make reasonable but less certain predictions about the effects that wolves would have on elk populations. Both sets of information were combined in a computer model to make projections of the dynamics of combined elk and wolf populations.

The projections of this model imply that the northern Yellowstone range could support about nine wolf packs, totaling approximately 75 animals. It was concluded that the elk population would decrease somewhat, but that the decrease would not exceed 10% under the conditions modeled. It was further concluded, assuming that other factors remain within normal bounds, that the relationship between predator and prey would be relatively stable and could therefore continue indefinitely.

This is an interim progress report. It is recognized that Yellowstone is a complex system which is difficult to represent with a model. Validation of the elk model, however, suggests that it captures important dynamics of the elk population during the past two decades. In addition, there will be several factors included in the final model which were excluded from

SOURCE: National Park Service. 1990. *Wolves for Yellowstone? A report to the United States Congress.* Volume I, executive summaries. Yellowstone National Park: National Park Service, pp. 23.

this draft that will afford added realism. For example, an area of concern in the wolf submodel is social class (young of the year; dominant pack members; and subdominant, nonbreeding helpers). Wolves that are not pack members (e.g., loners and dispersers) are not included in the present model but will be included in the final model. Likewise, we have not included information on the impact of wolf predation on the populations of mule deer (*Odocoileus hemionus*), bighorn sheep (*Ovis canadensis*), pronghorn (*Antilocapra americana*), moose (*Alces alces*), and bison (*Bison bison*) occupying the same winter range; this information will be evaluated in the final model.

CHAPTER 23
ESTIMATES OF THE POTENTIAL
INTERACTIONS BETWEEN HUNTER
HARVEST AND WOLF PREDATION
ON THE SAND CREEK, IDAHO, AND
GALLATIN, MONTANA, ELK POPULATIONS

DAVID J. VALES AND JAMES M. PEEK,
UNIVERSITY OF IDAHO

1. Estimates of the potential effects of gray wolf (*Canis lupus*) predation on the Gallatin, Montana, elk (*Cervus elaphus*) herd, and the Sand Creek, Idaho, elk herd are presented. These populations occupy Yellowstone National Park for a portion of the year, and are hunted when they occur outside of the park in fall and winter. Special hunts for both herds are used to control populations and prevent damage by elk on their winter ranges. We assumed that hunter harvest was accurately measured for these populations, and concluded that both population sizes are underestimated.

2. In the Gallatin elk herd, we estimated that up to 10 adult wolves could be supported at current elk population levels if hunter harvest were reduced from the 1983–1985 average of 436 elk to 300–400 elk, if harvest were restricted primarily to bulls, and if elk constituted between 75% and 90% of the wolf diet. If five wolves were present, harvest rates on antlerless (cow and calf) elk could be sustained at approximately half the current estimated level and produce a hunter harvest ranging from 350 to 450. This assumes no change from current population size. A compensatory response in the form of a 5% increase in survival of all sex/age classes of elk was of insufficient magnitude to change these conclusions.

3. If wolf predation on the Sand Creek population is confined to elk using Yellowstone National Park for 150 days, a hunter harvest of between 170 and 270 elk could be sustained on this population segment if ten wolves were present, but only by reducing cow harvest and increasing bull harvest. This harvest is similar to the 1980–1988

SOURCE: National Park Service. 1990. *Wolves for Yellowstone? A Report to the United States Congress.* Volume I, executive summaries. Yellowstone National Park: National Park Service, pp. 25

average of 219 elk. If wolves were allowed outside of southwest Yellowstone National Park, hunter harvest of Sand Creek elk could range from 640 to 770 with ten wolves on this population segment, a slight reduction from the 1980–1988 average of 738.

4. Our investigations suggested that heavily hunted elk populations can support wolves only if hunting pressure is directed primarily at bulls. We also believe these elk populations are larger than estimated, if the estimated harvest levels are reasonably accurate. It should be obvious that both predator and prey will have to be more intensively monitored than at present if both hunters and wolves are to occur together. Potential compensatory responses between the mortality factors and survival will be a major area for study if wolves again occupy this region.

CHAPTER 24
POPULATION MODELS FOR ELK,
MULE DEER, AND MOOSE ON
YELLOWSTONE'S NORTHERN
WINTER RANGE

JOHN A. MACK AND FRANCIS J. SINGER,
NATIONAL PARK SERVICE

1. With recent developments on the proposed wolf reintroduction in Yellowstone National Park, a need has arisen for estimating elk, mule deer, and moose numbers on Yellowstone's Northern Winter Range. We developed population models for these ungulates using harvest, mortality, and classification data in a PC–based software program, POP–II. Advantages of using POP–II are (1) it is relatively inexpensive, (2) it utilizes existing population trend and harvest data, and (3) it operates on a personal computer.

2. Apart from existing, provisional, sightability model estimates, we produced a second population estimate for Northern Range elk. Our estimates showed the elk population continually increased during the 1970's to a peak of about 21,000 animals in winter 1987–88. The population then declined to about 17,000 elk in winter 1989–90.

3. We produced first-time population estimates for Northern Range mule deer. We estimated the mule deer population increased during the mid-1970's to a peak of about 3,300 in late winter 1987–88. The mule deer population then declined to about 2,600 in late winter 1989–90.

4. We produced a first-time population model for Northern Range moose. Our estimates show the Northern Range moose population slowly increased from approximately 366 animals in winter 1975–76 to 432 in winter 1989–90.

5. POP–II models are flexible and can be easily updated so managers can vary mortality and recruitment according to several scenarios and predict the possible outcomes to the population in question. Using the

SOURCE: J. D. Varley and W. Brewster, eds. 1992. *Wolves for Yellowstone? A Report to the United States Congress.* Volume III, executive summary. Yellowstone National Park: National Park Service, p. 39.

POP–II models we described, wildlife managers can predict what effects hunter harvests, reproduction, and additional mortality (i.e., wolf predation) may have on elk, mule deer, and moose populations inhabiting Yellowstone's Northern Range.

CHAPTER 25
PREDICTED EFFECTS OF WOLF
PREDATION ON NORTHERN RANGE
ELK, MULE DEER, AND MOOSE
USING POP-II MODELS

JOHN A. MACK AND FRANCIS J. SINGER,
NATIONAL PARK SERVICE

1. Elk, mule deer, and moose population models were used to predict some effects a wolf reintroduction in Yellowstone National Park (YNP) may have on these 3 ungulate populations associated with Yellowstone's Northern Winter Range. We evaluated the effects of wolf predation plus observed human harvests on elk, mule deer, and moose. We also estimated the effects of wolf predation and lowered human harvests on the 3 big game species.

2. For 78 or 100 wolves inhabiting the Northern Range, our models suggested the antlerless elk harvest would have to be reduced 27% to allow for an increasing elk population. Likewise, antlerless mule deer and antlerless moose harvests would have to be reduced 50% or eliminated to sustain a recovered wolf population and maintain mule deer and moose populations above or near present levels.

3. Our models did not include functional and density-dependent predator-prey responses. We did not speculate on how or to what degree these predator–prey responses may occur, but if they did, Northern Range ungulate populations may be larger than we estimated and hunter opportunities and harvests may not be affected to the degree proposed in our models. Our estimates concerning the effects of wolf predation on Northern Range mule deer may be inaccurate because observed data are lacking for this species. However, if wolves establish on Yellowstone's Northern Range, we recommend a conservative antlerless deer harvest, at least until more mule deer population data can be gathered and analyzed for this herd. Existing population data were limited for our provisional

SOURCE: J. D. Varley, and W. Brewster, eds. 1992. *Wolves for Yellowstone? A report to the United States Congress.* Volume III, executive summaries. Yellowstone National Park: National Park Service, pp. 41–43.

moose model. We suggest obtaining better information on moose to more accurately estimate wolf predation effects on this population.

4. To investigate wolf effects on elk, mule deer, and moose, we assumed 12 wolves were hypothetically reintroduced in YNP in 1980 and the modeled wolf population rapidly increased. Two wolf population models, having either a maximum of 78 or 100 wolves, were used to determine a range of effects on the ungulate populations. Each wolf population was limited to Yellowstone's Northern Range and preyed only on wild ungulates.

5. For each wolf population, we used 3 scenarios, having different wolf predation rates (9, 12, and 15 ungulates/wolf/year), to predict the range of effects wolf predation may have had on elk, mule deer, and moose during the 1980's. We estimated numbers of elk, mule deer, and moose killed by wolves according to relative ungulate abundance, ungulate vulnerability to wolf predation, and age/sex class (young, females, and males) vulnerability to wolf predation.

6. For elk, we developed 2 population models, a Prefire Scenario and a Postfire Scenario. The Prefire Scenario ran from 1975–89 and estimated elk numbers using observed elk classification and hunter harvest data. During the 1980's, high antlerless elk harvests were used to reduce the Northern Range elk population, but even with these antlerless harvests, we estimated the Prefire Scenario elk population increased from 16,000 in 1980 to 21,000 in winter 1987–88 and then, because of the severe drought, fires, and high hunter harvest in 1988, declined to about 17,000 in 1989. The Postfire Scenario ran from 1975 to 1994. We incorporated into this model the positive reproductive benefits the 1988 fires were expected to have on the elk population. The model used observed harvest and classification data for years 1975–89. Average hunter harvest data from the late 1980's was used for the 1990–94 harvests. Compared to reproduction observed in the late 1980's, higher reproduction (26–36 calves/100 cows) was used for 1990–94. Postfire Scenario elk population estimates were the same as the Prefire Scenario up to 1989. For the Postfire Scenario elk numbers increased from about 17,000 in 1990 to 21,000 in 1994.

7. Our mule deer and moose models, without wolves, used observed hunter harvest and classification data to estimate population numbers from 1975–89. During the 1980's, we estimated mule deer increased to about 3,200 in 1988 and then declined to 2,600 in 1989. Throughout the 1980's we estimated the moose population remained stable or increased slightly to about 400 animals.

8. The Northern Range elk population appeared unable to sustain 78 wolves and the observed hunter harvests of the 1980's. Using ob-

served hunter harvests, Prefire Scenario elk numbers were 27–43% smaller in 1989 with 78 wolves than when wolves were absent. With 78 wolves and the human antlerless elk harvests reduced 27%, the estimated elk population was 5–18% smaller in 1989 compared to the elk population without wolves.

9. The Northern Range elk population also could not sustain 100 wolves and the observed hunter harvests of the 1980's. With observed hunter harvests and 100 wolves, Prefire Scenario elk numbers were 31–51% smaller in 1989 compared to the elk population without wolves. When the human antlerless elk harvests were reduced 27%, the estimated elk population was 11–30% smaller compared to population estimates without wolves.

10. With 78 wolves and the human antlerless elk harvests reduced 27%, Postfire Scenario elk population estimates were 5% (20,287 elk) to 41% (12,561 elk) lower in 1994 than population estimates without wolves. With 100 wolves and the antlerless elk harvests reduced 27%, the estimated elk population increased to about 17,000 under the first wolf-predation-rate scenario of 9 ungulates/wolf/year, remained relatively stable at about 14,000 elk under the second scenario of 12 ungulates/wolf/year, and rapidly declined in the 1990's under the third scenario of 15 ungulates/wolf/year.

11. The only condition in which our modeled mule deer population was able to support wolf predation under the 3 predation rate scenarios was when the human antlerless harvest was eliminated. For these wolf predation and hunter harvest scenarios, the modeled mule deer population ranged from 0 to 36% larger in 1989 compared to the deer population estimates with observed hunter harvests and no wolf predation.

12. The modeled moose population could not sustain observed human harvests of the 1980's and wolf predation. For 78 wolves and human bull and cow moose harvests reduced 50%, the modeled moose population was 5% smaller to 12% larger compared to moose population estimates without wolves. Using the same reduced moose harvests and having 100 wolves, the moose population estimates ranged from 13% smaller to 7% larger compared to no wolf predation. When the high bull harvests of the 1980's were maintained in our models but the cow harvests were eliminated, the modeled moose populations with wolf predation were nearly the same as moose population estimates having wolf predation and observed hunter harvests reduced 50%.

CHAPTER 26
WOLVES IN YELLOWSTONE, JACKSON
HOLE, AND THE NORTH FORK OF THE
SHOSHONE RIVER: SIMULATING
UNGULATE CONSEQUENCES
OF WOLF RECOVERY

MARK S. BOYCE AND JEAN-MICHEL GAILLARD,
UNIVERSITY OF WYOMING

This report summarizes the results of an expansion of the wolf–ungulate simulation model for Yellowstone National Park, conducted by M. S. Boyce in 1990, to encompass Jackson Hole and areas along the North Fork of the Shoshone River in northwestern Wyoming. In addition, the revised program enlists some new mathematical structures, e.g., a different functional response. The following conclusions may be reached based upon the behavior of this spatially explicit computer model:

1. Expanding the model to encompass areas outside the park has the effect of stabilizing fluctuations in wolf and ungulate numbers, and increasing the probability for long-term persistence of a wolf population.
2. A revised functional response equation has the effect of increasing the consequences of wolf predation on moose and mule deer wintering in Yellowstone National Park. Yet, as in the original model, there is no combination of management choices where wolf predation has devastating consequences to ungulate populations in the Greater Yellowstone Ecosystem.
3. Wolf predation under the most likely default assumptions is predicted to cause a reduction in the number of elk, bison, mule deer, and moose in the Greater Yellowstone Ecosystem. Mean elk numbers may be expected to be 5–20% lower if wolf recovery is accomplished. Fewer bison are expected to be killed by wolves, but the proportionate consequences to population size may be comparable to the effect of

SOURCE: J. D. Varley and W. Brewster, eds. 1992. *Wolves for Yellowstone? A Report to the United States Congress.* Volume III, executive summaries. Yellowstone National Park: National Park Service, pp. 45–46.

predation on elk. Moose and mule deer may be affected even more than elk in certain localities. We assume that wolves will have minor consequences to other vertebrates including bighorn sheep and pronghorns.

4. Wolf recovery in the Greater Yellowstone Ecosystem is not contingent upon discontinuing hunting for ungulates in areas near the parks. However, continued hunting when combined with wolf recovery will result in smaller ungulate populations. Elimination of elk hunting is not viewed as a viable option in Jackson Hole because of winter feeding programs which nearly eliminate over-winter mortality. Reduced moose hunting in Montana may be necessary to sustain wintering moose populations on the Northern Range.

5. Wolf recovery should reduce the need to cull elk in Grand Teton National Park.

6. Wolf numbers are expected to fluctuate substantially, but should eventually reach 50–170 animals, with population size largely depending upon management actions outside of the parks. Wolf populations along the North Fork of the Shoshone River may not be secure, but are expected to be quickly repopulated by dispersers from Yellowstone should they be locally extirpated.

7. To refine predictions of the model, research is needed to obtain detailed information on plant-herbivore dynamics, moose and deer populations, seasonal dynamics, and the functional response of wolf predation. Implementation of wolf recovery should be accompanied by a carefully designed monitoring program.

CHAPTER 27
ESTIMATING THE SIZE OF THE
NORTHERN YELLOWSTONE ELK HERD
FROM FIXED–WING AIRCRAFT
AND HELICOPTER SURVEYS—
A PROGRESS REPORT

Francis J. Singer,
National Park Service, and
Edward O. Garton, University of Idaho

1. Recent studies in western North America suggest visibility of elk is only 0.59–0.66 during aerial surveys. Therefore, population models of the predicted effects of a wolf recovery into Yellowstone National Park based upon uncorrected counts may provide biased prediction of wolf effects. The purpose of this investigation was to estimate the numbers of elk actually missed during aerial counts and to compare the efficiency of fixed-wing versus helicopter counts.

2. Helicopter surveys were 7% more efficient for observing elk than were fixed-wing surveys. The probability of detecting radiocollared elk was 0.75 during early winter and 0.50 during late winter from fixed-wing aircraft. The probability of detection from helicopter was 0.83 during early winter and 0.70 during late winter.

3. Sightability of elk from aircraft in Yellowstone's Northern Range was the highest yet reported from the western United States, apparently because of the extensive open grasslands and large concentrations of elk.

4. Multivariate step-wise logistic regression analysis of sightability variables is yet to be completed. A final report is expected during the fall of 1992.

Source: J. D. Varley and W. Brewster, eds. 1992. *Wolves for Yellowstone? A report to the United States Congress*. Volume III, executive summaries. Yellowstone National Park: National Park Service, p. 47.

CHAPTER 28
POTENTIAL IMPACTS OF YELLOWSTONE
WOLVES ON CLARKS FORK ELK HERD
EDWARD O. GARTON, ROBERT L. CRABTREE,
BRUCE B. ACKERMAN, AND GERALD WRIGHT,
UNIVERSITY OF IDAHO

1. Simulation modelling implies that approximately 3 wolf packs would occupy the summer range of the Clarks Fork elk herd within Yellowstone National Park (YNP).
2. These packs could remain resident within YNP or become migratory moving outside of YNP to occupy the winter range of the Clarks Fork elk herd during winter.
3. The simulated elk population remained stable under the combined influence of wolf predation and hunter harvest at current levels.
4. A resident wolf population would reduce numbers and annual harvest of the Clarks Fork elk herd by approximately 3%.
5. A migratory wolf population would reduce numbers and annual harvest of the Clarks Fork elk herd by approximately 15%.

SOURCE: J. D. Varley and W. Brewster, eds. 1992. *Wolves for Yellowstone? A report to the United States Congress.* Volume III, executive summaries. Yellowstone National Park: National Park Service, p. 49.

PART TWO

SECTION FOUR
OTHER EFFECTS OF WOLF
REINTRODUCTION

Throughout the debates over wolf restoration, concerns were expressed about numerous other aspects of wolf activity in and near Yellowstone National Park. The park, for example, is already home to a very famous threatened species, the grizzly bear. What would the addition of a new and powerful predator mean to the future of the grizzly bear population? The national forests and private lands around Yellowstone National Park are grazed by a variety of livestock, and the lore of the west is full of stock-killing wolves. How would a restored wolf population affect livestock? Wolves, like all wild animals, are susceptible to a variety of diseases, and regional lore included fears that rabies, brucellosis, and tuberculosis could be spread by wolves. Yellowstone is home to a wide variety of smaller mammals, both carnivores and herbivores. What would wolves mean for them? The chapters in this section address these and other questions.

These studies went a long way toward calming at least some fears about unknown aspects of wolf restoration. By taking the concerns past the level of vague fear and analyzing them, based on a wide experience by wolf managers elsewhere, these investigators were able to provide some reasonable context for the issues. The most notable of these issues may have been the fear of widespread destruction of livestock by wolves; a review of wolf-livestock interactions in other areas indicated that some concern was justified, because some wolves may kill livestock, but that widespread livestock depredation was not going to occur.

CHAPTER 29
SOME PREDICTIONS CONCERNING
A WOLF RECOVERY INTO YELLOWSTONE
NATIONAL PARK: HOW WOLF RECOVERY
MAY AFFECT PARK VISITORS, UNGULATES,
AND OTHER PREDATORS

FRANCIS J. SINGER,
NATIONAL PARK SERVICE

1. It is predicted that 7–9 grey wolf (*Canis lupus*) packs with fixed territories could occupy Yellowstone's northern winter range; another 1–2 packs could occupy the park's other winter ranges, and another 3–4 packs could be supported, but only if the latter packs were migratory or semimigratory. Overall, the park could support 8–11 wolf packs and portions of the territories of another 3–4 packs.

2. Opportunity for park visitors to view wild ungulates could decline slightly after wolf reoccupation of Yellowstone National Park, but viewing of habituated elk (*Cervus elaphus*), those that frequent developed areas, may increase since wolves will avoid these areas. Even though adult female ungulates with young change their habits due to wolf presence, they are typically shy and infrequently observed by park visitors even in the absence of wolves. Any changes in the distribution or behavior of other adult ungulates and older young are predicted to be minor.

3. The average relative abundance of ungulates on Yellowstone's northern range during the 1980's was 100 elk:10 mule deer (*Odocoileus hemionus*):2 bison (*Bison bison*):2 pronghorn (*Antilocapra americana*):1 bighorn sheep (*Ovis canadensis*):1 moose (*Alces alces*). Published studies indicate that the most to least vulnerable ungulates during winter would be pronghorn > bighorn sheep > mule deer > white-tailed deer > elk > bison > moose. However, since few mule deer, pronghorn or white-tailed deer winter within the park, and bighorns occupy steep rocky escape terrain, wolves are predicted to kill ungulates during

SOURCE: National Park Service. 1990. *Wolves for Yellowstone? A report to the United States Congress*. Volume I, executive summaries. Yellowstone National Park: National Park Service, pp. 27–28.

winter on the northern range as follows: elk > bison > mule deer > moose > pronghorn > bighorn sheep.

4. Ungulates on three other ranges within Yellowstone National Park occur in a ratio of about 100 bison:95 elk:5 moose:1 mule deer. Wolves are predicted to kill ungulates during winter on these other ranges in the following order: elk ~ = bison > moose > mule deer.

5. Young ungulates of all species are vulnerable to wolves during summer. Parkwide ungulate ratios during summer are 100 elk:16+ mule deer:8 bison:3+ moose:3 bighorn sheep:1 pronghorn:<1 white-tailed deer or mountain goat (*Oreamnos americanus*). Wolves are predicted to kill ungulates during summer in the order of most to least: elk > mule deer > bison > moose > bighorn sheep > pronghorn > mountain goat.

6. Wolves may limit the numbers of a more vulnerable, less abundant prey species when wolf numbers are set by a less vulnerable, more abundant prey species. This potential exists for mule deer, pronghorns, and bighorn sheep. Each of these species is substantially less abundant than elk and is more vulnerable to wolves than elk in snow. However, these more vulnerable species are not predicted to be greatly reduced by wolves since mule deer and pronghorn winter near or north of Gardiner, Montana, where sustained pack activity by wolves is unlikely, and bighorn sheep are relatively secure from wolves near steep, cliffy terrain. Moose are of special concern since they are already harvested by humans at high levels on the northern range. White-tailed deer status should change little since whitetails generally occupy areas distant from likely wolf occupation areas. Bison on the northern range should be less vulnerable than other ungulates, but more vulnerable on the Mary Mountain and Pelican winter ranges due to deeper snows in these areas.

7. Yellowstone Park ungulates that winter in scattered thermal areas of a few hectares in size on the plateaus of the park's interior could be vulnerable to wolves since wolves could chase the ungulates into adjacent deep snows. Conversely, ungulates in the larger, relatively snow-free thermal areas should not be as vulnerable to wolves, since they will have more opportunity to outrun wolves.

8. Yellowstone Park's coyotes (*Canis latrans*) will probably decline and red fox (*Vulpes vulpes*) will probably increase after wolf recovery. Black bears (*Ursus americanus*) and wolves usurp carcasses from each other, and wolves occasionally prey upon black bears, but no published information suggests either species would be significantly affected at the population level. Wolverines (*Gulo gulo*) can be killed by wolves, but they can also escape from wolves by climbing trees which are numerous in Yellowstone Park. Little published information was available on possible competition between wolves and wolverines at

carcasses. Minor effects upon grizzly bears (*Ursus arctos*) and mountain lions (*Felis concolor*) are predicted.

9. Humans disrupt activity at wolf dens which can cause wolves to move their pups. To avoid this disturbance many parks close the area surrounding wolf dens to human activity. Closures around wolf den sites tend to be smaller in forested habitats than in open areas. Closures vary from 2.6 km^2 in Voyageurs National Park and 13 km^2 in Isle Royale National Park (forested areas) to 41 km^2 in the tundra habitat of Denali National Park. In Yellowstone, den site closures will probably vary from no additional measures for dens in remote forested areas or in existing bear management zones to small closures at more accessible den sites.

CHAPTER 30
POSSIBLE EFFECTS OF A RESTORED
WOLF POPULATION ON GRIZZLY
BEARS IN THE YELLOWSTONE AREA

CHRISTOPHER W. SERVHEEN,
U.S. FISH AND WILDLIFE SERVICE, AND
RICHARD R. KNIGHT,
INTERAGENCY GRIZZLY BEAR STUDY TEAM

Brown bears (*Ursus arctos*) and gray wolves (*Canis lupus*) coexist throughout much of North America and Eurasia. A review of available literature on wolves and brown bears from the limitation of brown bear numbers by wolves or reports of limitation of wolf numbers by brown bears. Letters were sent to numerous scientists in the Soviet Union and Europe to solicit any opinions or unpublished information of wolf–brown bear interactions. None of those who responded indicated that wolves could pose a significant threat to brown bear populations. Reports of observed wolf–grizzly bear interactions from Alaska were summarized and did not indicate and significant detriment to either species due to interactions. In general, information indicates that the two species will interact over food sources but at few other occasions. Most interactions are characterized by mutual avoidance. Few instances of direct mortality to either species as a result of interactions are available.

In the Yellowstone area, wolves will change the numbers and distribution of ungulates that are used by grizzly bears as food. The significance of this change is speculative at this time. It is likely that any change to the ungulate population as a result of wolves would be gradual and grizzly bears would successfully adapt to this change over time. This change in ungulate numbers and distribution would be the most important impact of an increasing wolf population to grizzly bears in the Yellowstone area. It seems reasonable to assume that grizzly bears would adapt to these changes with little detrimental effect to grizzly numbers or survival.

SOURCE: National Park Service. 1990. *Wolves for Yellowstone? A report to the United States Congress*. Volume I, executive summaries. Yellowstone National Park: National Park Service, p. 29.

CHAPTER 31
EFFECTS OF RESTORING WOLVES ON YELLOWSTONE AREA BIG GAME AND GRIZZLY BEARS: OPINIONS OF FIFTEEN NORTH AMERICAN EXPERTS

Barbara Koth, David W. Lime,
Jonathan Vlaming, Cooperative Park
Studies Unit, University of Minnesota

The opinions of 15 North American gray wolf (*Canis lupus*) and wolf–prey researchers known for their studies of the interrelations among wolves, grizzly bears (*Ursus arctos*) and prey species were examined. Panelists addressed questions relating to the potential effects of a reintroduction of wolves to Yellowstone National Park on 1) wolf prey in the park, 2) the population of Yellowstone grizzly bears, and 3) big game hunting in areas surrounding the park.

A modified Delphi technique was used to conduct the study. This approach called for questions to be answered by experts followed by a collation of responses by project coordinators. Subsequent follow-up questionnaires were sent to the experts for further inquiry. Between late September and late December 1989, panelists were contacted three times and asked both general and specific questions about the issues. With each successive contact, their opinions were compiled, and new or more probing questions were addressed. The end product represented the panelists' best judgments on a variety of concerns and topics regarding the reintroduction of wolves to Yellowstone National Park. The following are the most salient results of their deliberations.

Major Findings:

1) Panelists unanimously agreed that wolves were part of the original Yellowstone National Park ecosystem.

Source: National Park Service. 1990. *Wolves for Yellowstone? A report to the United States Congress.* Volume I, executive summaries. Yellowstone National Park: National Park Service, pp. 31–36.

2) The core wolf population should be centered in Yellowstone National Park, but the application of artificial or political boundaries might not sustain recovery levels.

3) A viable wolf population of about a dozen wolf packs that spend the majority of their time within Yellowstone National Park seemed realistic after the population has stabilized (within 20 years after reintroduction).

4) If wolves are reintroduced, extinction of any prey species, elk (*Cervus elaphus*), mule deer (*Odocoileus hemionus*), moose (*Alces alces*), bison (*Bison bison*), pronghorn (*Antilocapra americana*), bighorn sheep (*Ovis canadensis*), and mountain goats (*Oreamnos americanus*) was thought to be extremely unlikely.

5) There should be relatively minor changes in prey species' behavior and distribution if wolves were reintroduced to Yellowstone National Park.

6) Elk and mule deer should be the primary prey for wolves—elk throughout the year, mule deer in summer. Other prey species should be relatively minor food sources.

7) Panelists unanimously agreed that wolves and grizzly bears can coexist. However, there were differing opinions about specific impacts of wolf reintroduction on grizzly bears, particularly whether wolf predation should provide grizzly bears with more protein from wolf–killed carcasses and a more consistent carrion supply. All panelists did call the overall impact on grizzly bears "slight" or "neutral."

8) Reduced big game hunting levels should not be an automatic requirement if wolves were restored to the greater Yellowstone ecosystem. Reduced hunting levels should be implemented only when necessary and then only in conjunction with wolf control measures and other prey population management tools.

9) More research is needed to better understand the interrelations among wolves, grizzly bears, prey species, and big game hunting in areas surrounding the park.

More specific findings addressed the following issues:

1) wolf numbers, 2) wolf movements, 3) general impacts of wolves on prey species, 4) specific impacts of wolves on large ungulates—elk, mule deer, moose, bison, pronghorn, bighorn sheep, and mountain goats, 5) impacts of wolves on grizzly bears, and 6) effects of reintroduced wolves on big game hunting in areas outside Yellowstone National Park.

Wolf Numbers:

1) Panelists estimated a mean of 13 wolf packs would spend the majority of their time in Yellowstone National Park after the wolf population was established.
2) To most panelists, a large number of packs (over 25) seemed unlikely.
3) Panelists estimated a mean pack size of seven to ten individuals.
4) Panelists estimated an average total in–park wolf population of 150 individuals would spend the majority of their time in Yellowstone National Park.
5) Panelists estimated five to ten additional packs would attempt to establish territories located primarily outside Yellowstone National Park.

Wolf Movements:

1) Wolves have the potential to locate nearly anywhere in Yellow-stone National Park, but the most likely area of wolf colonization would be in the north-central region; some areas would be lightly occupied, if at all.
2) A stable territorial mosaic of wolf packs should develop within 20 years after reintroduction. Territories should change in response to changing prey distributions, prey abundance, and pack size and dominance.
3) In summer, most wolves should be within park boundaries and wolf activity should concentrate around den sites and should take advantage of calving by mule deer, elk, bison, and moose within Yellowstone National Park.
4) In winter, wolf packs should hunt mainly in areas of low elevation where ungulates, particularly elk, aggregate.
5) A consensus could not be reached concerning when packs might leave the winter range, how often packs would visit major prey areas within their territories in winter, and whether winter hunting would commonly occur as a pack or periodically as a subunit of the pack.

General Impacts of Wolves on Ungulates:

1) Ungulate species, in the order of most to least vulnerable, were as follows: elk, mule deer, moose, bison, pronghorn, bighorn sheep, and mountain goats.
2) Elk were expected to be the primary prey species for wolves in all seasons. Secondary prey would be mule deer, moose, and bison.
3) Most distribution changes of prey populations should be relatively local changes in animal movements, implying little geographical and behavioral distribution impacts.

Impacts of Wolves on Elk:

1) Elk were expected to be the primary prey for wolves in all seasons.
2) There should be moderate or little change in elk behavior and distribution if wolves were reintroduced to Yellowstone National Park.
3) Wolf predation should induce an initial decline in elk numbers that should reduce nutritional stress and improve reproduction.
4) Ten years after wolf reintroduction, assuming a wolf population of ten packs of ten wolves each, a reduction in the elk population of less than 20% was expected.

Impacts of Wolves on Mule Deer:

l) Mule deer might be a primary prey for wolves during the summer and a secondary prey for the rest of the year.
2) There should be moderate or little change in mule deer behavior and distribution if wolves were reintroduced to Yellowstone National Park.
3) Ten years after wolf reintroduction, assuming a stable wolf population of ten wolf packs of ten wolves each, a reduction in the mule deer population of between 20% and 30% was expected.

Impacts of Wolves on Moose:

1) Moose were considered potential prey for wolves, although panelists felt there was not enough information to formulate an opinion on whether moose would provide an important prey base for wolves.
2) There should be moderate or little change in moose behavior and distribution if wolves were reintroduced to Yellowstone National Park.
3) Ten years after wolf reintroduction, assuming a stable wolf population of ten wolf packs of ten wolves each, a reduction in the moose population of between 10% and 15% was expected.

Impacts of Wolves on Bison:

1) Panelists held widely varying opinions about the level of utilization of bison as wolf prey. Wolves might prey on bison only occasionally, but bison also had the potential to be major prey depending upon a variety of factors such as type of wolf reintroduction and hunting skills developed over time.
2) There should be little or no change in bison behavior and distribution if wolves were reintroduced to Yellowstone National Park.
3) Ten years after wolf reintroduction, assuming a stable wolf population

of ten wolf packs of ten wolves each, a reduction in the bison population of less than 20% was expected.

Impacts of Wolves on Pronghorn, Bighorn Sheep, and Mountain Goats:

1) Pronghorn, bighorn sheep, and mountain goats would be available prey for wolves but would not likely be an important food source for them.

Impacts on Grizzly Bears:

1) Wolves would provide some carrion for grizzly bears, and some occasional wolf– bear conflicts might arise during competition for carcasses. Direct interspecies killing should be insignificant.
2) Grizzly bear distribution and behavior were not expected to change if wolves were reintroduced to Yellowstone National Park.
3) The omnivorous food habits of grizzly bears mean that grizzly bear densities are not strongly linked to ungulate densities.

Impacts of Wolves on Big Game Hunting in Areas Surrounding the Park:

1) Panelists were evenly split over whether reduced hunting levels would be a necessary concession that comes with wolf restoration.
2) Elk harvest levels might be reduced after wolf restoration, but, at present, elk are generally hunted below maximum sustained yield. No consensus was reached regarding mule deer, bison, and moose hunting. Projections indicated that harvest levels for pronghorn, bighorn sheep, and mountain goats would not need to be reduced.
3) According to the majority of panelists, sport hunting for any prey species should not have to be eliminated, even at higher pack levels (25 packs or more).
4) All panelists agreed that it cannot be assumed that a reduction in hunting would simply make up for wolf kills in an additive manner, because sport hunting and predation target different animals.
5) Hunting and wolf population control must be discussed as integrated factors. The objective outside Yellowstone National Park should be wolf population control, not eradication.

CHAPTER 32
LIVESTOCK GRAZING ON NATIONAL FORESTS AND NATIONAL PARKS WITHIN THE GREATER YELLOWSTONE AREA

JOHN A. MACK, WAYNE G. BREWSTER, AND
NORMAN A. BISHOP,
NATIONAL PARK SERVICE

1. The location, size, distribution, numbers and type of livestock, and grazing season were compiled and evaluated for the 1991 grazing season for livestock grazing allotments on Grand Teton National Park and national forests adjacent to Yellowstone National Park (YNP). Both Geographical Information System and descriptive data sets were developed for managers to use in defining livestock grazing programs or evaluating alternatives regarding wolf management.

2. Of 440 grazing allotments, 392 (89%) are active and they comprise 16,531 km² (45%) of the total national forest area of approximately 36,825 km². Fifty percent of all allotments were on the Bridger-Teton and Targhee National Forests.

3. A total of 77,362 cattle, 105,051 sheep, and 1,272 horses were authorized for grazing on national forests and Grand Teton National Park. Forty–two percent of the cattle were grazed on the Bridger-Teton National Forest and 49% of the sheep were grazed on the Targhee National Forest. The Bridger-Teton and Targhee National Forests account for 90% of all sheep grazed in the Yellowstone area.

4. Livestock were authorized to graze on allotments an average of 98 days, varying from 84 to 129 days. Median dates livestock were allowed on national forest allotments ranged from 25 June to 1 July. Median dates livestock were removed from allotments ranged from 15 September to 25 October. For most national forests, livestock were removed from allotments during the second or third week in October.

SOURCE: J. D. Varley and W. Brewster, eds. 1992. *Wolves for Yellowstone? A report to the United States Congress*. Volume III, executive summaries. Yellowstone National Park: National Park Service, p. 53.

5. Nearly all active grazing allotments are not adjacent to the YNP boundary. Livestock grazing occurs closest to YNP on the northwestern and southwestern corners of the park. Grazing allotments are most distant from the north, east, and south boundaries of YNP. Allotments ranged from 0 to 59.7 km and averaged from 16.6 to 36.2 km from the park boundary in the 4 cardinal directions (north, east, south, and west).

6. Large areas within the study area, including Yellowstone and Grand Teton National Parks, have no domestic livestock grazing and comprise approximately 30,659 km^2.

CHAPTER 33
A REVIEW OF WOLF DEPREDATION
ON LIVESTOCK AND IMPLICATIONS
FOR THE YELLOWSTONE AREA

JOHN A. MACK AND WAYNE G. BREWSTER,
NATIONAL PARK SERVICE,
AND STEVEN H. FRITTS,
U.S. FISH AND WILDLIFE SERVICE

1. We summarized data regarding wolf depredation on domestic live-
    stock in northwestern Montana, Minnesota, and Alberta and British
    Columbia, Canada. Data collected (for as many as 17 years) included
    number of cattle and sheep (young and adults) verified as wolf dep-
    redations, livestock numbers in wolf range, and wolf population
    numbers. We attempted to use this data to develop predictive mod-
    els of livestock losses on public lands surrounding Yellowstone Na-
    tional Park.

2. Calves comprised between 68% and 85% of wolf depredation on
    cattle, possibly because they are smaller than adults. Annual depre-
    dation on cattle averaged 4 adults and 23 calves in Minnesota, 76
    adults and 159 calves in Alberta, and 44 adults and 93 calves in
    British Columbia. In northwestern Montana, wolf depredation aver-
    aged 3 cattle annually. Annual wolf depredation rates (losses/1,000
    livestock available) on cattle averaged 0.12/1,000 in Minnesota, 0.87/
    1,000 in Alberta, 0.23/1,000 in British Columbia, and 0.04/1,000 in
    northwestern Montana.

3. Wolf depredation on sheep annually averaged 50 in Minnesota, 33 in
    Alberta, and 26 in British Columbia. An average of 2 sheep were lost
    to wolves annually in northwestern Montana. For the data provided,
    wolves did not select for lambs over adult sheep in depredation
    situations. Sheep losses versus sheep available to wolf depredation
    averaged 2.37/1,000 in Minnesota and 0.54/1,000 in British Colum-
    bia and averaged 5–10 times higher than for cattle. We could not
    calculate sheep depredation rates in Alberta because we could not

SOURCE: J. D. Varley and W. Brewster, eds. 1992. *Wolves for Yellowstone? A
report to the United States Congress.* Volume III, executive summaries.
Yellowstone National Park: National Park Service, pp. 55–56.

obtain estimates of sheep numbers in wolf range. In northwestern Montana, wolf depredation on sheep averaged 0.21/1,000 available.

4. Wolf numbers in Minnesota, Alberta, and British Columbia are several times larger than what others believe could inhabit Yellowstone National Park or the surrounding area. Larger wolf populations may have more individuals preying on livestock. In most areas where wolves and livestock live together, wolf numbers were unavailable or crudely estimated, and we were unable to investigate whether livestock losses were related to wolf numbers. In one small experimental study area (152 km²) on the Simonette River in Alberta, wolf numbers were accurately known but too few years data existed to predict a relationship between wolf numbers and livestock losses (additionally, wolf control was not conducted during the first 4 of this 6 year study).

5. Using data from Minnesota, we found no significant relationships between cattle or sheep losses and their respective availability. Cattle and sheep losses were also not related to total land area of farms within wolf range. Lack of a significant loss-availability relationship for the Minnesota data may suggest that depredation rates (losses/ 1,000 available) from other areas should not be used to predict numbers of possible livestock losses on public lands in the Yellowstone area. However, the data do suggest livestock losses will likely be relatively low on a large scale.

6. Wolf control in northwestern Montana, Minnesota, Alberta, and British Columbia likely contributed to the relatively low incidence of wolf depredation on livestock. However, individual livestock producers may experience persistent or large losses and these potential losses support having responsive and effective wolf control strategies.

7. In addition to lethal control measures, wolf control plans can include non-lethal strategies such as improved animal husbandry or livestock guarding dogs (although guarding dog effectiveness may be limited in deterring wolf depredations). From our review, wolf depredation on livestock was highly variable both among years and among areas experiencing depredations. Wolf control and improved animal husbandry can both work directly and indirectly in reducing the incidence of wolf depredation on livestock.

CHAPTER 34
THE POTENTIAL ROLE OF RABIES
IN RELATION TO POSSIBLE YELLOWSTONE
WOLF POPULATIONS
MARK R. JOHNSON, NATIONAL PARK SERVICE

1. Rabies in wolves was of significant concern in Europe during the seventeenth and eighteenth centuries. Rabid wolves have been significantly more abundant in Europe than in North America.

2. In the United States, prior to the late 1950's, rabies was predominantly a disease of domestic animals with dogs as the primary carriers. Since the late 1950's, when rabies control programs were established, rabies has decreased in dogs, cats, horses, cattle, and humans, and has steadily increased in wildlife.

3. Less than 1 person per year is infected with rabies within the United States and Canada.

4. In the United States and Canada, the predominant wildlife species infected with rabies are those which are primary carriers. The skunk, raccoon, bat, and fox comprise 98% of reported rabies cases in wildlife.

5. In North America, there are 5 distinct strains of terrestrial rabies. Each strain is specialized for a particular host and each strain can be distinguished from the others using laboratory techniques with monoclonal antibodies. Associated with each of these 5 strains are 5 outbreaks (expanding areas) of rabies currently in the United States and Canada. The 5 principal outbreaks in the United States and Canada are:

    A. Skunk rabies in northcentral states, southcentral Canada, and California.
    B. Skunk rabies in southcentral states.
    C. Raccoon rabies in mid-Atlantic and southeastern states.

SOURCE: J. D. Varley and W. Brewster, eds. 1992. *Wolves for Yellowstone? A report to the United States Congress*. Volume III, executive summaries. Yellowstone National Park: National Park Service, pp. 57–58.

    D. Arctic fox rabies in Alaska, Northwest Territories, and southeast-
       ern Canada.

    E. Gray fox rabies in a small area of Arizona.

6. Idaho essentially has no terrestrial rabies, only bat rabies. All wildlife
rabies cases in Idaho have been in bats.

7. In Montana and Wyoming, skunk rabies is enzootic. Skunks comprise over 50% of rabies cases. All other animals are infected as
"spillover" from exposure to skunks.

8. In Alaska, where the fox strain of rabies is enzootic, 4 wolves, from
an estimated population of 6,000 to 8,000 wolves, have been reported
with rabies in the last 5 years. In Minnesota, where the skunk strain
of rabies is enzootic, no free-ranging wolves, from an estimated
population of 1,700 wolves, have been reported with rabies.

9. Rabies has never been diagnosed in Yellowstone National Park.

10. Since skunk rabies occurs in areas where skunk densities are high, it
is extremely unlikely that rabies will extend into Yellowstone National Park where skunk densities are very low.

11. North American wolves and coyotes are not primary carriers of rabies and therefore do not play a significant role in the spread of
rabies and infrequently become infected with rabies.

12. The addition of the wolf to the Greater Yellowstone Area would not

contribute any additional risks associated with rabies to humans, livestock, or wildlife.

CHAPTER 35
THE DISEASE ECOLOGY OF BRUCELLOSIS AND TUBERCULOSIS IN POTENTIAL RELATIONSHIP TO YELLOWSTONE WOLF POPULATIONS

MARK R. JOHNSON,
NATIONAL PARK SERVICE

BRUCELLOSIS (*BRUCELLA* SPP.)

1. Wild canids, such as foxes, coyotes, and wolves can be naturally infected with bovine brucellosis (*B. abortus*), rangiferine brucellosis (*B. suis*, biovar 4), and possibly canine brucellosis (*B. canis*).
2. Wild canids become infected with brucellosis from eating abortion or calving materials, such as fetuses or fetal membranes, from infected primary hosts such as cattle, bison, or reindeer.
3. In general, wild canids do not become clinically ill due to *Brucella* infections. Reproductive disorders in wild canids due to brucellosis are rarely observed.
4. Wild canids can shed *Brucella* bacteria if enough infected material is originally ingested. Bacteria are shed in very low numbers, often in lower numbers than the infective dose for cattle.
5. Wild canids may be considered to be mechanical vectors (which only transport the disease for a limited time from one place to another), rather than biological vectors (which grow, maintain, and shed organisms in greater numbers than which it was originally infected).
6. In large undeveloped areas, such as national parks, wild canids may actually play a positive role in the disease ecology of brucellosis. By ingesting *Brucella*–infected material, especially during calving season, and excreting less bacteria than they eat, canids would reduce the amount of abortion or calving material capable of infecting other bison or elk.

SOURCE: J. D. Varley and W. Brewster, eds. 1992. *Wolves for Yellowstone? A report to the United States Congress*. Volume III, executive summaries. Yellowstone National Park: National Park Service, pp. 59–60.

TUBERCULOSIS (*MYCOBACTERIUM* SPP.)

7. The 3 principal types of tuberculosis affecting wildlife are *M. tuberculosis*, *M. bovis*, and *M. avium* complex.
8. Tuberculosis in humans and domestic animals in industrialized countries has been almost eradicated. The predominant reservoirs of this disease are now captive exotic and North American wildlife especially in primate colonies, game farms, and zoological parks.
9. Tuberculosis in wildlife is difficult to diagnose due to a lack of test methods validated for wildlife. Necropsy is the most reliable method when complemented with histopathology and bacterial cultures.
10. Canids, including foxes, coyotes, and wolves, can be infected with tuberculosis. The disease in canids is similar to that in other animals.
11. Free–ranging canids are rarely reported with tuberculosis due to limited exposure that canids have to tuberculosis, limited investigations, and lack of proven diagnostic methods.
12. Wild canids do not act as reservoirs of tuberculosis. Tuberculosis is not a population limiting factor for canids.

CHAPTER 36
SPRING BEAR USE OF UNGULATES IN
THE FIREHOLE RIVER DRAINAGE OF
YELLOWSTONE NATIONAL PARK
DAVID J. MATTSON AND RICHARD R. KNIGHT,
INTERAGENCY GRIZZLY BEAR STUDY TEAM

1. The Interagency Grizzly Bear Study Team studied spring bear use of ungulates in the Firehole River drainage, 1985–90. Data were collected from a total of 646 ungulate carcasses concerning location, species, sex-age cohort, and bear use. These data could serve as a basis for a comparative study after wolf establishment or reintroduction, to determine relationships among wolves, ungulates, and bears on the Firehole winter range.

2. Between 6 and 401 ungulate carcasses were found annually on transect routes. Mortality of adult elk varied most and mortality of adult bison least among years. Most mortality occurred between Julian dates (JD) 60 and 104, with bison mortality more prolonged than elk mortality. Most (44–75%) ungulate mortality was judged to be from under– nutrition and disease. Both coyote and bear predations were infrequent.

3. Bears made proportionally heaviest use of ungulates that died between JD 60 and 104; in areas greater than 5 km from the Old Faithful development and greater than 400 m from the Norris Junction–Old Faithful road; and within 50 m of the forest–nonforest edge, especially near human facilities. Adult female bison were the most heavily scavenged ungulate species and sex–age cohort by bears. Frequency of carcass use by grizzly bears on transect routes reached a maximum when greater than or equal to 100 carcasses were available. This number was exceeded only 1 of the 6 study years, during 1989.

4. Only 9% of bear track sets found were made by black bears. Of the grizzly bear track sets, 82% were in the range of adult females and subadult and adult males. Density of grizzly bear track sets peaked

SOURCE: J. D. Varley and W. Brewster, eds. 1992. *Wolves for Yellowstone? A report to the United States Congress.* Volume III, executive summaries. Yellowstone National Park: National Park Service, pp. 61–62.

between JD 90 and 104, while density of black bear track sets peaked after JD 119. We were ca. 17× as likely to find grizzly bear track sets greater than compared to less than or equal to 5 km from the Old Faithful development.

5. Reintroduced or established wolves could affect bear use of carcasses by (1) effects on ungulate populations and consequent effects on winterkill, (2) annual variation in availability of ungulate carrion, (3) redistribution of carcasses with respect to human facilities, (4) redistribution with respect to forest-nonforest edges, and (5) availability of carrion on large-bodied carcasses, especially adult female bison. Considerable uncertainty exists over likely effects of reintroduced wolves on spring grizzly bear use of ungulates in the study area.

CHAPTER 37
A PRELIMINARY ASSESSMENT OF THE
NON-UNGULATE PREY BASE FOR WOLVES
IN YELLOWSTONE NATIONAL PARK
ROBERT L. CRABTREE,
MONTANA STATE UNIVERSITY

1. Although ungulates comprise a large majority of the wolf diet, non-ungulate mammal prey (shrews to beaver) can be important.
2. Studies indicate that small mammal prey is an important alternative to ungulate prey in the non-winter seasons.
3. Six small mammal prey species present on the Northern Range (primary historic wolf range) were identified as potentially important for wolves: beaver, marmots, ground squirrels, snowshoe hare, pocket gophers, and voles.
4. It is predicted that small mammal prey will comprise only a small portion of the wolf diet on the Northern Range; however, ground squirrels (including marmots), voles and pocket gophers, and snowshoe hare will be important seasonally.
5. Small mammal prey will be utilized by wolves during the spring and late summer months when young ungulates are not as available or vulnerable and when wolves are energetically stressed due to need to provide food for pups.
6. Small mammal prey, or lack of it, could play a significant role in a wolf restoration attempt if there is a relationship between decreased ungulate vulnerability and late summer pup starvation.
7. It is recommended to continue the development of a small mammal prey inventory and monitoring method.

SOURCE: J. D. Varley and W. Brewster, eds. 1992. *Wolves for Yellowstone? A report to the United States Congress.* Volume III, executive summaries. Yellowstone National Park: National Park Service, p. 63.

PART TWO

SECTION FIVE:
SOCIOLOGY AND ECONOMICS

As already mentioned, public attitude (rather than scientific knowledge) is the most important force influencing the course of wolf recovery. Many studies have been conducted to learn how the public feels about wolves. These studies, summarized in Chapters 38 and 39, seem to lay to rest one traditional regional view, that a majority of Americans still do not like wolves. These surveys indicate that even in the region around Yellowstone National Park, a majority of people favor wolf recovery. In fact, if recovery were to be decided by a simple vote of American citizens, it would be approved by a landslide. Likewise, there has long been concern that regional economies, especially traditional land-based ones, would suffer if wolves were restored. When it was first published, the study summarized in Chapter 40 may have made more headlines than any other wolf-related study because it suggested that wolves would not only not hurt the economy of the region, they would help it.

CHAPTER 38
IDENTIFICATION AND DOCUMENTATION
OF PUBLIC ATTITUDES TOWARD
WOLF REINTRODUCTION IN
YELLOWSTONE NATIONAL PARK

ALISTAIR J. BATH, MEMORIAL UNIVERSITY, ST.
JOHN'S, NEWFOUNDLAND

1. Nationwide data suggests the U.S. public likes the wolf; within the Rocky Mountain region 50% like the wolf while 30% dislike the animal. Visitors to the park also overwhelmingly support wolf reintroduction. In 1987, a statewide survey of the Wyoming general public (n = 371) randomly selected, revealed most Wyoming residents (48.5%) favored wolf reintroduction while 34% were opposed and 17% had no opinion.

2. Surveys were mailed to randomly selected residents of Montana and Idaho. The response rate for Montana was 61.2% (n = 672) and 57.2% (n = 618) for Idaho. The research instrument was divided into 4 sections: (1) attitude toward the wolf, (2) knowledge of the wolf, (3) willingness to reintroduce the animal, and (4) sociodemographic characteristics.

3. Eight attitudinal items were used to compute an attitude toward the wolf score. A score of 1.0 indicated a "strong dislike" of the wolf while a score of 5.0 indicated a "strong like" of the wolf. The Montana statewide general public received a mean score of 3.05 indicating an attitude of "neither like nor dislike" of the wolf (3.0). The Idaho statewide general public sample received a mean score of 3.31 indicating an attitude between "neither like nor dislike" of the wolf (3.0) and "like" of the wolf (4.0). The Wyoming statewide general public received a mean score of 3.15 indicating an attitude that also lies between "neither like nor dislike" of the wolf and "like" of the wolf.

4. Knowledge scores were also computed. All groups, the Wyoming statewide public, the Idaho statewide public, and the Montana state-

SOURCE: J. D. Varley and W. Brewster, eds. 1992. *Wolves for Yellowstone? A report to the United States Congress*. Volume III, executive summaries. Yellowstone National Park: National Park Service, pp. 23–24.

wide public, answered less than half of the knowledge items correctly. This indicates that much is still to be learned by the general public about the wolf. Results indicate that those respondents with higher knowledge about the wolf tend to have more positive attitudes toward the animal.

5. Most respondents from Wyoming, Montana, and Idaho stated they were in favor of wolf reintroduction in Yellowstone National Park. Most Montana residents (43.7%) were in favor of wolf reintroduction with 40.3% opposed and 16.0% having no opinion. Idaho residents supported wolf reintroduction significantly more than Montana residents with 56.0% in favor, 27% against, and 17% had no opinion. The Wyoming general public also supports wolf reintroduction (48.5%) with 34% opposed and 17% no opinion. This research suggests that most residents of the 3-state region bordering Yellowstone National Park support reintroduction of the wolf into the park.

CHAPTER 39
PUBLIC ATTITUDES ABOUT WOLVES:
A REVIEW OF RECENT INVESTIGATIONS

Public attitudes toward wolves in America, both in general and in relation to Yellowstone National Park, have been surveyed by numerous investigators. This paper presents a chronological summary of surveys, including both Yellowstone-related ones and those involving other areas of the country. All such surveys are included, whether they involve Yellowstone or not, in order to more fully portray American attitudes about wolves, and trends in those attitudes.

Minn (1977) studied attitudes toward wolf recovery in Rocky Mountain National Park, Colorado, and found that 74.2% of respondents favored wolf restoration, and 25.8% did not.

Kellert (1985b) found that in Minnesota, there was "a strong positive perception of the timber wolf among all sample groups except farmers," and that all groups agreed that the timber wolf was "symbolic of nature's wonder and beauty."

In a survey of attitudes among members of the National Cattlemen, American Sheep Producers, National Trappers Association, and members of the public in the Rocky Mountains and Alaska, Kellert (1985a) found that in the Rocky Mountain region, 50% liked wolves and 30% did not.

McNaught (1985), in a survey of Yellowstone National Park visitors, found that they favored reintroduction 3 to 1, and that they believed, 6 to 1, that "a presence of wolves would improve the Yellow-stone experience."

Bath (1987a) surveyed various Wyoming interest groups, and found that 91.2% of members of the Wyoming Stock Growers were not in favor wolf reintroduction in Yellowstone National Park; 89.2% of Defenders of Wildlife members were in favor of wolf reintroduction, as were 66.8% of Wyoming Wildlife Federation members.

Source: U.S. Fish and Wildlife Service. 1994. *Final Environmental Impact Statement: The reintroduction of gray wolves to Yellowstone National Park and central Idaho.* Helena: U.S. Fish and Wildlife Service, pp. 6–32 to 6–35.

Bath (1987b) surveyed the public in Wyoming counties around the park, and found that 51% opposed wolf reintroduction in Yellowstone National Park, and 39% favored it. Bath also found that those opposing wolf reintroduction had a poorer knowledge level about wolves than those favoring it.

Bath (1987c) surveyed the Wyoming general public, and found that 48.5% favored wolf reintroduction into Yellowstone National Park, 34.5% opposed it, and 17% had no opinion.

Lenihan (1987) surveyed Montana residents, and found that 65% believed that wolves belong in the state; 78% of people living in the state's most populous counties agreed, while 54% of rural Montanans agree. Of those surveyed, 78% believed that "ranchers should be able to shoot wolves that attack livestock on their own property." A majority (52%) approved of reintroduction of wolves into areas of Montana, Idaho, and Yellowstone Park, but 56% of those from rural counties did not approve. A majority (59%) believed that ranchers should be compensated for livestock lost. Lenihan found that the 2 most important rationale for support of wolf reintroduction were that wolves were an important member of the ecological community (41%), and wolves were historically present (40%). The most important rationale for opposition was that livestock losses would be unacceptably high (57%).

A survey conducted by the Idaho Environmental Science Teachers (1987) through the University of Idaho Wildlife Issues Course found that 78% of Idahoans agreed with the statement that "I would like to see wild populations of wolves exist in Idaho," while 12% disagreed and 10% had no opinion.

Tucker and Pletscher (1989) surveyed hunters and residents of Flathead County (northwestern Montana), and found that 71.5% of the residents of the North Fork area and 58.3% of the hunters in Flathead County hoped that wolves would continue to inhabit the area and "should be allowed to spread beyond this area." They also concluded that "support [for wolves] could dwindle if restrictions on recreational and commercial uses were introduced to promote recovery."

Bath and Buchanan (1989) surveyed attitudes of 5 different interest groups in Wyoming: members of the Wyoming Stock Growers, of Defenders of Wildlife, of Wyoming Wildlife Federation, of the statewide public, and of counties near the proposed recovery area. They found that "extremes of the issues were defined by the stock growers and members of Defenders of Wildlife. Most members of the Wyoming Wildlife Federation and the statewide public had positive attitudes toward wolf-restoration, although the public in counties surrounding the wolf-recovery site held more negative attitudes."

Bath and Phillips (1990) and Bath (1991) surveyed the Montana and Idaho general public, and found that 43.7% of Montanans, 48.5% of Wyomingites and 56% of Idahoans favored wolf reintroduction into Yellowstone National Park, while 40.3% of Montanans, 34.5% of Wyomingites, and 27% of Idahoans were opposed. No opinion on wolf reintroduction was held by 16% of Montanans, 17% of Wyomingites, and 17% of Idahoans.

Kellert (1990) surveyed Michigan public attitudes. Of Upper Peninsula residents, 64% favored wolf restoration, 15% opposed it, and 21% were uncommitted. Of Lower Peninsula residents, 57% favored restoration, 9% opposed it, and 34% were uncommitted.

Bath and Phillips (1990) noted that the primary reason for opposition among Idaho and Montana residents to wolf reintroduction was the cost of the program, which agreed with Bath's (1987c) survey of Idaho residents. Bath and Phillips asked survey subjects if they would change their minds if a variety of conditions were met (including financial compensation for livestock losses, keeping livestock losses to less than 1%, and keeping wolves in the park and surrounding wilderness areas), and concluded that "most respondents who do not favor reintroducing the wolf would not change their opinion regardless of the options presented to them. On the other hand, if wolves could be monitored effectively and be restricted within the park and surrounding wilderness areas, an additional 27% (Montana) and 25% (Idaho) would be in favor of wolf reintroduction."

The Wyoming Game and Fish Department (Thompson 1991) surveyed Wyoming residents on wolf reintroduction, and found that 44% were in favor of Yellowstone Park wolf reintroduction, while 34.5% were opposed and the remaining 21.5% were undecided or had no opinion. This was very similar to Bath's (1987c) findings, but in other respects the 2 studies differed. For example, Thompson found that more than 30% (compared to 16.2% of Bath's respondents) of respondents would change their opposition to wolf restoration if wolves could be kept in the park and adjacent wilderness areas. Thompson also found that 14% of those opposed to wolf restoration (compared to 6.3% of Bath's respondents) would change their opinion if there was a compensation program for wolf restoration. On the other hand, Bath and Thompson's respondents agreed quite closely, 58.5% and 56.8% respectively, that wolves that killed livestock should be killed.

Freemuth (1992) asked Idahoans, "Do you favor or oppose having wolves in the wilderness and roadless areas of central Idaho?" He found that 72.4% favored wolves, 22.1% opposed them, and 5.4% did not know or had no opinion.

Eisenstein (1992) conducted an attitudinal survey analysis of 52 representative individuals regarding wolf restoration in Yellowstone National Park. He was seeking detailed responses on concerns and issues, rather than quantifiable yes-or-no expressions of positions. Thus his work does not statistically analyze public opinion, but summarizes and presents great amounts of personal position and opinion. His conclusions included the following general statement about wolves: "The interviews revealed not only polarization, but gross misunderstandings and misconceptions concerning the wolf and the program. It was clear that people still do believe in the horror stories of the wolf and 'Little Red Riding Hood.' Many respondents stated as fact that they *know* wolves kill people."

Duffield et al. (1992) surveyed American citizens nationally and found that "while GYA [Greater Yellowstone Area] respondents are nearly evenly divided in their opinion on wolf reintroduction, the US respondents are heavily in favor of reintroduction . . . Almost everyone in the GYA has an opinion on this issue with only 7 percent saying they 'don't know.' The national sample shows a strong majority favoring wolf recovery—by about a 2:1 margin." When asked to respond to the statement, "I dislike even the idea of wolves being present in Yellowstone Park," 25% of the Yellowstone area respondents strongly agreed, while 4–6% of US-wide respondents agreed.

Public approval of wolf reintroduction in Yellowstone National Park is high. Nationally, the public is very strongly in favor of reintroduction, while regionally there is at least a slight majority in favor of reintroduction. There is still some public concern over safety risks, that is, over the possibility that wolves might attack people. McNaught (1985) found that 19.7% of his respondents would be afraid to hike in Yellowstone Park if wolves were present.

There is a great concern among potentially affected stockgrowers that wolves will kill their stock, and any losses are unacceptable to them. There is strong public support for a compensation program to protect livestock owners from financial losses due to wolf depredation. There was likewise strong public concern over the need to control wolf distribution, in whatever management scenario is ultimately adopted. The public does not want wolves to have unlimited freedom to range on public and private lands, and wants wolf control measures to be stringent and promptly enacted.

The surveys do not agree on whether the public considers wolves a serious threat to wildlife populations, but among the surveys there is a consistent level of public concern over possible impacts on wildlife, especially as those might affect hunter harvest. There is significant public concern over the monetary costs of implementing a reintroduction program.

REFERENCES CITED

Bath, A. J. 1987a. Attitudes of various interest groups in Wyoming toward wolf reintroduction in Yellowstone National Park. MS Thesis, University of Wyoming. 124pp.

———. 1987b. Countrywide survey of the general public in Wyoming in counties around the park toward wolf reintroduction in Yellowstone National Park. A report submitted to the National Park service. 97pp.

———. 1987c. Statewide survey of the Wyoming general public attitude toward wolf reintroduction in Yellowstone National Park. A report submitted to the U.S. National Park Service. 95pp.

———. 1990. Public attitudes in Wyoming, Montana, and Idaho toward wolf restoration in Yellowstone National Park. Trans. 56th N.A. Wildl. & Nat. Res. Conf. 91–95.

———, and T. Buchanan. 1989. Attitudes of interest groups in Wyoming toward wolf restoration in Yellowstone National Park. Wild. Soc. Bull. 17:519–525.

———, and C. Phillips. 1990. Statewide surveys of Montana and Idaho resident attitudes toward wolf reintroduction in Yellowstone National Park. Report submitted to Friends for Animals, National Wildlife Federation, U.S. Fish and Wildlife Service, and U.S. National Park Service. 38pp.

Eisenstein, W. 1992. Wolf reintroduction into Yellowstone National Park, an attitudinal survey analysis. MA thesis, Montana State University, Bozeman. 85pp.

Freemuth, J. 1992. Public opinion on wolves in Idaho: results from the 1992 Idaho policy survey. Boise State University. 3pp.

Idaho Environmental Science Teachers. 1987. Attitude survey (wolf) in McCall. University of Idaho Wildlife Issues Course, unpublished. 6pp.

Kellert, S. R. 1985a. The public and the timber wolf in Minnesota. Unpublished report, Yale University. 175pp.

———. 1985b. Public perception of predators, particularly the wolf and coyote. Biological Conservation 31:167–189.

———. 1990. Public attitudes and beliefs about the wolf and its restoration in Michigan. Yale University and HBRS, Inc. 118pp.

Lenihan, M. L. 1987. Montanans ambivalent on wolves. The Montana Poll. Bureau of Business & Economic Research, School of Bus. Admin., University of Montana. 6pp.

McNaught, D. A. 1985. Park visitor attitudes toward wolf recovery in Yellowstone National Park. MS Thesis, University of Montana. 103pp.

Minn. B. P. 1977. Attitudes toward wolf reintroductions in Rocky Mountain National Park. MS Thesis, Colorado State University. 70pp.

Thompson, T. 1991. Attitudes of Wyoming residents on wolf reintroduction and related issues. Wyoming Game and Fish Department, Cheyenne. 43pp.

Tucker, P., and D. H. Pletscher. 1989. Attitudes of hunters and residents toward wolves in northwestern Montana. Wildlife Society Bulletin 17:507–514.

CHAPTER 40
AN ECONOMIC ANALYSIS OF WOLF
RECOVERY IN YELLOWSTONE: PARK
VISITOR ATTITUDES AND VALUES
JOHN W. DUFFIELD,
UNIVERSITY OF MONTANA

1. This study addresses the question of whether the benefits of wolf recovery in Yellowstone National Park (YNP) exceed the costs. The benefits of wolf recovery are the values that park visitors and others place on knowing that wolves are present in the Yellowstone ecosystem and on the opportunity to possibly see and hear wolves. Costs are associated with reduced populations of elk, deer, and moose which would affect viewing of animals in the park as well as hunting of animals migrating out of the park in fall and winter. Other costs are associated with livestock predation by wolves. The basic finding of this study is that the net social benefits for 20 years of wolf recovery in YNP are large and positive, on the order of $110 million.

2. This study also examines the impact of wolf recovery on the regional (Montana, Idaho, and Wyoming) economy. Sales of goods and services out of state and nonresident tourism expenditures in YNP and the adjoining states of Montana, Idaho, and Wyoming may increase by $19 million annually due to wolf recovery. This is because YNP visitation may increase by about 5% for out of region visitors. Increased nonresident tourism expenditure by YNP visitors will far outweigh an estimated total loss of $0.2 million per year in reduced nonresident hunting expenditures and reduced livestock exports. Using a simple export base model of regional economic development, this implies an annual positive net economic impact of $43 million for the regional economy. It is assumed that the impact of wolf recovery on other regional natural resource based industries is negligible.

3. The estimated benefits of wolf recovery to YNP visitors is based on the responses of 762 YNP visitors initially contacted at entrance stations in June 1991. A high response rate of 87% was achieved through

SOURCE: J. D. Varley and W. Brewster, eds. 1992. *Wolves for Yellowstone? A report to the United States Congress.* Volume III, executive summaries. Yellowstone National Park: National Park Service, pp. 25–28.

3 followup mail contacts with study participants. Based on the response to a hypothetical trust fund question, the typical respondent who favored wolf recovery would be willing to make a one-time donation of $23 for wolf recovery. Similar results were obtained for a separate sample of 612 YNP visitors surveyed in August–September 1990. About 1/3 of this value is associated with the recreational benefits of hearing or seeing wolves; the remainder is the existence value of knowing wolves are present in YNP. For YNP visitors opposed to wolf recovery, the typical respondent was willing to make a one-time donation of about $2 to prevent wolf recovery. The primary motivation for visitors opposed to wolf recovery was found to be expected reductions in hunting opportunities, which accounted for about 4/5 of the total expected donation.

4. There are about 2.8 million visits to YNP in the May–October summer season. Based on survey data corrected for oversampling of more frequent visitors, this implies a total of about 900,000 individual adult visitors who would participate in a wolf recovery trust fund and about 420,000 adult visitors who would participate in a trust fund opposing wolf recovery. The net social benefits of wolf recovery to park visitors at current visitation levels total $19 million in the first year and $118 million present value over 20 years. Assuming that the number of adult visitors is a known constant, the 90% confidence interval for the first year value is $14.8 to $23.6 million and $93 to $144 million for the 20-year present value. The donations in future years are based on one-time donations by first time YNP visitors who would not have been contacted in previous years. These values may be conservative by a factor of 3 given that individual values are based on typical (median) willingness to pay rather than mean (or average) willingness to pay. Additionally, possible net social benefits associated with increased YNP visitation are not included in this estimate.

5. Reduced hunter harvest of elk, mule deer, and moose in the Greater Yellowstone Area (GYA) due to wolf recovery could result in lost net social benefits on the order of $0.4 to $0.6 million per year or a present value of $2.9 to $4.7 million over 20 years. These estimates are probably high in that they are not adjusted for hunter use of substitute hunting opportunities. Average willingness to pay per hunter day for hunting districts adjoining YNP is derived from previous economic studies of Montana big game hunting. The hunter harvest of big game species on the Northern Yellowstone Range may be reduced by about 20% for elk, 14% for mule deer, and 30% for moose. If these reductions are primarily achieved through reductions in existing special permit hunts for antlerless animals, current big game populations on this range could remain at about current levels. The

exception is that elk populations may be about 12% lower with wolves than without wolves. Elk hunter harvest may be reduced by about 20% for the Gallatin herd and 5% for the Sand Creek herd. It is assumed that reduction of hunter harvest of other types of big game due to wolf recovery would be negligible.

6. Expected impacts of wolves in the GYA on livestock are based on actual livestock losses in recent years in Alberta (population of 5,000 wolves), Minnesota (1,700 wolves), and northwest Montana (currently 40–50 wolves). All of these areas have programs for compensation of livestock owners for verifiable wolf kills. The average annual losses of livestock in these areas (inflated to 1991 dollars and corrected to full market value) are $97,600 in Alberta (for 1981–89), $50,830 in Minnesota (for 1979–91), and $2,682 in Northwest Montana (for 1987–91). Extrapolating these findings to a population of 150 wolves in YNP leads to estimated annual loss of $3,000 to $11,000 per year. The lost market value to livestock producers in the GYA is likely to be small because of the relatively small projected population of wolves, the separation of wolves from livestock concentrations, and because wolves will probably be managed as a nonessential experimental population. Animal damage control (ADC) costs for wolves are expected to be no more than $25,000 to $40,000 per year based on ADC costs in Minnesota and the estimate that 15–25 wolves per year may disperse from a recovered YNP wolf population. These estimated costs assume that every wolf that disperses will be a problem wolf. In fact based on evidence from Alaska and Minnesota, wolves that disperse will suffer high mortality due to human causes.

7. About 70% of all respondents favor wolf recovery. There were significant differences in attitudes across population strata. Hunters were less likely to favor recovery than nonhunters; the same held for regional residents (Montana, Wyoming, and Idaho) compared to out of region visitors. About 82% of overnight visitor respondents said that they would prefer visiting the park with wolves reintroduced. This is similar to the findings of the only other survey of YNP visitors concerning attitudes of park visitors toward wolf recovery. The latter study sampled only overnight visitors and found that 86% felt that the presence of wolves would improve the YNP visitor's experience.

8. Multivariate statistical models were developed to see if the respondent reported willingness to pay for wolf recovery was consistent with economic theory. As one would expect, individual willingness to pay was significantly and positively correlated to income, previous familiarity with trust funds, measures of attitudes toward wildlife and the environment, and respondent reported measures of personal benefits from wolf recovery. As an example, the expected donation

increases about 5% for every 10% increase in reported income. Similar consistency is shown in a model of willingness to pay for the subsample opposed to wolf recovery. These findings indicate that responses to the trust fund question are not random but are a predictable function of the respondents socioeconomic characteristics and attitudes. The general validity of willingness to pay measures derived from these types of survey techniques has been supported by actual cash transaction experiments for nonmarket goods such as access to public hunting areas.

9. The scope of this analysis is limited. While the costs of wolf recovery in the GYA in terms of possible reduced hunting and increased livestock predation are examined, benefit estimates are limited to those likely to be realized by park visitors. Benefits of wolf recovery to the 200 plus million U.S. residents who will not visit YNP in the next 20 years have not been estimated. Management costs of the wolf recovery program have not been estimated.

10. Assumptions regarding the biological and physical impacts of wolf recovery are required by the economic analysis. The assumptions used are based where possible on findings in *Wolves for Yellowstone?* It is expected that 7–9 wolf packs with fixed territories could occupy Yellowstone's Northern Range; another 1–2 fixed packs could occupy the park's other winter ranges; and another 3–4 packs might be supported, but only if the latter were migratory. If each wolf pack plus loners averaged 10 wolves, this implies 110–150 wolves for YNP. Ten breeding pairs could lead to these population levels in 10 years. Depending on the management of hunter harvests of big game in the GYA, a recovered population of up to 150 wolves is expected to reduce populations of most ungulate prey species, including elk, deer, moose, and bison by 20% or less. No species will become extinct in YNP due to wolf recovery.

PART TWO

SECTION SIX:
CONTROL AND MANAGEMENT OF WOLVES

Both advocates and opponents of wolves recognized that wolves can and will cause some trouble, especially with livestock. Managers agree that even if those problems are relatively infrequent, as predicted, they must be addressed vigorously and effectively. That issue is only part of a bigger issue, though, involving the whole process by which wolves arrive in Yellowstone, and where they choose to go (or are allowed to go) once they arrive. Chapters 41, 42, and 43 address aspects of these questions, including the long-disputed matter of what subspecies of wolf is "appropriate" for Yellowstone.

CHAPTER 41
MANAGEMENT OF WOLVES INSIDE
AND OUTSIDE YELLOWSTONE NATIONAL
PARK AND POSSIBILITIES FOR WOLF
MANAGEMENT ZONES IN THE
GREATER YELLOWSTONE AREA
STEVEN H. FRITTS,
U.S. FISH AND WILDLIFE SERVICE

1. The need for control of wolves (*Canis lupus*) within Yellowstone National Park is expected to be negligible and limited mainly to occasional control of nuisance animals.
2. Any control is likely to be controversial. Some control will be needed outside the park to address occasional depredations on livestock and, possibly, to control excessive predation on ungulates.
3. The situation appears to be suited for reintroduction under Section 10(j) of the Endangered Species Act as a nonessential experimental population.
4. If a reintroduced population was classified as experimental *and* nonessential per Section 10(j) of the Endangered Species Act, federal agencies would only have to confer informally with the U.S. Fish and Wildlife Service (FWS) on activities that might jeopardize the species (except in national parks and national wildlife refuges). A jeopardy ruling by the FWS would not prohibit the federal agency from committing resources to the proposed activity. Therefore, land-use restrictions are not expected to be major issues.
5. Discussions with the Office of the Solicitor, Department of Interior, and review of the legislative history of Section 10(j) of the Endangered Species Act reveal that Congress intended broad flexibility for controlling experimental populations in order to make more reintroductions possible. The full extent of control possible under Section 10(j) has not been tested.
6. The court case of Sierra Club et al. vs. Clark et al. (1985) in Minnesota *did not pertain to experimental populations* and therefore will not affect

SOURCE: National Park Service. 1990. *Wolves for Yellowstone? A report to the United States Congress*. Volume I, executive summaries. Yellowstone National Park: National Park Service, pp. 3–4.

the management of wolves in the greater Yellowstone area (GYA).

7. The experimental population designation was recently used to successfully reintroduce the red wolf (*Canis rufus*) to the wild; an account of that case with discussion of control methods used is provided.

8. Presence of wolves in Yellowstone National Park would not preclude usual recreational activities in the park or surrounding lands. Wolves would not be a significant threat to human safety.

9. If wolves were to colonize the GYA (including Yellowstone National Park) on their own, the opportunity for management flexibility via experimental population designation would be lost, and wolves would receive the full protection of the Endangered Species Act.

10. The purpose of this report was not to make specific recommendations about wolf control and management zones for wolves in the GYA but to identify and give advantages and disadvantages of some of the numerous options available. Various scenarios are discussed, ranging from intensive control with public involvement to no control or minor control conducted by state or federal officials. In general, less control means increased potential for conflicts but reduced risk to the wolf population, reduced time to recovery (10 breeding pairs) and delisting, and greater probability of reaching recovery level. Conversely, more control means fewer conflicts but increased risk to the wolf population, more time required to reach recovery and delisting, and reduced chance of achieving recovery level. The opportunity exists to craft management that will both allow wolf recovery and address the potential conflicts in the GYA.

11. An integral question to the management (and therefore, to establishment of management zones) of wolves in the GYA is how much area wolves would require for a secure population to be established. No research, short of placing wolves in the park, can answer that question without conjecture.

CHAPTER 42
REINTRODUCTIONS AND TRANSLOCATIONS
OF WOLVES IN NORTH AMERICA:
AN ANALYSIS

STEVEN H. FRITTS,
U.S. FISH AND WILDLIFE SERVICE

1. Only 6 previous relocations of gray wolves have occurred. These
   have involved both captive-raised and wild-captured wolves. Three
   attempts have been made to reestablish wild populations of gray
   wolves, and 2 efforts have been made to resolve management problems by translocation of problem wolves. An intensive effort is in
   progress to reestablish red wolves of captive origin into certain areas
   of the southeastern United States by reintroduction.
2. Releases are broadly characterized as "hard" or "soft." Hard release
   refers to the immediate and direct release of wolves into a new environment. Soft release refers to the release of wolves into a temporary
   enclosure at the release site where they receive food and water, possibly live prey; are disturbed as little as possible; and generally given
   time to be calmed, monitored, and conditioned prior to release. Mat-
   ing, denning, and whelping in the enclosure could be a part of the
   process. Gray wolf releases to date have been mostly hard releases; a
   soft release procedure is used with red wolves.
3. Captive-raised gray wolves that were socialized to humans approached humans after release, leading to their deaths. Use of
   captive-born wolves presents different problems than use of wild-
   captured wolves.
4. None of the adult gray wolves remained at their release site, but in no
   case was there a serious attempt to acclimate them to the release site
   by holding for an extended period (soft release). Released adult gray
   wolves have tended to travel extensively; most have attempted to
   return home; and a few have succeeded. Limited data suggest that
   gray wolves have difficulty homing if the distance they are moved is

SOURCE: J. D. Varley and W. Brewster, eds. 1992. *Wolves for Yellowstone? A
report to the United States Congress.* Volume III, executive summaries.
Yellowstone National Park: National Park Service, pp. 31–32.

>64 km. Pups tended to become sedentary in the vicinity of the release sites. With the procedures used so far, even parents and offspring have tended to separate after release. Adult wild-captured wolves were able to kill ungulate prey in their new surroundings. Survival rates of adults and pups have been good.

5. Translocation of problem wolves was usually successful at arresting depredations by individuals. However, extensive post–release movements often brought individuals through areas where the potential for conflicts was high and they may have been attracted to livestock (possibly carrion) or to the type of habitat where they were originally captured.

6. An acclimation period of several weeks or months at the release site in a large enclosure will likely be necessary to overcome homing and extensive post-release movements of reintroduced gray wolves. Some of the procedures used in red wolf reintroductions appear to be applicable to gray wolves in the northern Rockies. Those procedures should be carefully evaluated for potential use.

7. Because of individual differences in wolf behavior and limited experience with wolf reintroductions, we should not expect reintroductions and translocations of wolves in the northern Rockies to proceed smoothly, particularly at first. Multiple releases over a period of years may be necessary to establish a viable population.

CHAPTER 43
TAXONOMY, GENETICS, AND STATUS OF THE GRAY WOLF, *CANIS LUPUS*, IN WESTERN NORTH AMERICA: A REVIEW

Wayne G. Brewster,
National Park Service
and Steven H. Fritts,
U.S. Fish and Wildlife Service

1. Early taxonomists named 24 subspecies of gray wolf (*Canis lupus*) in North America based on skull characteristics, body size, and color. The 24 subspecies were based largely on the work of E. A. Goldman and other taxonomists during the first half of the 20th century. These early taxonomists did not employ statistical analyses and, of course, did not have access to improved modern taxonomic methods. They had access to very few specimens from some areas, and some of the subspecies recognized were based on as few as 5 specimens. The naming of wolf subspecies occurred during a period in history when it was fashionable to name many subspecies.

2. Wolves vary in size, color, and in minor skull measurements within their vast geographic range. Except for color, these differences are minor, and when geographic differences in North American wolf populations have been shown, it was with the aid of extremely sensitive techniques, such as multivariate statistical methods. Most evaluations have shown little difference.

3. Wolves from different areas are not distinct in any one characteristic. Subspecific names usually represent only *averages* or *trends* that supposedly occur in a geographic area but almost universally intergrade over substantial distances with neighboring designations and there is usually considerable overlap between the characteristics of neighboring subspecies. Highly sensitive analyses usually are needed to distinguish differences in morphology of populations. Some specimens found well within the range of one named group may be practically identical to some specimens from the ranges of other named groups.

Source: J. D. Varley and W. Brewster, eds. 1992. *Wolves for Yellowstone? A report to the United States Congress*. Volume III, executive summaries. Yellowstone National Park: National Park Service, pp. 33–36.

4. More recent taxonomic work using multivariate analysis and larger sample sizes suggests that this number of subspecies is unwarranted, with 5 North American subspecies possibly being more reasonable; yet the 24 named subspecies persist in the literature.

5. Genetic studies of wolves using molecular techniques suggest genetic differentiation among North American populations too small to justify many subspecies. Genetic mixing of all but geographically isolated wolf populations is facilitated by genetic exchange among local and distant populations through dispersal and colonization of new areas. Dispersal (implying gene flow) over large distances has been documented for wolves, including across multiple alleged subspecific ranges. Therefore, genetic divergence among even widely separated populations is limited.

6. Wolves were essentially eradicated in the Rocky Mountains south of central Canada by the 1930's, and thus any characteristics peculiar to the populations in that area of the continent were lost. Since then wolves most likely from Alberta and British Columbia (B.C.) began appearing in the northwestern U.S., and within the past decade established a breeding population.

7. Evidently no populations of wolves remained in the area of western North America ascribed to *C. l. irremotus*, including Yellowstone and central Idaho, by about 1930. By 1940 wolves had been eliminated from nearly the entire western half of the U.S., and for some 700 km northward into Canadian provinces in the lower elevation settled areas. From the 1930's to the 1950's the wolf recolonized much of southwestern Canada but was again intensively controlled and the expansion stopped. Since that time populations in Alberta and B.C. have continued to colonize southward, reoccupying much of the southern parts of the provinces, with the exception of the prairie biome, and a wolf population has begun recolonizing northwestern Montana and possibly Idaho and Washington. Increased wolf observations in the early 1950's and the mid- to late-1970's corresponded to increased wolf numbers and range expansion in Alberta and B.C. A pattern of sporadic, yet persistent reports, with an occasional wolf killed, persisted throughout western Montana, northern and central Idaho; in northwestern Wyoming infrequent reports persisted but no specimens were recorded. No persuasive evidence of reproduction was obtained from 1940 to 1986 in the western U.S. This would be consistent with very low wolf numbers, probably individuals dispersing from Canada possibly supplemented by occasional reproduction.

8. It is significant that skulls of wolves examined that have been killed in the northwestern U.S. from 1941 to 1991, including the wolf from central Idaho in 1991, fall within the morphological grouping of

wolves from Canada. First, it shows that wolves dispersing from packs probably several hundred kilometers away were reaching the northwestern U.S. during that era. Second, it strongly suggests that no "original" wolves were left in the northern Rockies of the U.S. One specimen killed in the area that resembled *C. l. irremotus* was killed a few kilometers north of Yellowstone National Park in 1988. This individual was killed close to a captive colony of wolves, the founders of which were from central Montana, and showed characteristics of captive rearing.

9. The subspecies of wolf that was described for the central Rocky Mountains, *C. l. irremotus*, was similar to other subspecies, especially those in the western U.S. and extreme southwestern Canada. Wolf populations that occurred in the northwestern U.S. and extreme southwestern Canada prior to eradication may be assignable to a "supergroup" that was distinguishable from another "supergroup" occupying most of Canada and interior Alaska.

10. The taxonomy of the gray wolf in North America is in need of revision. Very possibly, there should never have been a *C. l. irremotus* named, as any difference between it and neighboring North American subspecies is small. The most recent thinking on subspecific differentiation of North American wolves, from a morphometric standpoint, suggests that approximately 5 subspecies might be appropriate, with affinities occurring mainly in an east–west direction and a pronounced character change in the area just north of the border between Canada and the U.S. This would be consistent with the current trend in taxonomy, which is to combine subspecies where there is no appreciable genetic difference and no evidence of geographic or behavioral isolation.

11. From the 17th through the 19th century, wolves in North America received an ecological jolt of epic proportions, perhaps akin to that of the Pleistocene but occurring in a mere 300 years. From about 1870 to 1920, a span of 50 years, wolves west of the Mississippi went from universally distributed robust populations to extermination. Whatever the genetic relationships of those original wolves to the remainder of the species, they are gone. Someday we may be able to reconstruct a better understanding of what the mosaic of variation was among wolves in western North America. Perhaps, as technology advances in analysis of genetic variation, aspects of this dimension can be reconstructed from preserved specimens.

12. Historic patterns of variation in wolves have not been static, but dynamic, with glaciation and human-related extirpation being major influences. There are areas of North America where in recent times a subspecies was recognized, was extirpated, and the area was

recolonized by wolves from the area of another recognized subspecies. Primarily, this occurred on islands and peninsulas where the probability of animal extinctions is known to be higher. Wolves are recolonizing northwestern Montana from another area, west central Canada. Any "original" wolves that have managed to survive in the northwestern U.S. will interbreed with those from more northerly stock. If any individual or small relict population of *C. l. irremotus* stock could have managed to survive, it would probably be suffering some loss of genetic variability due to small population size. The "original stock" undoubtedly was a dynamic entity with long distance dispersal in and out of the area and with local extinctions and recolonizations. We need to dismiss the typological thinking of local types and recognize that local extinctions and recolonization from distant areas occurs constantly in nature. It is the rule, not the exception.

13. In view of the information presented above, we conclude that if *Canis lupus* is to be recovered in the western U.S. it *is appropriate* to reintroduce wolves to the Yellowstone area. If taken from southwestern Canada, reintroduced wolves will be of the same genetic stock from which natural dispersers no doubt immigrated into the original Yellowstone population, the same stock as those currently recolonizing Montana and Idaho, and the same stock that, given enough time, may get to Yellowstone without human help.

14. Indications are that wolves of current southwest Canadian stock will continue to expand their range southward and reproduce in the northwestern U.S. Given enough time they will likely become established in the Yellowstone area. Therefore, obtaining wolves from southern British Columbia or Alberta for reintroduction into Yellowstone and/or central Idaho would only accelerate an ongoing process and need not be viewed as compromising the "natural" or "historic" taxonomic arrangement of wolves in the area.

Part III
___

Law and Policy

T he evolution of the national park idea is fascinating, and is made all the more so by the obvious pace at which that evolution is continuing today. Some of the driving principles and ideas of the modern conservation movement were essentially nonexistent when the first national parks were created; park managers have repeatedly had to adjust their goals to accommodate new information and changing public attitudes. The wilderness movement, ecosystem management, biodiversity, and other ideas and ideals have arisen since Yellowstone was created in 1872, and with each new element, park protection became a more involved business. Predator management has been one of the most challenging and interesting of those elements.

One of the least persuasive rhetorical flourishes of modern conservation debates is the one that makes a plea for a certain action in the national parks so that these lands can serve us "in the way their founders intended." Their founders' intentions were so slightly expressed, and so poorly formed, that our society has spent the past century and more in an often painful exercise of "establishing" Yellowstone and the other parks by a process of trial and error, experiment and guesswork, and an ever more heated public dialogue. The laws and policies upon which modern park management is built provide an intriguing and revealing window on this great continuing experiment in public land management.

It may be that the wolf recovery program in Yellowstone will have benefits far beyond restoring an important predator to the park. Recovery of rare and endangered species is controversial partly because of the complexity of the legal process and the public perception that the process simply cannot work or is too awkward and expensive to be worth the trouble. Yellowstone wolf recovery, because of its high visibility, represents an important opportunity to change that perception. An often-expressed goal of the wolf project leader, Mike Phillips, for example, is to bring the project to completion ahead of schedule and under budget. An achievement like that could have great benefits for endangered species issues throughout the country.

CHAPTER 44
THE YELLOWSTONE PARK ACT OF 1872

In terms of setting management direction or outlining a philosophy by which parks should be cared for, the legislation that created Yellowstone National Park is distinguished by its vagueness. This pioneering piece of legislation left almost every detail concerning the management of Yellowstone to the discretion of the Department of the Interior, the staff of which usually had many more pressing things to do besides paying attention to some obscure, remote parcel of land far off in the mountains. Almost from the beginning, the formulation and evolution of park policy—the process by which philosophical inclinations are turned into actual management guidelines—was driven by local needs and pressures. This from-the-ground-up management structure has made the national parks different from almost all other federal agencies, in that many units in the system emerged with a surprisingly autonomous management style. None demonstrate that tendency as strongly as does Yellowstone.

Notice that the act does mandate the protection of park animals from "wanton destruction" and from commercial exploitation. What was unsaid was that hunting by park visitors, both for sport and for subsistence, was regarded as an appropriate activity. In the park's early years, the few concession facilities were primitive and inadequate, and visitors had their choice of bringing their own food or hoping to kill park wildlife to feed themselves.

CHAP. XXIV.—An act to set apart a certain Tract of Land lying near the Head–waters of the Yellowstone River as a public Park.

Be it enacted by the Senate and House of Representatives of the United States of America in Congress assembled, that the tract of land in the Territories of Montana and Wyoming, lying near the head–waters of the Yellowstone river, and described as follows, to wit, commencing at the junction of Gardiner's river with the Yellowstone river, and running east to the meridian passing ten miles to the eastward of the most eastern point of Yellowstone lake; thence south along said meridian to the parallel of

Source: U.S. Statutes at Large, Vol. 17, ch. 24, pp. 32–33, as reprinted in L. C. Cramton, 1932. *Early history of Yellowstone National Park and its relation to national park policies.* Washington: U.S. Government Printing Office, pp. 76–77.

latitude passing ten miles south of the most southern point of Yellowstone lake; thence west along said parallel to the meridian passing fifteen miles west of the most west point of Madison lake; thence north along said meridian to the latitude of the junction of the Yellowstone and Gardiner's rivers; thence east to the place of the beginning, is hereby reserved and withdrawn from settlement, occupancy, or sale under the laws of the United States, and dedicated and set apart as a public park or pleasuring-ground for the benefit and enjoyment of the people; and all persons who shall locate or settle upon or occupy the same, or any part thereof, except as hereinafter provided, shall be considered trespassers and removed therefrom.

Sec. 2. That said public park shall be under the exclusive control of the Secretary of the Interior, whose duty it shall be, as soon as practicable, to make and publish such rules and regulations as he may deem necessary or proper for the care and management of the same. Such regulations shall provide for the preservation, from injury or spoliation, of all timber, mineral deposits, natural curiosities, or wonders within said park, and their retention in their natural condition. The Secretary may in his discretion, grant leases for building purposes for terms not exceeding ten years, of small parcels of ground, at such places in said park as shall require the erection of buildings for the accommodation of visitors; all of the proceeds of said leases, and all other revenues that may be derived from any source connected with said park, to be expended under his direction in the management of the same, and the construction of roads and bridle–paths therein. He shall provide against the wanton destruction of the fish and game found within said park, and against their capture or destruction for the purposes of merchandise or profit. He shall also cause all persons trespassing upon the same after the passage of this act to be removed therefrom, and generally shall be authorized to take all such measures as shall be necessary or proper to fully carry out the objects and purposes of this act.

Approved March 1, 1872

CHAPTER 45
1883 LETTER FROM SECRETARY
OF THE INTERIOR H. M. TELLER
PROHIBITING PUBLIC HUNTING IN
YELLOWSTONE NATIONAL PARK

The 1870's were a time of fabulous waste of western wildlife. Commercial hunters killed bison, elk, and other large mammals by the millions. Yellowstone National Park, underfunded and almost without protection, was not spared. Park administrators, visiting officials, and literally hundreds of local citizens decried the slaughter of park wildlife, reporting that thousands of elk were killed for their hides some years.

By the early 1880's, a number of forces conspired to lessen the slaughter. These forces included a probable reduction in available animals, changing markets for hides, growing public disapproval of such behavior, and even an occasional improvement in the ability of park administrators to enforce regulations against commercial hunting. Among the leading voices in the campaign to save Yellowstone's wildlife were a number of sportsmen-conservationists, who helped persuade the Department of the Interior simply to ban all hunting in the park. Though established primarily to preserve beautiful landscapes and unique geothermal features, Yellowstone National Park very quickly became perceived as an important "game preserve," one of the early symbols of wildlife conservation. Sportsmen took a leading role in this process, because, as they explained, as long as the wildlife in the park was protected, Yellowstone would serve as a perpetual reservoir of animals that would regularly migrate beyond park boundaries to restock depleted hunting grounds.

Secretary of the Interior Teller's letter is revealing in many ways. Besides listing a few species (including goat, pheasant, and quail) that did not even occur in the park, it ignores almost all of the predators; it lists only a few carnivorous furbearers of obvious commercial value. At this early date, most people saw any animal that lived by killing, or competed with humans for elk, deer, or other respected game species, as vermin undeserving of any protection. The idea of providing those species with legal protection would not have occurred to most managers and certainly not to the Washington, D.C., political appointee who probably drafted the letter, which was published in a number of periodicals in the first few weeks after it was written.

SOURCE: Letter to the Superintendent, Yellowstone National Park, January 15, 1883, from the Secretary of the Interior, reprinted under the heading of "Game in the park," in the Bozeman (MT) *Avant Courier*, February 22, 1883.

Department of the Interior,
Washington, January 15, 1883

To the Superintendent of the Yellowstone National Park:

Sir:—The regulations heretofore issued by the Secretary of the Interior in regard to killing game in the Yellowstone National Park are amended so as to prohibit absolutely the killing, wounding, or capturing at any time of any buffalo, bison, moose, elk, black tailed or white tailed deer, mountain sheep, Rocky Mountain goat, antelope, beaver, otter, martin, fisher, grouse, prairie chicken, pheasant, fool hen, partridge, quail, wild goose, duck, robin, meadow lark, thrush, goldfinch, flicker or yellow-hammer, blackbird, oriole, jay, snowbird, or any of the small birds commonly known as the singing birds.

The regulations in regard to fishing in the Park are amended so as to prohibit the taking of fish by means of seines, nets, traps, or by the use of drugs, or any explosive substances or compounds, or in any other way than by hook and line.

All cutting of timber in the Park, except upon special permission from the Department of the Interior, is prohibited.

You will please see that all persons coming within the limits of the Park are notified, so far as possible, of these regulations, and that they observe the same.

You will report to this Department any infraction of the regulations.

Very respectfully,
H. M. Teller, Secretary

CHAPTER 46
THE LACEY ACT

Known among Yellowstone residents as the Lacey Act, this law should not be confused with the later and much more famous act by the same name, which was passed in 1900 to prohibit the interstate trade in wild animals and thus stop much of the commercial marketing of wildlife. Yellowstone's Lacey Act (both acts were the work of Iowa Congressman John Lacey, an enthusiastic defender of the park) was the result of a notorious bison-poaching incident, in which the poacher got away without punishment because park regulations were essentially "toothless"; they prohibited killing wildlife, but provided no penalty for doing so beyond expulsion from the park.

Although this act did not deal specifically with the issue of predators or predator control, it is one of the pillars of law enforcement, and therefore of wildlife management, in Yellowstone.

CHAP. 72.– An Act To protect the birds and animals in Yellowstone National Park, and to punish crimes in said park, and for other purposes.

Be it enacted by the Senate and House of Representatives of the United States of America in Congress assembled, That the Yellowstone National Park, as its boundaries now are defined, or as they may be hereafter defined or extended, shall be under the sole and exclusive jurisdiction of the United States; and that all the laws applicable to places under the sole and exclusive jurisdiction of the United States shall have the force and effect in said park: *Provided, however,* That nothing in this act shall be construed to forbid the service in the park of any civil or criminal process of any court having jurisdiction in the States of Idaho, Montana, and Wyoming. All fugitives from justice taking refuge in said park shall be subject to the same laws as refugees from justice found in the State of Wyoming.

Sec. 2. That said park, for all the purposes of this Act, shall constitute a part of the United States judicial district of Wyoming, and the district and circuit courts of the United States in and for said district shall have jurisdiction of all offenses committed within said park.

Sec. 3. That if any offense shall be committed in said Yellowstone

Source: U.S. Statutes at Large, Vol. 28, p. 73, as reprinted in L. C. Cramton, 1932. *Early history of Yellowstone National Park and its relation to national park policies.* Washington: U.S. Government Printing Office, pp. 78–81.

National Park, which offense is not prohibited or the punishment is not specially provided for by any law of the United States or by any regulation of the secretary of the Interior, the offender shall be subject to the same punishment as the laws of the State of Wyoming in force at the time of the commission of the offense may provide for a like offense in the said State; and no subsequent repeal of any such law of the State of Wyoming shall affect any prosecution for said offense committed within said park.

SEC. 4. That all hunting, or the killing, wounding, or capturing at any time of any bird or wild animal, except dangerous animals, when it is necessary to prevent them from destroying human life or inflicting an injury, is prohibited within the limits of said park; nor shall any fish be taken out of the waters of the park by means of seines, nets, traps, or by the use of drugs or any explosive substances or compounds, or in any other way than by hook and line, and then only at such seasons and in such times and manner as may be directed by the Secretary of the Interior. That the Secretary of the Interior shall make and publish such rules and regulations as he may deem necessary and proper for the management and care of the park and for the protection of the property therein, especially for the preservation from injury or spoliation of all timber, mineral deposits, natural curiosities, or wonderful objects within said park; and for the protection of the animals and birds in the park, from capture or destruction, or to prevent their being frightened or driven from the park; and he shall make rules and regulations governing the taking of fish from the streams or lakes in the park. Possession within said park of the dead bodies, or any part thereof, of any wild bird or animal shall be prima facie evidence that the person or persons having the same are guilty of violating this Act. Any person or persons or stage or express company or railway company, receiving for transportation any of the said animals, birds, or fish so killed, taken, or caught shall be deemed guilty of a misdemeanor, and shall be fined for every such offense not exceeding three hundred dollars. Any person found guilty of violating any of the provisions of this Act or any rule or regulation that may be promulgated by the Secretary of the Interior with reference to the management and care of the park, or for the protection of the property therein, for the preservation from injury or spoliation of timber, mineral deposits, natural curiosities or wonderful objects within said park, or for the protection of the animals, birds and fish in the said park, shall be deemed guilty of a misdemeanor, and shall be subjected to a fine of not more than one thousand dollars or imprisonment not exceeding two years, or both, and be adjudged to pay all costs of the proceedings.

That all guns, traps, teams, horses, or means of transportation of every nature or description used by any person or persons within said park limits when engaged in killing, trapping, ensnaring, or capturing such wild beasts, birds, or wild animals shall be forfeited to the United States, and may be seized by the officers in said park and held pending the prosecution of any person or persons arrested under charge of violating the provisions of this Act, and upon conviction under this Act of such person or persons using said guns, traps, teams, horses, or other means of transportation such forfeiture shall be adjusted as a penalty in addition to the other punishment provided in this Act. Such forfeited property shall be disposed of and accounted for by and under the authority of the Secretary of the Interior.

Sec. 5. That the United States circuit court in said district shall appoint a commissioner, who shall reside in the park, who shall have jurisdiction to hear and act upon all complaints made, of any and all violations of the law, or of the rules and regulations made by the Secretary of the Interior for the government of the park, and for the protection of the animals, birds, and fish and objects of interest therein, and for other purposes authorized by this Act. Such commissioner shall have power, upon sworn information, to issue process in the name of the United States for the arrest of any person charged with the commission of any misdemeanor, or charged with the violation of the rules and regulations, or with the violation of any provision of this Act prescribed for the government of said park, and for the protection of the animals, birds, and fish in the said park, and to try the person so charged, and, if found guilty, to impose the punishment and adjudge the forfeiture prescribed. In all cases of conviction an appeal shall lie from the judgment of said commissioner to the United States district court for the district of Wyoming, said appeal to be governed by the laws of the State of Wyoming providing for appeals in cases of misdemeanor from justices of the peace to the district court of said State; but the United States circuit court in said district may prescribe rules of procedure and practice for said commissioner in the trial of cases and for appeal to said United States district court. Said commissioner shall also have power to issue process as hereinbefore provided for the arrest of any person charged with the commission of any felony within the park, and to summarily hear the evidence introduced, and, if he shall determine that probable cause is shown for holding the person so charged for trial, shall cause such person to be safely conveyed to a secure place for confinement, within the jurisdiction of the

United States district court in said State of Wyoming, and shall certify a transcript of the record of his proceedings and the testimony in the case: *Provided*, That the said commissioner shall grant bail in all cases bailable under the laws of the United States or of said State. All process issued by the commissioner shall be directed to the marshal of the United States for the district of Wyoming; but nothing herein contained shall be construed as preventing the arrest by any officer of the Government or employee of the United States in the park without process of any person taken in the act of violating the law or any regulation of the Secretary of the Interior: *Provided*, That the said commissioner shall only exercise such authority and powers as are conferred by this Act.

SEC. 6. That the marshal of the United States for the district of Wyoming may appoint one or more deputy marshals for said park, who shall reside in said park, and the said United States district and circuit courts shall hold one session of said courts annually at the town of Sheridan in the state of Wyoming, and may also hold other sessions at any other place in said State of Wyoming or in said National Park at such dates as the said courts may order.

SEC. 7. That the said commissioner provided for in this Act shall, in addition to the fees allowed by law to commissioners of the circuit courts of the United States, be paid an annual salary of one thousand dollars, payable quarterly, and the marshal of the United States and his deputies, and the attorney of the United States and his assistants in said district, shall be paid the same compensation and fees as are now provided by law for like services in said district.

SEC. 8. That all costs and expenses arising in cases under this Act, and properly chargeable to the United States, shall be certified, approved, and paid as like costs and expenses in the courts of the United States are certified, approved, and paid under the laws of the United States.

SEC. 9. That the Secretary of the Interior shall cause to be erected in the park a suitable building to be used as a jail, and also having in said building an office for the use of the commissioner, the cost of such building not to exceed five thousand dollars, to be paid out of any moneys in the Treasury not otherwise appropriated upon the certificate of the Secretary as a voucher therefor.

SEC. 10. That this Act shall not be construed to repeal existing laws conferring upon the Secretary of the Interior and the Secretary of War certain powers with reference to the protection, improvement, and control of the said Yellowstone National Park.

Approved, May 7, 1894.

CHAPTER 47
NATIONAL PARK SERVICE ACT, 1916

By 1916, Yellowstone was one of several national parks, and their administration was handled by a hodgepodge of offices and bureaus scattered here and there throughout Washington, D.C. For several years, there had been interest in organizing them into a small agency of their own and in straightening out the peculiarities of their management. Some, including Yellowstone, were under the protection of the U.S. Army, which did not especially want the assignment.

A small book could be written around a line-by-line analysis of the National Park Service Act, but a few points will do. Notice in Section One, following the salary standards, the mission of the agency. The National Park Service (NPS) was to both promote and regulate the use of the parks; though today most conservationists agree that the last thing parks need is more promotion, it was seen as essential by early administrators, whose most urgent need was more visitors to convert into park defenders and political allies.

Then, notice the things to be protected. First is scenery, second is natural and historic objects, and third is wildlife. This ordering was no accident; the parks were still perceived as picturesque landscapes more than as wildlife sanctuaries.

Then, notice that the NPS was to protect these park features in such a way as to keep them unimpaired for future generations. This, it has often been observed, was the first time that protection of the park's wonders was put on such equal footing with their use. Yes, they were to be used, but they were not to be used in a way that would diminish their use by future visitors.

Last, notice that this law specifically authorized park managers to kill "detrimental" animal life if necessary. The authority to kill animals has never been questioned; what has changed is the perception of what should be killed.

An Act To establish a National Park Service, and for other purposes approved August 25, 1916 (39 Stat. 535)

Be it enacted by the Senate and House of Representatives of the United States of America in Congress assembled, That there is hereby created in the Department of the Interior a service to be called the National Park Service, which shall be under the charge of a director, who shall be appointed by

Source: U.S. Statutes at Large, 39(1916):535–536.

the Secretary and who shall receive a salary of $4,500 per annum. There shall also be appointed by the Secretary the following assistants and other employees at the salaries designated: One assistant director, at $2,500 per annum; one chief clerk, at $2,000 per annum; one draftsman, at $1,800 per annum; one messenger, at $600 per annum; and, in addition thereto, such other employees as the Secretary of the Interior shall deem necessary: *Provided*, That not more than $8,100 shall be expended for salaries of experts, assistants, and employees within the District of Columbia not herein specifically enumerated unless previously authorized by law. The service thus established shall promote and regulate the use of the Federal areas known as national parks, monuments, and reservations hereinafter specified by such means and measures as conform to the fundamental purpose of the said parks, monuments, and reservations, which purpose is to conserve the scenery and natural and historic objects and the wild life therein and to provide for the enjoyment of the same in such manner and by such means as will leave them unimpaired for the enjoyment of future generations. (U.S.C., title 16, sec. 1)

SEC. 2. That the director shall, under the direction of the Secretary of the Interior, have the supervision, management, and control of the several national parks and national monuments which are now under the jurisdiction of the Department of the Interior, and of the Hot Springs Reservation in the State of Arkansas, and of such other national parks and reservations of like character as may be hereafter created by Congress: *Provided*, That in the supervision, management, and control of national monuments contiguous to national forests the Secretary of Agriculture may cooperate with said National Park Service to such extent as may be requested by the Secretary of the Interior. (U.S.C., title 16, sec. 2)

SEC. 3. That the Secretary of the Interior shall make and publish such rules and regulations as he may deem necessary or proper for the use and management of the parks, monuments and reservations under the jurisdiction of the National Park Service, and any violations of any of the rules and regulations authorized by the Act shall be punished as provided for in section fifty of the Act entitled "An Act to codify and amend the penal laws of the United States," approved March fourth, nineteen hundred and nine, as amended by section six of the Act of June twenty–fifth, nineteen hundred and ten (Thirty-sixth United States Statutes at Large, page eight hundred and fifty-seven). He may also, upon terms and conditions to be fixed by him, sell or dispose of timber in those cases where in his judgment the cutting of such timber is required in order to control the attacks of insects or diseases or otherwise conserve the scenery or the natural or historic objects in any such park, monuments, or reservation. He may also provide in his discretion for the destruction of such animals and of such plant life as may be detrimental to the use of any of said parks, monuments, or reservations. He may also grant privileges, leases, and permits for the use of land for the accommodation of visitors in the various parks, monuments, or other reservations herein provided for, but for periods not exceeding twenty years; and no natural curiosities, wonders, or objects of interest shall be leased, rented, or granted to anyone on such term as to interfere with free access to them by the public: *Provided, however,* That the Secretary of the Interior may, under such rules and regulations and on such terms as he may prescribe, grant the privilege to graze live stock within any national park, monument, or reservation herein referred to when in his judgment such use is not detrimental to the primary purpose for which such park, monument or reservation was created, except that this provision shall not apply to the Yellowstone National Park. (U.S.C. title 16, sec. 3)

SEC. 4. That nothing in this Act contained shall affect or modify the provisions of the Act approved February fifteenth, nineteen hundred and one, entitled "An Act relating to rights of way through certain parks, reservations, and other public lands." (U.S.C., title 16, sec. 4)

CHAPTER 48
THE NATIONAL PARK SERVICE'S POLICY
ON PREDATORY MAMMALS
HORACE ALBRIGHT

Predator control in the national parks was endemic by the 1920's, Until 1925, when NPS Director Stephen Mather reduced the list, National Park Service staff members in various parks were authorized to kill not only wolves, mountain lions, and coyotes but also lynx, bobcat, foxes, mink, weasel, fisher, otter, marten, and a number of predatory birds. It is interesting to note that early National Park Service administrators justified these killings partly on the grounds that they had a responsibility to prevent the parks from becoming breeding grounds for predators that would leave the park and cause trouble for livestock operations nearby.

But public and scientific attitudes were changing. In the 1920's, the National Park Service was pressured by a variety of organizations, including the American Society of Mammalogists, the New York Zoological Society, and the Boone and Crockett Club to curtail unnecessary predator killing. Because of its peculiar mission to preserve natural settings, the National Park Service was more vulnerable to criticism over the killing of predators than were most other federal agencies, who saw their missions as simpler.

Horace Albright, superintendent of Yellowstone National Park from 1919 to 1929 and director of the National Park Service from 1929 to 1933, issued this policy statement shortly before leaving the federal government. It reveals the halting evolution of predator management in the parks. In this policy statement, Albright seemed to take a determined stand on the appropriateness of predators in national parks. The policy was fairly adventurous for the time (compared to many other management agencies) in recognizing that predators belonged somewhere on the public lands, but it also gave managers ample room to continue predator control. Though predators were now seen as something other than wholly evil, their effects on more popular wildlife were still largely—sometimes wildly—overestimated.

The year this policy was published in the Journal of Mammalogy, *Yellowstone staff members killed 145 coyotes and did not stop the killing until after 1935, when they killed 110. Between 1907 and 1935, 4,352 coyotes were killed in Yellowstone, but a milestone study of Yellowstone coyote ecology by Adolph Murie, published in 1940, showed that the coyotes were not the killing machines many people imagined them to be. Of course, the killing of wolves and mountain lions in Yellowstone had*

SOURCE: *Journal of Mammalogy* 12:185–186.

ceased in the 1920s (see Chapter 1), perhaps more because managers ran out of wolves and mountain lions to kill than because they became more enlightened about the need to kill them.

The National Park Service is attempting to put the parks to their highest use. Every policy developed is an attempt to meet the purposes for which the parks were formed: First, the national parks must be maintained in absolutely unimpaired form for the use of future generations as well as those of our own time; second, they are set aside for the use, observation, health, pleasure, and inspiration of the people; and third, the national interest must dictate all decisions affecting public or private enterprise in the parks.

Certainly, one of the great contributions to the welfare of the nation that the national parks may make is that of wild life protection. It is one of the understood functions of the parks to give total protection to animal life. A definite policy of wild life protection is being developed with the result that fine herds of game are presented "as a spectacle" for the benefit of the public, and these same herds furnish the best opportunity for scientific study. Many disappearing species are to be found within park areas, so that in some instances we may speak of the parks as providing "last stands."

Of late there has been much discussion by the American Society of Mammalogists and other scientific organizations relative to predatory animals and their control. The inroads of the fur trapper and widespread campaigns of destruction have caused the great reduction of some and the near disappearance of several American carnivores. The question naturally arises as to whether there is any place where they may be expected to survive and be available for scientific study in the future.

The National Park Service believes that predatory animals have a real place in nature, and that all animal life should be kept inviolate within the parks. As a consequence, the general policies relative to predatory animals are as follows:

1. Predatory animals are to be considered an integral part of the wild life protected within national parks, and no widespread campaigns of destruction are to be countenanced. The only control practiced is that of shooting coyotes or other predators when they are actually found making serious inroads upon herds of game or other animals needing special protection.

2. No permits for trapping within the borders of a park allowed. A resolution opposing the use of steel traps within a park was passed sev-

Soldiers at the Soda Butte Soldier Station, 1905, with coyote skin. After the army left the park in 1918, the National Park Service continued to kill coyotes by the hundreds until the mid-1930's. Concerns over the effects of coyotes on ungulate populations, and being a good neighbor to nearby ranchers, made it more difficult for park administrators to embrace new ecological perspectives on the role of predators in wilderness. NPS photo.

eral years ago by the superintendents at their annual meeting, and they are used now only in emergencies.

3. Poison is believed to be a non-selective form of control and is banned from the national parks except where used by Park Service officials in warfare against rodents in settled portions of a park, or in case of emergency.

Though provision is made for the handling of special problems that may arise, it is the intention of the Service to hold definitely to these general policies. It can be seen, therefore, that within the national park system definite attention is given to that group of animals which elsewhere are not tolerated. It is the duty of the National Park Service to maintain examples of the various interesting North American mammals under conditions for the pleasure and education of the visitors and for the purpose of scientific study, and to this task it pledges itself.

CHAPTER 49
SUGGESTED NATIONAL PARK
POLICY FOR THE VERTEBRATES
George M. Wright, Joseph S. Dixon,
and Ben H. Thompson

George Wright was one of the great pioneers of ecological thinking in national park management. He and his colleagues issued this proposal as part of their 1933 report Fauna of the national parks of the United States, No. 1, *one of the first attempts to address the complex issues of national parks as ecological preserves. It was informally adopted soon after publication and was made official policy in 1936. Although published at about the same time as the Albright statement, Wright's proposal was a significant advance, requiring considerably more justification for killing of any predators than did Albright.*

Every tenet covering the vertebrate life in particular must be governed by the same creed which underlies administration of wild life in general through the national parks system, namely:

That one function of the national parks shall be to preserve the flora and fauna in the primitive state and, at the same time, to provide the people with maximum opportunity for the observation thereof.

In the present state of knowledge, and until further investigations make revision advisable, it is believed that the following policies will best serve this dual objective as applied to the vertebrate land fauna. Without further comment, inasmuch as the supporting reasons have been developed in the preceding sections [of the report *Fauna of the National Parks of the United States*], it is proposed:

Relative to areas and boundaries—

1. That each park shall contain within itself the year-round habitats of all species belonging to the native resident fauna.

Source: G. M. Wright, J. S. Dixon, and B. H. Thompson. 1933. *Fauna of the national parks of the United States.* Washington: U.S. Government Printing Office, pp. 147–148.

2. That each park shall include sufficient areas in all these required habitats to maintain at least the minimum population of each species necessary to insure its perpetuation.

3. That park boundaries shall be drafted to follow natural faunal barriers, the limiting faunal zone, where possible.

4. That a complete report upon a new park project shall include a survey of the fauna as a critical factor in determining area and boundaries.

Relative to management—

5. That no management measure or other interference with biotic relationships shall be undertaken prior to a properly conducted investigation.

6. That every species shall be left to carry on its struggle for existence unaided, as being to its greatest ultimate good, unless there is real cause to believe that it will perish if unassisted.

7. That, where artificial feeding, control of natural enemies, or other protective measures, are necessary to save a species that is unable to cope with civilization's influences, every effort shall be made to place that species on a self-sustaining basis once more; whence these artificial aids, which themselves have unfortunate consequences, will no longer be needed.

8. That the rare predators shall be considered special charges of the national parks in proportion that they are persecuted everywhere else.

9. That no native predator shall be destroyed on account of its normal utilization of any other park animal, excepting if that animal is in immediate danger of extermination, and then only if the predator is not itself a vanishing form.

10. That species predatory upon fish shall be allowed to continue in normal numbers and to share normally in the benefits of fish culture.

11. That the numbers of native ungulates occupying a deteriorated range shall not be permitted to exceed its reduced carrying capacity and, preferably, shall be kept below the carrying capacity at every step until the range can be brought back to original productiveness.

12. That any native species which has been exterminated from the park area shall be brought back if this can be done, but if said species has become extinct no related form shall be considered as a candidate for reintroduction in its place.

13. That any exotic species which as already become established in a

park shall be either eliminated or held to a minimum provided complete eradication is not feasible.

14. That the threatening invasion of the parks by other exotics shall be anticipated; and to this end, since it is more than a local problem, encouragement shall be given for national and State cooperation in the creation of a board which will regulate the transplanting of all wild species.

Relative relations between animals and visitors—

15. That presentation of the animal life of the parks to the public shall be a wholly natural one.

16. That no animal shall be encouraged to become dependent upon man for its support.

17. That problems of injury to the persons of visitors or to their property or to the special interests of man in the park, shall be solved by methods other than those involving the killing of the animals or interfering with their normal relationships, where this is at all practicable.

Relative faunal investigations—

18. That a complete faunal investigation, including the four steps of determining the primitive faunal picture, tracing the history of human influences, making a thorough zoological survey and formulating a wild–life administrative plan, shall be made in each park at the earliest possible date.

19. That the local park museum in each case shall be repository for a complete study skin collection of the area and for accumulated evidence attesting to original wild–life conditions.

20. That each park shall develop within the range department a personnel of one or more men trained in the handling of wild-life problems, and who will be assisted by the field staff appointed to carry out the faunal program of the Service.

CHAPTER 50
NATURAL PREDATION, FROM
THE LEOPOLD REPORT

A. STARKER LEOPOLD

Perhaps no document in the history of the parks has been more frequently in-voked, heralded, and reconsidered than the Leopold Report of 1963. In this report, "Wildlife management in the national parks," ecologist A. Starker Leopold (son of Aldo Leopold; see Chapter 8) and his colleagues presented the Secretary of the Inte-rior with a philosophical blueprint for restoring and maintaining ecological integrity in the parks. Some of its perspectives have been dated by later research, but the Leopold Report remains one of the most influential and profoundly expressed state-ments of the values of national parks. In this brief excerpt, Leopold pushed "equal rights" for predators even further than had Wright thirty years earlier. Note, how-ever, that by the 1960's there was a conviction among these experts that ungulate populations were in some sense out of control (this was the common belief in Yellowstone) and that even healthy predator populations could not control them. The notion that predators are the only significant natural control over ungulates in Yellowstone, though in some respects now disproven (many researchers now regard available winter food to be the primary controlling force), is still commonly held, and has been a major element in wolf-recovery dialogues.

NATURAL PREDATION

Insofar as possible, control through natural predation should be en-couraged. Predators are now protected in the parks of the United States, although unfortunately they were not in the early years and the wolf, grizzly bear, and mountain lion became extinct in many of the national parks. Even today, populations of large predators, where they still occur in the parks, are kept below optimal level by programs of predator con-trol applied outside the park boundaries. Although the National Park Service has attempted to negotiate with control agencies of federal and

SOURCE: A. S. Leopold, S. A. Cain, C. M. Cottam, I. N. Gabrielson, and T. L. Kimball. 1963. Wildlife management in the national parks. *Trans. North Am. Wildl. Conf.* 24:28–45.

local governments for the maintenance of buffer zones around the parks where predators are not subject to systematic control, these negotiations have been only partially successful. The effort to protect large predators in and around the parks should be greatly intensified. At the same time, it must be recognized that predation alone can seldom be relied upon to control ungulate numbers, particularly the larger species such as bison, moose, elk, and deer; additional artificial controls frequently are called for.

CHAPTER 51
THE NORTHERN ROCKY MOUNTAIN
WOLF RECOVERY PLAN, 1987

The recovery plan, approved on August 3, 1987, was prepared by the U.S. Fish and Wildlife Service, working with the Northern Rocky Mountain Wolf Recovery Team. The team was a group of eleven people, including representatives of the relevant state and federal agencies, the scientific community, the stockgrowers, and the conservation community. Required under the terms of the Endangered Species Act, the plan, as explained below, provide the blueprint for wolf recovery and management. The excerpts that follow provide some of the clearest, most comprehensive statements of the goals of the program as those goals were mandated by law.

PREFACE

As enacted by Congress, the purposes of the Endangered Species Act are to provide a program for the conservation of such endangered and threatened species as well as a means whereby the ecosystems upon which such species depend may be conserved. The Act also mandates that the Secretary of the Interior shall develop and implement plans for the conservation and survival of endangered and threatened species. It is further declared to be the policy of Congress that all Federal departments and agencies shall seek to conserve endangered and threatened species and shall utilize their authorities in furtherance of the purposes of the Act.

The Northern Rocky Mountain Wolf Recovery Plan outlines steps for recovery of gray wolf (*Canis lupus*) populations in portions of their former range in the Northern Rocky Mountains of the United States. Historical evidence documents the presence of gray wolves throughout the Northern Rocky Mountains of the contiguous United States. This subspecies (*Canis lupus irremotus*) was a predator on native ungulates under pristine conditions and later, as European Americans spread west-

SOURCE: U.S. Fish and Wildlife Service. 1987. Northern Rocky Mountain Wolf Recovery Plan. U.S. Fish and Wildlife Service, Denver, CO, pp. iv–vi, 9–11.

ward, on domestic livestock. Substantial declines in wolf numbers resulted from control efforts to reduce livestock and big game depredations. Currently, no viable populations of wolves occur in the Rocky Mountains south of Canada, however, at least one pack and several individual animals are known to be present.

This plan emphasizes gray wolf recovery through natural processes (dispersal southward from western Canada) where possible. Where this is not possible because of distance from "seed" populations, translocation is the only known way to establish a population. Either philosophy necessitates conservation of suitable habitat in appropriate recovery areas. Establishing and maintaining wolf populations in three separate areas is believed necessary for recovery at this time. The probability of recovery through natural recruitment is high in northwestern Montana, moderate in Idaho, and remote in Yellow-stone National Park. Characteristically, the recovery areas that have been identified are large and remote, where the potential for conflict situations would generally be limited to their periphery. However, resolution of such conflicts is requisite to successful natural reestablishment and thus is an essential element for recovery.

This recovery plan is intended to provide direction and coordination for recovery efforts. State responsibility for many plan items is proposed because the Endangered Species Act (Act) of 1973, as amended, provides for responsibilities outlined in the implementation schedule are suggestions contingent upon appropriations, priorities, and personnel and funding constraints.

The plan is a guidance document that presents conservation strategies for the Northern Rocky Mountain wolf. It is not a decision-making document. Implementation of some tasks outlined in the plan, such as the reintroduction of wolves, will require further analysis under the National Environmental Policy Act as well as public involvement.

EXECUTIVE SUMMARY

The Northern Rocky Mountain Wolf Recovery Plan represents a "road map" to recovery of the gray wolf in the Rocky Mountains. The primary goal of the plan is to remove the Northern Rocky Mountain wolf from the endangered and threatened species list by securing and maintaining a minimum of 10 breeding pairs of wolves in each of the three recovery areas for a minimum of three successive years.

The three recovery areas identified for the Northern Rocky Mountain

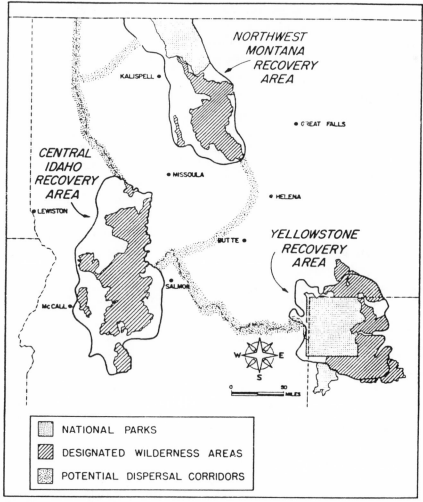

Wolf recovery areas as described in the Northern Rocky Mountain Wolf
Recovery Plan, *1987.*

wolf include northwest Montana, central Idaho, and the Greater
Yellowstone Area. Each recovery area will be stratified into wolf management zones. Zone I is the area where wolf recovery will be promoted
due to the low potential for conflict with other land uses. Zone III (all
land area outside the recovery area) is the area where wolf recovery will
not be promoted due to the high potential for conflict with existing land
uses. Zone II represents a buffer between Zone I and Zone III.

Management guidelines will be developed for the different wolf management zones. These guidelines will then be applied to Federal lands in order to coordinate multiple use activities with wolf management objectives.

Recovery through natural recolonization will be relied upon for the northwest Montana and central Idaho recovery areas. If monitoring efforts in these recovery areas do not indicate satisfactory progress (two breeding pairs) toward recovery through natural recolonization within five years after approval of the recovery plan, other conservation strategies will be identified and implemented.

Due to its geographic isolation from areas with established wolf populations, recovery in the Yellowstone area will likely involve the reintroduction of wolves into Yellowstone National Park. However, before any reintroduction effort is initiated, the appropriate National Environmental Policy Act documents will be prepared with full public involvement. In addition, a proposed rulemaking must be developed and finalized to designate the Yellowstone population as an "experimental population." Such designation will increase the Fish and Wildlife Service's flexibility to manage these translocated populations. Under such designation, experimental populations of species otherwise listed as endangered may be treated as threatened with regard to specific take provisions of the Act and promulgation of special rules. Designation of an experimental population involves preparation and publication in the Federal Register of a proposed rule detailing the geographic location of the experimental population and identifying procedures to be utilized in its management. The rule may also authorize activities designed to contain the population within designated boundaries or to remove nuisance animals.

A control plan(s) will be developed for resolving wolf depredation problems. The goal of the control program is to reduce and prevent livestock losses to wolves while removing the minimum number of wolves necessary to resolve the conflict yet still progress toward recovery. Control will include live—capturing and relocating, holding in captivity, or killing the offending animal(s). If initial efforts to trap a problem wolf are unsuccessful and depredations continue, or if transplanted wolves return, lethal control using approved methods may be used. If predation on big game herds is determined to be in significant conflict with management objectives of a State wildlife agency, wolf control that would not jeopardize recovery will be considered.

A program of research and monitoring will be implemented to track the progress of recovery, gather information upon which to base management decisions, and determine the impacts upon ungulate populations. Public information and education will be an important aspect of the recovery effort and are key to the overall success of the program.

FACTORS AFFECTING RECOVERY

A few places, mostly National Parks and other wild areas, still exist in the Northern Rocky Mountains where wolves can survive. Although maintenance and improvement of suitable habitat may be the key long-term factor in wolf conservation, an important factor limiting wolf recovery in the Northern Rocky Mountains is human-induced mortality. The wolf traditionally has been feared and maligned by many people. If wolves increase in the Northern Rocky Mountains and livestock depredations occur, immediate steps must be taken to alleviate the problem.

As proposed by this plan, control actions will be undertaken to trap and relocate depredating wolves (or, if this is not possible, lethal control may be used as a last resort) only in the case where verified wolf depredation occurs on lawfully present domestic livestock. Control actions will serve to enhance the overall survival of the wolf by demonstrating to those concerned about the impact of wolf recovery on the livestock industry that responsible Federal agencies will act quickly to alleviate depredation problems. Timely response to depredation problems will serve to alleviate the perception of government inaction that often results in the indiscriminate killing of wolves. In addition, control actions will focus on removal of only offending wolves, and in doing so will resolve wolf-human conflicts by taking the minimum number of wolves necessary. Thus, by enhancing the survival chances of those non-offending animals now present in Montana, the control program will actually contribute to the ultimate recovery of the wolf in the Northern Rocky Mountains.

An information and education program based on factual information concerning wolves is requisite to public acceptance and support of the recovery effort. Such programs should stress that a few remaining wild areas do still exist where wolves and wolf habitat can be maintained or enhanced in conjunction with the balanced use of other resources. Recovery of the wolf, whether through natural reestablishment or translocation, cannot succeed without public support and acceptance. In the past, fear, lack of knowledge of wolf ecology, and misinformation have been very real factors in inhibiting wolf recovery. Livestock operators and the industry as a whole will not support such a program without some assurance that depredating wolves can and will be controlled. Wolf recovery areas should not be superimposed over major livestock-producing areas, and provisions should be established for controlling problem wolves. Development and implementation of wolf management zones and a specific wolf control plan are necessary elements for wolf recovery in the Northern Rocky Mountains.

Recent studies have shown gray wolves, especially juveniles, are susceptible to canine parvovirus and distemper. Because survival of juvenile wolves is critical to successful recovery, developing a comprehensive health monitoring program for translocated and naturally-reestablishing wolves is essential to minimize the risk of diseases adversely affecting recovery.

WOLF-HUMAN INTERACTIONS

Until 1944, when Adolph Murie's *The Wolves of Mount McKinley* was published, no unbiased ecological treatise on wolves existed. Even "scientific" works mixed science with folklore (Lopez 1978). Although Native Americans admired and emulated wolves, Europeans seemed universally to associate wolves with the Devil, pagan worship, evil, and man's bestial nature. Wolves, along with werewolves, became tied to man's baser emotions with debauchery, sacrilege, witchcraft and sorcery. This traditional view of the wolf came to the New World with the first colonists and persists in television productions today.

The natural reestablishment of wolves in Glacier National Park and wilderness areas in Montana, Wyoming, and Idaho, and reintroduction of the wolf into Yellowstone National Park raise the question of how wolves and humans will interact in wild country visited by large numbers of recreationists. Researchers in Denali (Mount McKinley) National Park, Alaska (Murie 1944), Algonquin Provincial Park, Ontario (Pimlott 1969), Prince Albert National Park, Saskatchewan, Jasper National Park, Alberta, Riding Mountain National Park, Manitoba (Carbyn 1974, 1980), and Isle Royale National Park, Michigan (Peterson 1979), all document that, far from being a threat to humans, healthy, wild wolves actually avoid humans. In fact, no case of modern North Americans being seriously injured by wolves can be documented (Mech 1970, Lopez 1978). The challenge, then, is to protect wolves from humans, rather than people from wolves.

In the last 40 years, after centuries of fantasy and superstition, wildlife research has yielded a new picture of the wolf as a social creature and an important member of natural ecosystems. Surveys of public attitudes in Minnesota show broad support, except among farmers, for protection and conservation of the wolf (Kellert 1985). Visitors to Yellowstone National Park, when questioned, overwhelmingly (six to one) indicated that having wolves would improve the Yellowstone experience (McNaught 1985).

SUMMARY

Occurrence of wolves in the Northern Rocky Mountains of the United States has recently been documented. A pack of 12 wolves is now known to occupy an area in northwestern Montana. Reproduction was documented in this area in 1982, 1985, 1986, and 1987. However, the prognosis for the species in this and other recovery areas remains uncertain. The plight of Canadian wolves in the border region will strongly influence the ecology and recovery of wolves in the United States. Proposed and ongoing development in the area threaten these wolves, which represent the only source for natural reestablishment into Montana and Idaho. Protection and improvement of habitat in recovery and corridor areas and north of the border is fundamental to the recovery effort as it will enhance wolf dispersal from western Canada as well as reintroduction efforts. Prevention of livestock depredations by wolves, public education regarding wolves and wolf management, and development of a control plan to deal with problem wolves are also essential if wolf recovery is to be accepted and coordinated with alternate resource uses.

The probability of natural reestablishment of wolves in the Yellowstone Ecosystem is extremely remote. Translocation of healthy wolves into the area appears to be the only viable method of establishing and recovering a population at this time. The 1982 Amendments to the Endangered Species Act (Pub. L. 97-304) provide for the designation of "experimental populations," a special category allowing endangered and threatened species to be reintroduced within their historic range with provisions for additional management flexibility. Such designation would include formulation of a special rule identifying procedures to be utilized in management of the species. These regulations may also authorize activities designed to contain the population within the original boundaries set out in the regulation and to remove problem animals.

LITERATURE CITED IN EXCERPTS

Carbyn, L. N. 1974. Wolf predation and behavioral interactions with elk and other ungulates in an area of high prey diveristy. Can. Wildl. Serv. Rpt. Edmonton, Alberta. 233pp.

———. 1980. Ecology and management of wolves in Riding Mountain National Park, Manitoba. Can. Wildl. Ser. final rpt. 184pp.

Kellert, S. R. 1985. The public and the timber wolf in Minnesota. Unpublished report, Yale University School of Forestry and Environmental Studies, New Haven, CT. 175pp.

Lopez, B. H. 1978. Of wolves and men. Charles Scribner's Sons, New York. 309pp.

McNaught, D. A. 1985. Park visitor attitudes toward wolf recovery in Yellowstone National Park. MS Thesis, Univ. of Montana. 103pp.

Mech, L. D. 1970. The wolf: The ecology and behavior of an endangered species. Nat. Hist. Press, Doubleday, NY. 389pp.

Murie, A. 1944. The wolves of Mt. McKinley. USDI NPS Fauna Ser. 5. 238pp.

Peterson, R. O. 1979. The wolves of Isle Royale—new developments. p. 3–18 in Klinghammer , E. (ed.), The behavior and ecology of wolves . Garland STPM Press, New York. 588pp.

Pimlott, D. H., J.A. Shannon, and G. B. Kolenosky. 1969. The ecology of the timber wolf in Algonquin Provincial Park. Ont. Dept. Lands For. Res. Rep. (Wildl.) 87. 92pp.

CHAPTER 52
WOLVES AND CONGRESS:
PROPOSED LEGISLATION

One of the questions facing proponents of Yellowstone wolf recovery was what part of the legal process should be put to work to accomplish it. Though eventually the National Environmental Policy Act, with its environmental impact statement process, was employed to bring wolves to Yellowstone, both proponents and opponents flirted for a few years with a more direct approach: passing a law.

The first of these proposed bills was submitted by Utah Congressman Wayne Owens, an outspoken advocate of wolf restoration. On September 30, 1987, in an attempt to stir up interest in the issue and serve notice that it was here to stay, Owens introduced H.R. 3378 "To require the National Park Service to reintroduce wolves into Yellowstone National Park." The Owens bill was referred to the Committee on Interior and Insular Affairs, from which it never emerged. But it did raise the issue and generated a great deal of attention among wolf restoration friends and enemies.

100TH CONGRESS 1ST SESSION, H.R. 3378
A BILL
To require the National Park Service to reintroduce wolves into Yellowstone National Park.

Be it enacted by the Senate and House of Representatives of the United States of America in Congress assembled,

SECTION 1. REINTRODUCTION OF WOLVES INTO YELLOWSTONE

The Secretary of the Interior, acting through the Director of the National Park Service, shall take such steps as may be necessary to reintroduce wolves into Yellowstone National Park. The project to carry out such reintroduction shall be commenced as expeditiously as practicable and shall be completed within 3 years after the date of enactment of this Act.

SOURCES: As given in the introduction of each selection.

Two years later, on June 28, 1989, Owens enlisted many colleagues to cosponsor a more expansively stated bill with the same goal. This time he addressed the issues involved more specifically, calling for an environmental impact statement and due consideration of all relevant concerns, such as the effects of wolves on livestock. Owens also surfaced a very controversial idea that was already part of the public dialogue: giving these restored wolves a special "experimental designation" that could exempt them from some terms of the Endangered Species Act, thus making them easier to control and, he hoped, making wolf recovery more palatable to livestock interests. This bill was not passed either and because of its mention of the experimental designation, was even criticized by some pro-wolf groups.

101ST CONGRESS 1ST SESSION, H.R. 2786
IN THE HOUSE OF REPRESENTATIVES
JUNE 28, 1989

Mr. Owens of Utah (for himself, Ms. Schneider, Mr. Fuster, Mr. Bates, Mr. Solomon, Mr. Kasich, Mr. Fish, Mr. Neal of North Carolina, Mr. Ford of Tennessee, Mr. DeFazio, Mr. Evans, Mr. Lewis of Georgia, Mr. Ford of Michigan, Mr. Anderson, Mr. Mineta, Mr. Ravenel, Mr. Henry, Mr. Bennett, Mr. Levine of California, Mr. Owens of New York, Mr. Pallone, Mr. Torres, Mr. Downey, Ms. Pelosi, Mr. Boucher, Mrs. Boxer, Mr. Scheuer, Mr. Green, Mr. Kastenmeier, Mr. Dixon, Mr. Smith of Florida, Mr. Miller of California, Mr. Boehlert, Mr. Lehman of California, Mr. McHugh, Mr. Weldon, Mr. Edwards of California, Mr. Kleczka, Mr. Brown of California, Mr. Crocket, Mr. Towns, Mr. Lipinski, Mr. Clement, Mr. Dellums, Mr. Weiss, Mr. Buechner, Mr. Kostmayer, Mr. Wolpe, Mr. de Lugo, Mr. Leland, Mr. Hughes, Mr. Hamilton, Mrs. Schroeder, and Mr. Skaggs), introduced the following bill; which was referred jointly to the Committees on Merchant Marine and Fisheries and Interior and Insular Affairs.

A BILL

To provide for a timely analysis of all factors relating to the restoration of gray wolves to Yellowstone National Park and surrounding public lands, and for other purposes.

Be it enacted by the Senate and House of Representatives of the United States of America in Congress assembled,

SEC. 1. FINDINGS.

The Congress finds that—
(1) the gray wolf, indigenous to the northern Rocky Mountains, was extirpated from this region by poisoning, trapping, and government control;
(2) the policy of the National Park Service is to restore ecosystem balance by reintroducing indigenous species extirpated by man;
(3) the gray wolf is listed as an endangered species in the conterminous United States (except in Minnesota where it is listed as threatened); therefore Federal agencies have a nondiscretionary mandate to effect wolf recovery;
(4) experts in wolf biology from North America have addressed wolf population viability and outlined criteria for prompt delisting from endangered species and threatened species status;
(5) the Northern Rocky Mountain Rocky [sic.] Recovery Plan states that translocation of wolves to the Greater Yellowstone Area is now timely;
(6) the Recovery Plan provides for wolf recovery in a manner that is consistent with the National Environmental Policy Act of 1969; and
(7) The Recovery Plan is now two years behind its proposed schedule for implementation.

SEC. 2. PURPOSE.

It is the purpose of this Act to provide for a timely analysis of all factors relating to the proposed restoration of gray wolves to the Greater Yellowstone Area without further delay through a process consistent with the National Environmental Policy Act of 1969 (42 U.S.C. 4321 et seq.).

SEC. 3. ENVIRONMENTAL IMPACT STATEMENT FOR WOLF RECOVERY.

(a) Preparation.—The Secretary of the Interior shall prepare an environmental impact statement in accordance with the National Environmental Policy Act of 1969 (42 U.S.C. 4321 et seq.) for the reintroduction of gray wolves to Yellowstone National Park and adjacent public lands, generally known as the(sic.) "the Greater Yellowstone Area" in accordance with the provisions of the Recovery Plan. The environmental impact statement shall be completed by December 31, 1991.

(b) EIS State Participation.—In preparing the environmental impact statement under subsection (a), the Secretary shall invite the specific views of the Governors and representatives from the State wildlife management agency and the State agriculture agency of each of the States of Wyoming, Montana, and Idaho to participate.

(c) Particular EIS Considerations.—In preparing the environmental impact statement under subsection (a), the team designated by the Secretary shall, among other things, consider—

(1)   the potential for wolves to leave the recovery area and cause damage to domestic livestock and evaluate measures to resolve conflicts;
(2)   the wildlife management responsibilities and objectives of the States of Wyoming, Montana, and Idaho; and
(3)   the possibility of reintroducing gray wolves as an experimental population under section 10(j) of the Endangered Species Act (16 U.S.C. 1539(j)).

SEC. 4. WOLF RECOVERY DECISION.

(a) Decision by Secretary.—Within 60 days after the completion of the environmental impact statement under section 3, the Secretary shall select an alternative consistent with the Endangered Species Act, the National Environmental Policy Act of 1969, and this Act.

(b) Implementation of Decision.—Within six months after the decision under subsection (a), the Secretary, in consultation with the Secretary of Agriculture and the Governors of the States of Wyoming, Montana, Idaho, shall begin the implementation of the decision.

(c) Financial Assistance For State Wolf Conservation and Management Plans.—In carrying out the Endangered Species Act (16 U.S.C. 1531 et seq.), the Secretary is authorized and directed to provide financial assistance to each of the States of Wyoming, Montana, and Idaho for the implementation of wolf conservation and management plans.

SEC. 5. DEFINITIONS.

For the purposes of this Act—

(1) the Greater Yellowstone Area shall comprise Yellowstone National Park and that area generally described for wolf restoration by the Recovery Plan, with such further modification as may be determined by the Secretary based on the environmental impact statement referred to in section 3;

(2) the term "Recovery Plan" means the Northern Rocky Mountain Wolf Recovery Plan (approved by the Secretary on August 3, 1987); and

(3) the term "Secretary" means the Secretary of the Interior.

The third attempt to legislate a resolution to the wolf recovery debate may have been the most interesting and in some ways the most influential. On May 22, 1990, Idaho Senator James McClure introduced S. 2674, which was something of a surprise to many participants in the wolf debates. For, although its goals were extremely modest in terms of how many wolves should be introduced, and although it was unacceptable to most conservationists because it required limiting the wolves' endangered status, it was still a remarkable gesture coming from a lifelong opponent of wolf recovery.

McClure's bill seems to have been pragmatic; he is now seen as having had the foresight to understand that one way or another, wolves were coming, and the people who didn't like it had best take part in the process by which they arrived. Like the Owens bills before it, the McClure bill came to nothing in terms of law, but is seen as a major political breakthrough in the public debate. The ranks of the very powerful anti-wolf congressional delegations in the three states around Yellowstone had been broken, and although McClure retired shortly afterward, the practical wisdom he displayed did not all leave with him.

Nevertheless, in 1990, for the third straight year, Congress toyed with the idea of funding an environmental impact statement and did not. Its next course of action is the subject of the next chapter.

A BILL

To provide for the reestablishment of the gray wolf in Yellowstone National Park and the Central Idaho Wilderness Areas.

Be it enacted by the Senate and the House of Representatives of the United States of America in Congress assembled, That this Act may be referred to as the "Northern Rocky Mountain Gray Wolf Restoration Act of 1990."

SEC. 2. Within two years from the date of enactment of this Act, the Secretary of the Interior is directed to introduce three Alpha pairs of gray wolves each into Yellowstone National Park and into the Idaho portion of the Selway–Bitteroot and River of No Return Wilderness areas within the areas designated as "Core Zone" on the map entitled "Wolf Core Zone—Idaho, Montana, Wyoming" dated May 17, 1990. Prior to introduction of such wolves, the Secretary shall consult with the Governors of Idaho, Montana, and Wyoming and the Secretary of Agriculture.

SEC. 3. Upon introduction, natural dispersal of the wolves shall be permitted and no effort may be taken to restrict such dispersal: *Provided,* That the Secretary shall immediately replace any wolves that do not remain within the core zones. Each wolf introduced pursuant to this Act shall be equipped with a radio collar for monitoring purposes. At such time as the Secretary determines that three pairs have established themselves within the core zone in Idaho for a period of three years, the Secretary shall restrict the boundaries of the core zone to coincide with the established territories.

SEC. 4. The Secretary is authorized and directed to permit the natural recolonization of gray wolves in the area designated as a "Natural Recovery Area" on the map entitled "Natural Recovery Area—Montana" dated May 22, 1990.

SEC. 5. Effective on the date of enactment, the gray wolf is hereby declared and determined not to be a threatened or endangered species within the meaning of the Endangered Species Act (P. L. 93–205, 87 Stat. 884, as amended) outside the areas designated as "Core Zone" on the map referred to in section 2 of this Act outside the area designated as a "Natural Recovery Area" on the map referred to in section 4 of this Act within the States of Idaho, Montana, and Wyoming and may not be so determined in the future other than by specific designation as such in an Act of Congress.

CHAPTER 53
WOLVES AND CONGRESS: THE WOLF MANAGEMENT COMMITTEE AND THE FUNDING OF THE EIS

On November 5, 1990, Congress tried another approach to breaking the deadlock over wolf restoration, directing the Secretary of the Interior to create a Wolf Management Committee to prepare a report on wolf restoration for both Yellowstone and the Central Idaho Wilderness.

The managers agree that the Secretary shall, within 30 days of enactment, appoint a 10 member Wolf Management Committee. The Committee's task shall be to develop a wolf– reintroduction and management plan for Yellowstone National Park and the Central Idaho Wilderness Area. The Committee shall consist of the following:

1. One representative from the Fish & Game Departments of each of the States of Idaho, Montana and Wyoming.
2. One representative from the National Park Service.
3. One representative from the U.S. Forest Service.
4. One representative from the U.S. Fish and Wildlife Service.
5. Two representatives from conservation organizations.
6. Two representatives from the livestock/hunting community.

The panel shall make available to the Secretary and the Congress by May 15, 1991 its completed plan along with its recommendations. The Committee's plan shall represent a consensus agreement of Committee members with at least six members supporting the plan.

An inside story of the work of this committee appears in a book by one of the members. Hank Fischer represented Defenders of Wildlife, and his 1995 book The Wolf Wars, *reviews the deliberations of the committee at some length. Here are the recommendations, which were issued on April 30, 1991.*

SOURCES: As given in the selections.

WOLF MANAGEMENT COMMITTEE RECOMMENDATIONS

1. Concurrent with the beginning of the development of the EIS, rulemaking, and State management plans, Congress will designate the area of Idaho, Montana, [and] Wyoming (with the exception of the Glacier Area as defined by the Committee) as a nonessential, experimental area for purposes of wolf recovery. This designation to remain in force until July 1, 1993. Until such time as the States' wolf management plans are implemented and the EIS and rulemaking processes are completed, the FWS intends to manage wolves in the experimental population area substantially in accord with the attached Wolf Management Plan Summary and accompanying text; and

2. at the same time, Congress will declare that the primary management authority for wolves outside of the defined Glacier Area and National Parks and National Wildlife Refuges will be under the jurisdiction of the States. To assume this authority, the States must have adopted wolf management plans agreed to buy the Secretary of the Interior and Secretary of Agriculture and the Governors of the involved States prior to release of wolves in Yellowstone National Park, but no later than July 1, 1993. The Committee recommends that the States follow the guidelines in the Wolf Management Plan Summary in developing State wolf management plans; and

3. at the same time, Congress will declare as basic components of any acceptable State wolf management plan, as described in the preceding paragraph: (a) the right of involved States to manage wolves and their unacceptable impacts on livestock, big game resources, and multiple land uses; and (b) the responsibility to pursue wolf recovery.

Congress chose not to act on the Wolf Management Committee's report, but the report did become a part of the environmental impact statement, which, after several years of being authorized in the House and then stopped in the Senate, was finally funded as follows.

102D CONGRESS
1ST SESSION
HOUSE OF REPRESENTATIVES
REPORT 102-256

MAKING APPROPRIATIONS FOR THE DEPARTMENT OF THE INTE-
RIOR AND RELATED AGENCIES, FOR THE FISCAL YEAR ENDING
SEPTEMBER 30, 1992, AND FOR OTHER PURPOSES

October 17, 1991.—Ordered to be printed

Mr. Yates, from the committee of conference, submitted the following
CONFERENCE REPORT
[To accompany H.R. 2686]

The managers have agreed to include language in the bill to prohibit
use of funds in this Act to reintroduce wolves into Yellowstone National
Park and Central Idaho. The managers further agree that:

1. The Fish and Wildlife Service is to prepare an environmental impact
   statement in consultation with the National Park Service and Forest
   Service. For this purpose, $348,000 is provided for the Fish and Wild-
   life Service and $150,000 is provided for the National Park Service.
   Forest Service needs are to be covered within funding for the agency's
   endangered species responsibilities.
2. The environmental impact statement is to cover a broad range of alternatives.
3. The draft environmental impact statement should be completed no
   later than 18 months after enactment of the 1992 Interior appropriations bill.
4. The Fish and Wildlife Service is to provide quarterly reports on the
   progress of the draft EIS.
5. The Fish and Wildlife Service should follow normal distribution patterns for EIS including appropriate Congressional distribution

*This language was repeated in the Congressional Record (House of Representa-
tives), October 17, 1991, H8075. President George Bush signed Public Law 102-154
on November 13, 1991, making the draft environmental impact statement due on
May 13, 1993.*

*In the meantime, two exchanges among lawmakers, from the Congressional
Record, bear on the wolf restoration process as they reflect specific concerns held by
regional delegations.*

Congressional Record — Senate, September 20, 1991, S13408

Wolves

Mr. BAUCUS. Mr. President, I have not been a supporter of artificial reintroduction of wolves into Yellowstone National Park. However, I have joined with Senator BURNS and my colleagues from Wyoming and Idaho in sponsoring this amendment because I believe that the preparation of an environmental impact statement on reintroduction of wolves to Yellowstone and central Idaho is the best means to get a full and fair look at the social, economic, and biological issues involved. This amendment requires only a study, and, in fact, prohibits any use of funds in fiscal year 1992 for the reintroduction of wolves to these areas.

I share the views of my colleague from Montana with respect to the scope of the alternatives to be considered by the environmental impact statement required by this amendment. It is my understanding that the preparation of this environmental impact statement does not mean that wolves will or will not be reintroduced to Yellowstone and central Idaho. The environmental impact statement is merely a means of exploring all possible alternatives and consequences concerning reintroduction of wolves to Yellowstone and central Idaho, including the possibility of taking no action and allowing wolves to return to these areas on their own if that is what happens. Further, it is my understanding that this amendment is not intended to either rule out consideration of alternatives in the environmental impact statement that would require changes to existing law or to encourage such changes.

I would ask the distinguished chairman of the Appropriations Committee if he shares my understanding of this amendment.

Mr. BYRD. I would respond to the senior Senator from Montana and chairman of the Subcommittee on Environmental Protection that I do share his views with respect to these matters.

Mr. BURNS. Mr. President, I would like to briefly discuss my understanding of the agreed upon amendment dealing with appropriating funds for a Fish and Wildlife Service environmental impact statement on the introduction of Rocky Mountain gray wolves in Yellowstone National Park and the Central Idaho Wilderness.

Although portions of Montana contain identified recovery areas for the gray wolf, no introduction is planned specifically for any area in Montana. This is because wolves are migrating into Montana and northern Idaho from Canada and naturally recolonizing those States. The wolf population in Montana has been increasing slowly for the past couple of years and appears to be increasing its range beyond the confines of the recovery area, concerns increase regarding the management of the wolf.

There are a number of people in Montana that would prefer not to have any wolves in the State. At the same time many others don't particularly care about wolves one way or the other as long as they are managed properly.

My understanding is that in addition to developing alternatives for the introduction of wolves into Yellowstone and central Idaho, the environmental impact statement will also address the concerns of management of wolves that are naturally recolonizing as well as the management of any wolves that are introduced. This would include an evaluation of any impact of wolves on areas surrounding Yellowstone and central Idaho, including the adjacent lands in Montana.

I have discussed this entire issue with the Senator from Idaho [Mr. CRAIG] and I believe I can say that he has the same understanding.

As a matter of standard procedure, the environmental impact statement should also contain an alternative that will consider allowing the natural recolonization of the wolf without additional introduction. This would be the so-called no action alternative. I believe that I speak for both Senator CRAIG and myself when I say that natural recolonization is the preferred option.

I wonder if the distinguished floor manager would agree that he has the same understanding?

Mr. BYRD. The Senator is correct.

Mr. CRAIG. Mr. President, I would like to clarify with the distinguished chairman and ranking member of the Interior and Related Agencies Appropriations Subcommittee an issue relevant to the amendment adopted on wolf reintroduction in Yellowstone National Park Park and central Idaho. I feel it is most important that there be a comprehensive analysis within the environmental impact statement that evaluates the social and economic aspects of each alternative. I am particularly interested that the costs of predation on livestock and the resulting effects on local and regional economies be fully evaluated and displayed.

Mr. BYRD. Mr. President, Senator Craig is correct it is the intention of the committee that a comprehensive analysis of the social and economic impacts of each alternative be included in the environmental impact statement.

Mr. NICKLES. I concur with the chairman's statement.

Congressional Record — Senate, October 31, 1991, S15674

Reintroduction of Wolves to Yellowstone

Mr. WALLOP. Mr. President, on page 16 of the statement of managers, the managers have agreed to include language which would direct the Fish and Wildlife Service to complete an environmental impact statement on the reintroduction of wolves to Yellowstone National Park. The managers further agreed that the environmental impact statement is to cover a broad range of alternatives. I would like to ask the chairman of the committee whether the wolf management report referred to in H.R. 2686 as passed by the Senate on September 19, 1991, is to be considered as one of the alternatives?

Mr. BYRD. The Senator is correct, and I believe my colleague, the distinguished ranking member of the subcommittee, concurs in my assessment.

Mr. NICKLES. If the Senator will yield for a moment.

Mr. BYRD. I yield to the Senator from Oklahoma.

Mr. NICKLES. I thank the Senator and would say to my colleague from Wyoming, the managers report language does not disagree with nor negate the language of the Senate-passed bill. The Senator from West Virginia is correct—a broad range of alternatives would include the recommendations of the Wolf Management Committee report published as and entitled "Reintroduction and Management of Wolves in Yellowstone National Park and Central Idaho Wilderness Area."

Mr. WALLOP. Mr. President, I thank both the Senator from West Virginia and the Senator from Oklahoma for their response and appreciate their assistance in this very important matter.

CHAPTER 54
CHRONOLOGY OF THE EIS

Once authorized, the EIS moved steadily ahead. It faced formidable hurdles in one of the most extensive public involvement processes in the history of wildlife management.

11/13/91	Congress directs FWS to prepare EIS on wolf reintroduction into Yellowstone National Park and central Idaho.
12/3/91	EIS team selections begin, continue through March 1992.
3/92	Idaho Legislature passes bill that allows Idaho Fish and Game to participate in EIS.
3/23/92	News release on issue scoping open houses issued.
3/25/92	Letter and poster requesting participation sent to over 2,500 groups or individuals that may be interested in EIS.
4/3/92	Notice of Intent to prepare EIS published in Federal Register. News release provided.
4/3/92	Issue scoping brochure sent to 10,000 people on mailing list.
4/6/92	Series of 34 issue scoping open houses (9 each in Wyoming, Montana, Idaho and 7 National) began, 1,730 people attended.
5/15/92	Issue Scoping Comment period closed. Nearly 4,000 comments received.
6/29/92	Notice of Hearings published in Federal Register.
7/8/92	Issue scoping report sent to 16,000 people on mailing list, includes alternative scoping open house schedule.
7/10/92	News release on issue scoping report issued.
7/17/92	News release announcing alternative scoping open houses issued.

SOURCE: U.S. Fish and Wildlife Service. 1994. *Final Environmental Impact Statement: The reintroduction of gray wolves to Yellowstone National Park and central Idaho.* Helena: U.S. Fish and Wildlife Service, pp. 6–26.

7/30/92	Alternative scoping brochure mailed to about 20,000 people on mailing list.
7/31/92	News release on alternative scoping hearings issued.
8/2/92	Brochure inserted in 230,000 Sunday newspapers in Wyoming, Idaho, and Montana.
8/3/92	Series of 27 alternative scoping open houses began, 491 people attended.
8/18/92	Series of 6 alternative scoping hearings begins, about 1,400 people attended and 430 testified.
9/4/92	Comment period for alternative scoping closed, nearly 5,000 comments received. News release issued.
11/18/92	Alternative scoping report sent to about 31,000 people on mailing list, representing all 50 states and 40 foreign countries.
1/4/93	DEIS is prepared.
4/93	DEIS progress report was sent to about 32,000 people remaining on mailing list.
6/93	DEIS completed and public review requested during 90 days public comment period.
8/93 and 9/93	16 public hearings conducted; 4 locations in each state of Idaho, Montana, and Wyoming and 4 in cities in other parts of the country. More than 1,500 people attended and about 700 presented testimony at these hearings.
11/26/93	Comment period on DEIS closed.
12/10/93	Analysis of over 160,000 public comments on DEIS completed.
3/94	Summary of public comment mailed to about 42,000 people and organizations on Gray Wolf EIS mailing list.
5/94	Final EIS released.

CHAPTER 55
THE RULES

Following revisions based on public comment, the final EIS was produced. The final rules are the guidelines for the restoration process now under way. As the previous chapter showed, the EIS was released in May 1994. The record of decision, which required that wolf recovery as described in the EIS be undertaken, was signed by Secretary of the Interior Bruce Babbitt on June 15 and by Secretary of Agriculture Mike Espy on July 19. The proposed rules were published on August 16 for public review, and the final rules were published as follows in the Federal Register *in November 1994.*

The text in the Federal Register *runs to 30 pages, and includes various summaries and responses to public comments. What follows is only the final section of this material: the amended rule providing for management of the recovery and the recovered wolves.*

It is worth emphasizing that this rule, like all prior stages in the recovery process, underwent public scrutiny far beyond that of almost all other wildlife management decision-making processes. Complaints persisted from some quarters that wolf recovery did not pay adequate attention to this or that viewpoint, but the level of public involvement, and the attention paid to all viewpoints, was extraordinary, perhaps even unprecedented, in the history of American wildlife management. The guidelines that emerged from that long and contentious process were unsatisfactory or less than perfect in the eyes of many participating groups, but all positions were heard, usually many times, during the dialogue.

An element of special importance in the final rules is the "experimental nonessential" designation. As a concession to those people who feared that full protection of wolves under the Endangered Species Act would hinder adequate management and control of wolves, the experimental-nonessential designation was instituted. This designation relaxed the customary restrictions on the removal of problem animals through a variety of closely regulated and carefully defined means. It represented a compromise between those seeking full protection for wolves as an endangered species, and those who, like Senator McClure (Chapter 52), were willing to have recovery proceed, but only if the wolves had no special protection under the Endangered Species Act. Yellowstone wolf recovery will provide an interesting and probably precedent–setting test of this designation.

SOURCE: *Federal Register*, Vol. 59, No. 224, Tuesday, November 22, 1994, pp. 60279– 60281.

50 CFR PART 17
ESTABLISHMENT OF A NONESSENTIAL EXPERIMENTAL POPU-
LATION OF GRAY WOLVES IN YELLOWSTONE NATIONAL
PARK IN WYOMING, IDAHO, MONTANA, CENTRAL IDAHO
AND SOUTHWESTERN MONTANA; FINAL RULES

§17.84 Special rules–Vertebrates.

(i) Gray wolf (Canis Lupus)

(1) The gray wolves (wolf) identified in paragraph (i)(7) of this section are nonessential experimental. These wolves will be managed in accordance with the respective provisions of this section.

(2) The Service finds that reintroduction of nonessential experimental gray wolves, as defined in (i)(7) of this section, will further the conservation of the species.

(3) No person may take this species in the wild in an experimental population area except as provided in paragraphs (i)(3), (7), and (8) of this section.

(i) Landowners on their private land and livestock producers (i.e. producers of cattle, sheep, horses and mules or as defined in State and tribal wolf management plans as approved by the Service) that are legally using public land (Federal land and any other public lands designated in the State and tribal wolf management plans as approved by the Service) may harass any wolf in an opportunistic (the wolf cannot be purposely attracted, tracked, waited for, or searched out, then harassed) and noninjurious (no temporary or permanent physical damage may result) manner at any time, *Provided* that such harassment is non–lethal or is not physically injurious to the gray wolf and is reported within 7 days to the Service project leader for wolf reintroduction or agency representative designated by the Service.

(ii) Any livestock producers on their private land may take (including to kill or injure) a wolf in the act of killing, wounding, or biting livestock (cattle, sheep, horses, and mules or as defined in State and tribal wolf management plans as approved by the Service), *Provided* that such incidents are to be immediately reported within 24 hours to the Service project leader for wolf reintroduction or agency representative designated by the Service, and livestock freshly (less than 24 hours) wounded (torn flesh and bleeding) or killed by wolves must be evident. Service or other Service authorized agencies will confirm if livestock were wounded or killed by wolves. The taking of any wolf without such evidence may be referred to the appropriate authorities for prosecution.

(iii) Any livestock producer or permittee with livestock grazing allotments on public land may receive a written permit, valid for up to 45 days, from the Service or other agencies designated by the Service, to take (including to kill or injure) a wolf that is in the act of killing, wounding, or biting livestock (cattle, sheep, horses, and mules or as defined in State and tribal wolf management plans as approved by the Service), *Provided* that six or more breeding pairs of wolves have been documented in the experimental population area and the Service or other agencies authorized by the Service has confirmed that the livestock losses were caused by wolves and have completed agency efforts to resolve the problem. Such take must be reported immediately within 24 hours to the Service project leader for wolf reintroduction or agency representative designated by the Service. There must be evidence of freshly wounded or killed livestock by wolves. Service or other Service authorized agencies will investigate and determine if the livestock were wounded or killed by wolves. The taking of any wolf without such evidence may be referred to the appropriate authorities for prosecution.

(iv) Potentially affected States and tribes may capture and translocate wolves to other areas within an experimental population area as described in paragraph (i)(7), *Provided* the level of wolf predation is negatively impacting localized ungulate populations at an unacceptable level. Such translocations cannot inhibit wolf population recovery. The States and tribes will define such unacceptable impacts, how they would be measured, and identify other possible mitigation in their State or tribal wolf management plans. These plans must be approved by the Service before such movement of wolves may be conducted.

(v) The Service, or agencies authorized by the service, may promptly remove (place into captivity or kill) any wolf the Service or agency authorized by the Service determines to present a threat to human life or safety.

(vi) Any person may harass or take (kill or injure) a wolf in self defense or in defense of others, *Provided* that such take is reported immediately (within 24 hours) to the Service reintroduction project leader or Service designated agent. The taking of a wolf without an immediate and direct threat to human life may be referred to the appropriate authorities for prosecution.

(vii) The Service or agencies designated by the Service may take wolves that are determined to be "problem" wolves. Problem wolves are defined as wolves that in a calendar year attack livestock (cattle, sheep, horses, and mules) or as defined by State and tribal wolf management plans approved by the Service or wolves that twice in a calendar year attack domestic animals (all domestic animals other than livestock). Authorized take includes, but is not limited to non-lethal measures such as: aversive conditioning, nonlethal control, and/or translocating wolves. Such taking may be done when five or fewer breeding pairs are established in an experimental population area. If the take results in a wolf mortality, then evidence that the mortality was nondeliberate, accidental, nonnegligent, and unavoidable must be provided. When six or more breeding pairs are established in the experimental population area, lethal control of problem wolves or permanent placement in captivity will be authorized but only after other methods to resolve livestock depredations have been exhausted. Depredations occurring on Federal Lands or other public identified in State or tribal management plans and prior to six breeding pairs becoming established in an experimental population area may result in capture and release of the female wolf with pups, and pups at or near the site of capture prior to October 1. All wolves on private land, including female wolves with pups, may be relocated or moved to other areas within the experimental population area if continued depredation occurs. Wolves attacking domestic animals other than livestock, including pets on private land, two or more times in a calendar year will be relocated. All chronic problem wolves (wolves that depredate on domestic animals after being moved once for previous domestic animal depredations) will be removed from the wild (killed or placed in captivity). The following three criteria will be used in determining the status of problem wolves within the nonessential experimental population area:

(A) There must be evidence of wounded livestock or partial remains of a livestock carcass that clearly shows that the injury or death was clearly caused by wolves. Such evidence is essential since wolves may feed on carrion which they found and did not kill. There must be reason to believe that additional livestock losses would occur if no control action is taken.

(B) There must be no evidence of artificial or intentional feeding of wolves. Improperly disposed of livestock carcasses in the area of depredation will be considered attractants. Livestock carrion or carcasses on public land, not being used as bait under an agency authorized control action, must be removed or otherwise disposed so that it will not attract wolves.

(C) On public lands, animal husbandry practices previously identified in existing approved allotment plans and annual operating plans for allotments must have been followed.

(viii) Any person may take a gray wolf found in an area defined in paragraph (i)(7), *Provided* that the take is incidental to an otherwise lawful activity, accidental, unavoidable, unintentional, and not resulting from negligent conduct lacking reasonable due care, and due care was exercised to avoid taking a gray wolf. Such taking is to be reported within 24 hours to a Service or Service designated authority. Take that does not conform with such provisions may be referred to the appropriate authorities for prosecution.

(ix) Service or other Federal, State, or tribal personnel may receive written authorization from the Service to take animals under special circumstances. Wolves may be live captured and translocated to resolve demonstrated conflicts with ungulate populations or with other species listed under the Act, or when they are found outside of the designated experimental population area. Take procedures in such instances would involve live capture and release to a remote area or placement in a captive facility, if the animal is clearly unfit to remain in the wild. Killing of wolves will be a last resort and is only authorized when live capture attempts have failed or there is clear endangerment to human life.

(x) Any person with a valid permit issued by the Service under §17.32 may take wolves in the wild in the experimental population area, pursuant to terms of the permit.

(xi) Any employee or agent of the Service or appropriate Federal, State, or tribal agency, who is designated in writing for such purposes by the Service, when acting in the course of official duties, may take a wolf from the wild within the experimental population area, if such action is for:

(A) Scientific purposes;

(B) To relocate wolves to avoid conflict with human activities;

(C) To relocate wolves within the experimental population areas to improve wolf survival and recovery prospects;

(D) To relocate wolves that have moved outside the experimental population area back into the experimental population area;

(E) To aid or euthanize sick, injured, or orphaned wolves;

(F) To salvage a dead specimen which may be used for scientific study; or

(G) To aid in law enforcement investigations involving wolves.

(xii) Any taking pursuant to this section must be reported immediately (within 24 hours) to the appropriate Service or Service-designated agency, which will determine the disposition of any live or dead specimens.

(4) Human access to areas with facilities where wolves are confined may be restricted at the discretion of Federal, State, and tribal land management agencies. When five or fewer breeding pairs are in an experimental population area, land-use restrictions may also be employed on an as-needed basis, at the discretion of Federal land management and natural resources agencies to control intrusive human disturbance around active wolf den sites. Such temporary restrictions on human access, when five or fewer breeding pairs are established in an experimental population area, may be required between April 1 and June 30, within 1 mile of active wolf den or rendezvous sites and would only apply to public lands or other such lands designated in State and tribal wolf management plans. When six or more breeding pairs are established in an experimental population area, no land-use restrictions may be employed outside of national parks or national wildlife refuges, unless wolf populations fail to maintain positive growth rates toward population recovery levels for 2 consecutive years. If such a situation arose, State and tribal agencies would identify, recommend, and implement corrective management actions within 1 year, possibly including appropriate land-use restrictions to promote growth of the wolf population.

(5) No person shall possess, sell, deliver, carry, transport, ship, import, or export by any means whatsoever, any wolf or part thereof from the experimental populations taken in violation of the regulations in paragraph (i) of this section or in violation of applicable State or tribal fish and wildlife laws or regulations or the Endangered Species Act.

(6) It is unlawful for any person to attempt to commit, solicit another to commit, or cause to be committed any offense defined in this section.

(7) The site for reintroduction is within the historic range of the species:

(i) The central Idaho area is shown on the map on the following page. The boundaries of the nonessential experimental population area will be those portions of Idaho that are south of Interstate Highway 90 and west of Interstate 15, and those portions of Montana south of Interstate 90, Highway 93 and 12 from Missoula, Montana west of Interstate 15.

(ii) The Yellowstone Management Area is shown on the map on page 269. The boundaries of the nonessential experimental population area will be that portion of Idaho that is east of Interstate Highway 15; that

Central Idaho Nonessential Experimental Population Area

portion of Montana that is east of Interstate Highway 15 and south of the Missouri River from Great Falls, Montana, to the eastern Montana border; and all of Wyoming.

(iii) All wolves found in the wild within the boundaries of this paragraph (i)(7) after the first releases will be considered nonessential experimental animals. In the conterminous United States, a wolf that is outside an experimental area (as defined in paragraph (i)(7) of this section) would be considered as endangered (or threatened if in Minnesota) unless it is marked or otherwise known to be an experimental animal; such a wolf may be captured for examination and genetic testing by the Service or Service-designated agency. Disposition of the captured animal may take any of the following courses:

(A) If the animal was not involved in conflicts with humans and is determined likely to be an experimental wolf, it will be returned to the reintroduction area.

(B) If the animal is determined likely to be an experimental wolf and was involved in conflicts with humans as identified in the management plan for the closest experimental area, it may be relocated, placed in captivity, or killed.

(C) If the animal is determined not likely to be an experimental animal, it will be managed according to any Service approved plans for that area or will be marked and released near its point of capture.

(D) If the animal is determined not to be a wild gray wolf or if the

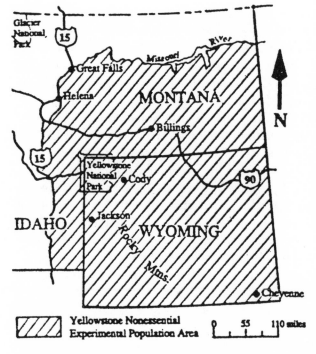

Yellowstone Nonessential
Experimental Population Area

Service or agencies designated by the Service determine the animal shows physical or behavioral evidence of hybridization with other canids, such as domestic dogs or coyotes, or of being an animal raised in captivity, it will be returned to captivity or killed.

(8) The reintroduced wolves will be monitored during the life of the project, including by the use of radio telemetry and other remote sensing devices as appropriate. All released animals will be vaccinated against disease and parasites prevalent in canids, as appropriate, prior to release and during subsequent handling. Any animal that is sick, injured, or otherwise in need of special care may be captured by authorized personnel of the Service or Service-designated agencies and given appropriate care. Such an animal will be released back into its respective reintroduction area as soon as possible, unless physical or behavioral problems make it necessary to return the animal to captivity or euthanize it.

(9) The status of the experimental population will be reevaluated within the first 3 years, after the first year of releases of wolves, to determine future management needs and if further reintroductions are required. This review will take into account the reproductive success and movement patterns of the individuals released in the area, as well as the overall health and fate of the experimental wolves. Once recovery goals are met for downlisting or delisting the species, a rule will be proposed to address downlisting or delisting.

(10) The Service does not intend to reevaluate the "nonessential experimental" designation. The Service does not foresee any likely situa-

tion which would result in changing the nonessential experimental status until the gray wolf is recovered and delisted in the northern Rocky Mountains according to provisions outlined in the Act. However, if the wolf population does not demonstrate positive growth toward recovery goals for 2 consecutive years, the affected States and tribes, in cooperation with the Service, would, within 1 year, identify and initiate wolf management strategies, including appropriate public review and comment, to ensure continued wolf population growth toward recovery levels. All reintroduced wolves designated as nonessential experimental will be removed from the wild and the experimental population status and regulations revoked when (i) legal actions or lawsuits change the wolves status to endangered under the Act or (ii) within 90 days of the initial release date, naturally occurring wolves, consisting of two breeding pairs that for 2 consecutive years have each successfully raised two offspring, are discovered in the experimental population area. The naturally occurring wolves would be managed and protected as endangered species under the Act.

Dated: November 15, 1994.
George T. Frampton, Jr.
Assistant Secretary for Fish and Wildlife and Parks
[FR Doc. 94–28747 Filed 11–18–94; 8:45am]

Part IV

Wolves Arrive

T he return of the wolf to Yellow-
stone National Park has been one of the great media events, and perhaps
one of the great symbolic events as well, of the modern conservation
movement. The legal struggles, the preparations in the park, the capturing program in Canada, the dramatic airplane flight and trailer ride of
the animals and their escort, and the colorful and controversial public
statements by the supporting and opposing advocacy groups led to a
level of tension and suspense that attracted national attention. National
media provided frequent reports of those final contentious days when a
team of biologists waited in Canada for clearance to bring the wolves
south (they were bringing them both to Yellowstone and Idaho, where
releases also occurred, but Yellowstone, perhaps predictably, got most of
the headlines).

As the saying goes, news is not history. It will be quite a while yet
before we can view the events of 1994 and 1995 with enough distance to
understand what it will mean to Yellowstone, to wolves, and to the
public. In the meantime, it is not too soon to hear some of the voices of
those most directly involved in the process.

CHAPTER 56
RETURN OF A PREDATOR:
WOLF RECOVERY IN MONTANA

ED BANGS

Wolf recovery in Yellowstone is part of a larger process of wolf recovery in the Northern Rockies. It is important to have some background on events to the north and west of the park in the years that Yellowstone wolf recovery was being debated. In this 1990 article, U.S. Fish and Wildlife Service biologist Ed Bangs, project leader for the Wolf EIS, reviews the recolonization of Montana by wolves in recent years and considers some of the social consequences of that event.

Very few people felt any regret when the last traces of a viable wolf population vanished from the West in the 1920s. Most were proud that the predator eradication program started in the 1890s had successfully extirpated at least one varmint.

As wolves return to their historic ranges in Montana today, the public viewpoint is not so unanimous. Polls indicate that although two out of three Montanans believe wolves should be allowed to return, one-third feel that modern Montana has no place left for wolves (Johnson 1987). Controversy about wolf population recovery has been around since 1973, when wolves were listed as endangered under the powerful Federal Endangered Species Act (ESA). The debate grew shrill as wolves began dispersing into and found a foothold in the state.

Wolves are large social predators that kill and feed upon ungulates. The benefit of living and hunting in social groups is the strategy employed by the three most widely distributed mammals on earth in recent history: Humans, wolves and lions made their living in closely related family units (tribes, packs and prides) hunting large ungulates (Nowak 1981). This cooperative lifestyle generally includes a well-defined social hierarchy, territorial defense and sharing of resources. It allowed wolves to occupy a wide variety of habitats in almost every part of North American north of Mexico City.

SOURCE: *Western Wildlands*, Spring, 1991, pp. 7–13.

As humans greatly expanded their niche through agriculture, conflicts with what were once "brothers in the hunt" led to extreme competition for the forage base. Agriculturists killed wild ungulates both for food and to reduce competition with their domesticated animals. Large predators responded to the disappearance of wild ungulates by killing livestock. The stage was set for conflict between rapidly expanding human populations and wild animals. The battle between man and nature reached its highest intensity with the persecution of large predators.

In North America, like many other areas, the removal of wildness—plant, animal and land—peaked near the end of the 19th century. Bison, elk, antelope, deer, mountain sheep, waterfowl and upland birds fared no better than predators. Some, such as the passenger pigeon, became extinct. The last large, wild areas of the United States were in the Rocky Mountains, so it is no surprise that wolves and other species held out longer there. However, by the 1920s, the few remaining large predators were the targets of aggressive federal predator-elimination programs. A few grizzly bears survived in the remote areas, but wolves were eliminated from Montana by 1930.

They were banished to the most remote parts of northern Canada and Alaska, where the land was unsuitable for agriculture and livestock production. Even there, wolves were killed to "control the spread of diseases" or to "protect big game populations." However, since the wolves no longer were competing for what humans considered their personal property, society did not manifest the fierce desire required to persecute wolves to extinction. Wolves became synonymous with remote wilderness because these were the only areas where viable populations persisted. This banishment lasted for almost 50 years.

Thoreau once said that, "To regret deeply is to live afresh." Remorse over the intense persecution of wolves has probably contributed to the large number of wolf recovery programs throughout the world today. Alaska and Canada led efforts to let wolves recolonize historic habitats. By the 1960s, wildlife management agencies in several western provinces and Alaska were protecting wolves to promote population recovery. As a result, wolves reoccupied several areas, including Alaska's Kenai Peninsula (Peterson et al. 1984), Vancouver Island in British Columbia (Hebert et al. 1982) and southern Alberta and British Columbia near the U.S. border (Ream and Mattson 1982).

Wolves can rapidly reoccupy historic habitat. On the Kenai Peninsula, a recolonizing wolf population grew from a founding pair in 1967 to about 180 wolves in nine years, an increase of more than 40 percent annually. Once the available habitat was fully occupied and hunting was again allowed, the wolf population stabilized. Wolves were so rare on Vancouver Island that British Columbia considered listing them as a threatened species in 1970. Because of favorable conditions, the population rapidly increased, and wolves were considered abundant by 1979. In one area of Minnesota, a recovering wolf population grew at a record rate of more than 80 percent a year (Mech 1986).

If history teaches anything, it shows that wolf recovery in Montana can occur rapidly under favorable biological conditions. The primary reason that wolf populations do not rapidly recolonize suitable habitat is human–caused mortality.

Wolves are very adept at finding new areas. They mate and look for two basic things when dispersing to find a place to form a new pack. The first is an area without resident wolves. Established packs advertise their presence, and strange wolves that ignore their territorial claims are killed. Second, dispersing wolves require food, in the form of ungulates. Wolves can successfully make a living on a wide variety of prey, from bison to deer; they do best in areas with abundant prey, but they can survive in areas with relatively few prey. Ungulate populations in Montana are now at record high levels, and virtually none of the thousands of square miles of potential wolf habitat contain wolves, so the state is biologically picture–perfect for rapid population growth.

In 1985, a pack of 10 wolves occupied an area in Montana along the U.S./Canadian border. If wolves in the border area increase at a rate of 40 percent a year, there could be more than 190 wolves by 1994. Almost now one believes that wolf numbers will increase that quickly, but the U.S. Fish and Wildlife Service now estimates that wolves may be abundant enough by 1997—that is, the state will have at least ten breeding pairs for three successive years—to allow their removal from ESA protection and to be managed entirely by state or tribal agencies.

In addition to protection under the ESA, wolves are also covered by the 1973 Montana Endangered Species Act. These laws prohibit the killing of wolves by the public. The ESA also mandates development of a wolf recovery plan to outline the tasks needed to increase populations until they no longer require federal protection. The 1987 Wolf Recovery Plan recognized the need to minimize conflicts with agricultural and outdoor-recreation interests if wolves were to be tolerated by people who raise livestock, hunt ungulates and/or recreate on the public lands where wolves would be allowed to live.

Participating in the plans as part of an interagency task force are managers and biologists from the Fish and Wildlife Service, U.S. Forest Service, National Park Service and the Bureau of Land Management, Animal Damage Control, Blackfeet Nation and Confederated Salish and Kootenai Tribes of the Flathead Nation; cooperators in the group's recovery programs are the University of Montana, Montana Department of Fish, Wildlife and Parks, Montana Department of State Lands and Montana Department of Livestock.

Wolf recovery entails four major tasks for wildlife management agencies: 1) Wolf numbers and distribution are monitored to determine how close the population is to the ten breeding pairs goal; 2) wolves that kill livestock are controlled to minimize conflicts; 3) research is conducted to learn more about wolves and ungulates for later management use; and 4) accurate information about wolves and the recovery program is provided to the public.

Monitoring. The program to determine wolf distribution and abundance in Montana includes detection, confirmation and monitoring (Day 1981). Detection enlists the aid of the public to report wolf activity. The public detection program has been in effect since 1972 and led to discovery of the wolves near Glacier National Park (Ream and Mattson 1982). This program was accelerated in 1989, when personnel from resource management agencies throughout northwestern Montana were introduced to wolf identification and recovery. Presentations, new releases, publications and posters were used to encourage the public to report any wolf activity.

Any time a cooperating agency in the wolf recovery effort receives a report of a wolf sighting, it forwards the information to the Fish and Wildlife Service office in Helena, where the reports are compiled. Individuals who report wolf sightings receive an annual report, describing that year's activities and summarizing all wolf observations. In 1989, 162 wolf observations were reported; 265 were received in 1990.

When the public detection system provides a pattern of reports that suggests wolf pack activity, the confirmation phase begins. The Fish and Wildlife Service contacts the nearest cooperator, which then asks its field crews in the reported area to be alert for wolf sign. Specific surveys are also conducted, in which biologists use common inexpensive techniques, such as snow tracking or howling, to search for wolves.

If wolf packs are discovered, surveys are repeated to determine how many wolves are involved. Snow tracking during February can determine whether an estrus female is in the area by detecting bloody urine;

paired scent markings can indicate that a breeding pair is forming and pups may be imminent.

The third phase, monitoring, begins after the presence of breeding pair is confirmed. The newly discovered pack is followed with standard wolf capture and radio telemetry techniques. Several wolves in the pack are captured in traps or tranquilized from helicopters; they are then immobilized, examined and fitted with radio transmitters. Examination allows biologists to determine whether the wolves are actually wild. Although wolf-dog hybrids and domesticated wolves have almost no chance of surviving in the wild because they depend on food supplied by humans, their abnormal behavior can affect local attitudes about wolves; if found, they are immediately removed.

Wild wolves are released on-site and monitored from the ground or aircraft with radio-location data. Blood analysis is used to determine whether wolves have been exposed to canid diseases. Radio telemetry allows biologists to document information important to recovery, including home range size, pack size, dispersal rates, mortality factors, food habits, conflicts with livestock, exposure to diseases and reproductive success.

Control. Wolf recovery in Montana will result in occasional losses of private property, just as increased numbers of elk, deer, antelope, mountain lions, grizzly bears and eagles have caused some human/wildlife conflicts. Wolves do not normally seek out livestock as prey, but they do attack livestock on occasion, and losses to individual owners can be significant if nothing is done. In North America, this means removing depredating wolves.

Wolf predation on livestock has been intensively studied in Minnesota (Fritts 1982, Fritts et al., in press) and some Western provinces (Gunson 1983). Surprisingly, these studies indicate that even when wolves are closely associated with livestock, they rarely use domestic animals as prey. About 1,500 wolves are interspersed with more than 7,000 farms and ranches in Minnesota. Each year, only three out of every 1,000 farms suffer confirmed losses to wolves. ADC specialists kill wolves that do feed on livestock. Livestock producers are paid for confirmed losses caused by wolves through a state program. In Canada, wolves that attack livestock are also killed, primarily by poisoning. Alberta and Ontario provide compensation to producers for losses caused by predators.

In the northern Rocky Mountains, ADC specialists are responsible for identifying livestock losses caused by wolves and capturing depredating wolves. When a wolf attacks livestock and further losses appear likely, the problem wolf is controlled. Because of the currently low numbers of wolves in Montana—less than six breeding pairs—problem wolves are translocated and given one more chance at living in the wild without attacking livestock. When six breeding pairs have been documented in the state, the occasional removal of problem wolves won't impede recovery, and translocations may not be required.

Wolves that attack livestock have been successfully controlled since 1987. In 1990, Congress provided additional funding for predator control activities for endangered and threatened species in the northern Rocky Mountains. The funds relieved the livestock producers' concerns about whether the costs of wolf control might affect other ADC programs like coyote removal.

Montana has no federal or state program to compensate livestock producers for losses caused by wolves. However, the environmental group Defenders of Wildlife has established a compensation program, funded entirely by private donations. The group relies on evidence collected by resource specialists to decide whether a producer should be compensated. The program compensates producers for 100 percent of the market price of livestock definitely lost to wolves and 50 percent of the price of livestock possibly lost to wolves. In the spring of 1990, for example, a producer reported wolf activity and wolf depredation on five calves at his ranch immediately after discovering the loss. The problem wolf was killed, and the Defenders program compensated the rancher at the price his calves sold for in the fall.

Research. The wolf recovery group has placed special emphasis on obtaining accurate information about wolves as they recolonize northwestern Montana. The first efforts to study wolves in the state was begun at the University of Montana by Dr. Robert Ream, who founded the Wolf Ecology Project in 1972. Its initial task was simply to determine whether there were any wolves in Montana. In 1979, the group captured and radio–collared a wolf near the U.S./Canada border in the North Fork of the Flathead River in British Columbia. Research efforts intensified as wolf numbers grew, and a wolf den was discovered in Montana in 1986 (Ream et al. 1987). Among other things, the research effort found that wolves are firmly established along the west side of Glacier National Park and that white-tailed deer and elk are their main prey. The average pack has 12 members, produces six pups a year, uses an area of 300 to 400 square miles and tends to avoid people.

In 1987, biologists began conducting research on the possible effect of wolf predation on ungulates (Peek and Vales 1989). Using computer modeling and a review of the information available on ungulates in Montana, the study's results suggested that high wolf predation rates in ungulate populations heavily hunted by humans would require wildlife managers to reduce hunting of female ungulates in order to maintain population levels. Ungulate populations that are not heavily hunted, the study stated, could absorb the additional mortality caused by wolves without a need to reduce human hunting levels.

Modeling exercises that evaluated the potential impacts of wolf recovery in Yellowstone National Park came to similar conclusions (Yellowstone National Park et al. 1990). Wolf predation would have minor impacts on ungulate populations. However, in some situations, particularly in areas of heavy hunting pressure, ungulate numbers would decline in the presence of wolves, unless mortality from other large predators or hunting was reduced.

Information. More than any other animal in North America, wolves have a long mythological history. Rumors and myths about wolves attacking people, decimating ungulate populations and frequently attacking livestock are still widely believed (Mader 1988).

In Montana, some older ranchers still can recall stories or incidents from their childhoods in which livestock were reported killed by the few remaining wolves or the death of the last "lobo" was celebrated. They are understandably apprehensive about wolves and may view them as cruel, vicious or cunning killers. Younger, urban residents of the state, on the other hand, grew up with stories and movies such as *Never Cry Wolf* and may believe that wolves have desirable human traits—being caring parents, loving mates and capable of "restoring balance in nature."

Both perceptions are biased and often have more to do with feelings about people's relationships to nature than with the characteristics of the animals themselves. Wolves, like most other creatures, can have both negative and positive effects on humans.

People's knowledge of wolves is the most important determinant of how well the animals are tolerated (Kellert 1987). Public polls indicate five basic, but often overstated reasons why people oppose wolf recovery. Some are concerned about the impacts of wolves on livestock production and big game populations, the cost of recovery and possible restrictions on use of public lands. The fifth and surprisingly common reason is the unfounded perception that wolves are a threat to human safety (Mech 1989).

The Montana wolf recovery program has made special efforts to incorporate public concerns. As mentioned, any wolves that prey on livestock are controlled, and livestock producers are compensated for losses probably and possibly caused by wolves. Although there is little evidence that the low number of wolves required to reach population recovery can significantly affect ungulate populations, the recovery team and its cooperators are continuing to monitor both wolves and ungulates to determine the interactions of the two populations.

Some people opposed to wolf recovery object to its costs. Presently, the total federal budget for wolf recovery in Montana runs about $260,000 annually. It includes salaries, travel, research, control, monitoring, equipment, office support and education programs in the Fish and Wildlife Service, Forest Service, Bureau of Land Management and National Park Service. Rapid wolf recovery would minimize total program costs because state-run management, which will take over one the wolf population is "delisted," is considerably less expensive; it requires only a small portion of the research and monitoring involved with management of an endangered species.

A commonly misunderstood factor is the level of management (that is, restrictions) required to achieve wolf recovery. The disappearance of wolves and their recent reappearance in Montana were both almost entirely functions of human-caused mortality, not habitat limitations. The state's biological environment is entirely suited for wolf recolonization. The abundant ungulate populations—considered overabundant in some areas—and abundant public lands can easily support many more than the approximately 100 wolves required to achieve recovery.

There are only two land–use restrictions associated with wolf recovery in Montana: 1) ADC personnel may not use non-selective controls—i.e., poison—to control predators in areas occupied by wolves, and 2) a one-mile area around recognized and active wolf dens and rendezvous sites are to be protected from intensive human use between March 15 and July 1. The latter is intended to protect wolf dens from disturbances that could convince the female to move her pups from the area prematurely, possibly causing their deaths.

Unless forced to act because of criminal activity, such as the illegal killing of wolves, neither federal nor state agencies plan to adopt any other restrictions on use of public lands because of wolf activity. However, all wildlife recovery programs require resource managers to develop land-use guidelines to assure recovery. In addition, the procedures that lead to "delisting" of a species require a state conservation program that ensures that the species to be delisted will not again become endangered or threatened. For that reason, high and persistent levels of illegal wolf kills could prevent Montana or tribal authorities from assuming sole management authority.

Wolves will undoubtedly recolonize northwestern Montana unless society reverses its current commitment to recovery. Wolves from Alberta and British Columbia have already made it apparent that dispersal into Montana is not unusual. Conservation efforts in those provinces have been designed to enhance wolf recovery in the state and have already produced several wolf packs. In 1990, at least four, and possibly six litters of wolves were born in Montana, and there are probably between 40 and 50 wolves in the state. Unless human–caused mortality is high, the wolf population should reach recovery levels by the turn of the century.

A commonly asked question is, "Why do we want wolves?" At the end of the 19th century, people's concerns in the West focused on taming the wildlands and strengthening civilization's ability to provide livelihoods in an expanding nation. Many people lived in rural agricultural communities and thought about the riches available in a seemingly endless frontier. The resulting national policies helped people achieve many of these economic and social objectives. They also displaced indigenous people and greatly reduced or eliminated many wildlife species and their habitats.

Today, most Americans live in an urban environment. There are many more of them, and almost all of the wild areas in their country have been conquered, most more than 70 years ago. Political and, to some extent, economic policies have begun to emphasize retaining and restoring our wildland heritage. While more controversial than many natural resource issues, wolf recovery is just one small example of an ongoing global, national and individual re-evaluation of how humans define what contributes to the quality of their lives.

Acknowledgments

The author wishes to acknowledge the contributions of the following wolf working group members: Joe Fontaine, a biologist with the U.S. Fish and Wildlife Service; Dale Becker, the wildlife program manager with the Confederated Salish and Kootenai Tribes of the Flathead Nation; Can Carney, a biologist with the Blackfeet Nation; Tad Day, a biologist with the Bureau of Land Management; Carter Niemeyer, the western district supervisor for Animal Damage Control; Wayne Brewster, the wolf coordinator for Glacier National Park; and Jim Claar, Cathy Bulchis, Don Godtel, Mike Hillis, Bob Summerfield, and Tom Wittinger, biologists with the U.S. Forest Service.

LITERATURE CITED

Day, B.L. 1981. The Status and Distribution of Wolves in the Northern Rocky Mountains of the United States. MS Thesis. University of Montana, Missoula.

Fritts, S.H. Wolf Depredation on Livestock in Minnesota. Resource Publication 145. U.S. Fish and Wildlife Service, Department of Interior, Washington, D.C.

Fritts, S.H., W.J. Paul, L.D. Mech, and D.P. Scott. In Press. Wolf-Livestock Conflicts in Minnesota, 1975–1986. Research Report. U.S. Fish and Wildlife Service, Department of Interior, Washington, D.C.

Gunson, J.R. 1983. Wolf Predation of Livestock in Western Canada. *In:* Wolves in Canada and Alaska: Their Status, Biology and Management (L.N. Carbyn, editor). Canadian Wildlife Service Report 45: 102–105. Edmonton, Alberta.

Hebert, D.M., J. Youds, R. Davies, H. Langin, D. Janz and G. Smith. 1982. Preliminary Investigations of the Vancouver Island Wolf (*Canis lupus crassodon*) Prey Relationships. *In: Wolves of the World* (F.H. Harrington and P.C. Paquet, editors). Noyes Publications, Parkridge, NJ.

Kellert, S.R. 1987. The Public and the Timber Wolf in Minnesota. *Anthrozoos* 1(2):100–109.

Johnson, M., S. Wallwork and M. Lenihan. 1987. The Montana Poll. The Bureau of Business and Economic Research (University of Montana) and Great Falls Tribune.

Mader, T.R. 1988. *Wolf Reintroduction into Yellowstone National Park: A Historical Perspective*. Common Man Institute, Gillette, WY.

Mech, L.D. 1986. Wolf Numbers and Population Trends in the Superior National Forest, 1967–1985. Research Paper NC–270. U.S. Forest Service, North Central Forest Experiment Station, St. Paul, MN.

Mech, L.D. 1989. Who's Afraid of the Big Bad Wolf? *Audubon* 92(2):82–85.

Nowak, R.M. 1981. A Perspective on the Taxonomy of Wolves in North America. *Canadian Wildlife Service Report* 45:10–19. Edmonton, Alberta.

Peek, J.M. and D.J. Vales. 1989. Projecting the Effects of Wolf Predation on Elk and Mule Deer in the East Front Portion of the Northwest Montana Wolf Recovery Area. Report to the U.S. Fish and Wildlife Service, Helena, MT.

Peterson, R.O., J.D. Wollington and T.N. Bailey. 1984. Wolves of the Kenai Peninsula, Alaska. Wildlife Monograph No. 88 U.S. Fish and Wildlife Service, Kenai, AK.

Ream, R.R., and U.I. Mattson. 1982. Wolf Status in the Northern Rockies. *In:*

Wolves of the World (F.H. Harrington and P.C. Paquet, editors). Noyes Publications, Parkridge, NJ.

Ream, R.R., M.W. Fairchild, D.A. Boyd and D.H. Pletscher. 1987. Wolf Monitoring and Research in and Adjacent to Glacier National Park. Final Report. Montana Cooperative Wildlife Research Unit, University of Montana, Missoula.

Tucker, P. and D.H. Pletscher. 1989. Attitudes of Hunters and Residents toward Wolves in Northwest Montana. *Wildlife Society Bulletin* 17(4):509–514.

Yellowstone National Park, U.S. Fish and Wildlife Service, University of Wyoming, University of Idaho, Interagency Grizzly Bear Study Team and University of Minnesota Cooperative Park Studies Unit. 1990. A Report to the United States Congress, Volume II, Research and Analysis. National Park Service, Yellowstone National Park, WY.

CHAPTER 57
OPERATION WOLFSTOCK: REPORTS
OF THE *WOLF TRACKER*

Operation Wolfstock was the name given to the process of preparing the acclimation pens for the new wolves, bringing the wolves down from Canada to Yellowstone, and caring for them once they arrived. Starting in October 1994, Yellowstone Center for Resources staff produced a monthly newsletter, the Wolf Tracker, *which was widely distributed in and near the park. Filled with the details of each month's activities, these updates may serve as a more immediate and personal account of the arrival of the new wolves.*

The original newsletters contained some material that most readers would find peripheral to the narrative of wolf recovery (employee profiles and a variety of procedural matters), which have not been included.

OCTOBER 1994
PREPARATIONS UNDERWAY FOR WOLF RESTORATION

After many years of discussion and public comment, Secretary of the Interior Bruce Babbitt signed the Record of Decision on the Final Environmental Impact Statement (FEDS) for reintroduction of gray wolves to Yellowstone National Park and central Idaho on June 15, 1994. As a result, staff from Yellowstone, the U.S. Fish and Wildlife Service (USFWS), as well as participating states and tribes, are now making preparations for wolf restoration to the park and central Idaho. The USFWS has drafted proposed rules outlining how wolves would be managed as a nonessential experimental population under section 10(j) of the Endangered Species Act. These proposed rules have been published in the Federal Register and are open for public comment until October 17, 1994. As outlined in the Record of Decision, the states and tribes are encouraged to implement and lead wolf management outside

SOURCE: The *Wolf Tracker* was a newsletter produced by the Yellowstone Center for Resources, National Park Service. The chief author and compiler was Resource Management Biologist Sue Consolo Murphy, and additional material was provided by other staff members.

283

the boundaries of national parks and wildlife refuges, within federal guidelines. The states have begun preparation of state wolf management plans outlining how they intend to undertake this responsibility.

In Yellowstone, numerous park staff have assisted with on-the-ground planning for a delayed release of wolves in the park. This technique, which has been used before for various species' restorations, such as with red wolves in the southeastern United States and swift fox in the Great Plains, involves the temporary holding of animals in an area of suitable habitat. The penning of the animals is intended to discourage immediate long-distance dispersal away from the desired reintroduction area.

In contrast, an immediate release technique, in which animals are free to disperse immediately wherever they choose, will be attempted in central Idaho. This is partly due to logistical problems related to the limited access in the central Idaho wilderness. It also provides for a comparison of the success of the two release methods over the course of the reintroduction program in the two recovery areas.

At three suitable sites in the Lamar Valley, park staff have completed site planning, archeological, and sensitive plant surveys. Sites were selected to have a dependable source of water and tree cover for the wolves, as well as reasonable access during the time of temporary holding. Design calls for enclosing approximately one acre at each site, with 9-gauge chain link fence in 10' × 10' panels. These can be dismantled and reconstructed an another site if necessary in future years. The fence will have a 2' overhang to discourage climbing over the fence, and a 4' chain link apron at the bottom to prevent digging under the enclosure. Each pen will have a small holding area attached in the rare case that a wolf would need to be separated from the group and handled. Several plywood security boxes will be inside the pen to provide shelter and allow a wolf to rest or escape from its pen mates, if necessary.

Construction of the panels is being contracted, but the on-site erection of the pens will be done by park staff, hopefully beginning in early October. It is estimated that each pen will take a week or so for completion.

The USFWS has the lead role in identifying and capturing wolves for reintroduction. They have contacted Canadian officials and are working together to try and provide wolves for both recovery areas. Tentative plans call for releasing wolves of dispersal age (1–2 years old) into Idaho and releasing pups of the year (7+ months old) into Yellowstone, together with one or more of the alpha pair (breeding adults). Pups of this

The capturing and handling of Alberta wolves for translocation to Yellowstone and central Idaho was a cooperative effort among the U.S. Fish and Wildlife Service, the National Park Service, and the Alberta Ministry of the Environment, Fish and Wildlife Branch. Photo by LuRay Parker.

age are likely to weigh 70–80 lbs, yet are less likely to have already established an affinity for a home range in Canada. The FEDS called for "adaptive management," or "learning by doing" during the gray wolf reintroduction. Until trapping begins, it is impossible to be certain about the numbers and ages of wolves that may be available for reintroduction, though the goal is to have 5–7 wolves from one social group together in each release pen.

Prior to being held here in the park, each wolf will be radio-collared. Ideally, each wolf will be collared as it is captured in Canada, to minimize the handling disturbance of the animals. For approximately 6–8 weeks while temporarily penned, the wolves will experience minimal human contact. Approximately once each week, they will be fed carcasses of elk, deer, or bison from the ecosystem. They will be guarded around the clock by commissioned rangers and other volunteers, who will minimize the amount of visual contact needed to insure security at each release site. Site attendants will use radio-telemetry to check on the

An extraordinary moment in the wolf recovery program, as more than a dozen tranquilized animals were spread out at the processing center in Hinton, Alberta, for final preparations for the flight to the United States. Photo by LuRay Parker.

welfare of wolves both in pens and subsequent to their release into the wild.

Although some persons have expressed concern about the wolves becoming habituated to humans or to the captive conditions, the temporary holding period is not long in the life of a wolf. In Alaska and Canada, wolves are seldom known to develop the habituated behaviors seen more commonly in grizzly bears. Wolves, while social among their own kind, typically avoid human contact. They are highly efficient predators and will not lose their predatory instincts during a short period of captivity. Their social structure and pack behavior minimizes their need to scavenge food or garbage available from human sources. Compared to a bear, whose diet is predominantly vegetarian, wolves have less specific habitat requirements. The wolves' primary need is for prey, which is most likely to be elk, deer, and other ungulates in these recovery areas.

Legal Developments

Jim and Cat Urbigkit of Pinedale, Wyoming, have filed a 60-day notice of intent to sue to stop wolf reintroduction into Yellowstone. The Sierra Club Legal Defense Fund has also filed a 60-day notice of intent to sue to stop wolf reintroduction in central Idaho only. The Endangered Species Act requires that anyone considering filing suit under this authority must give 60 days notice prior to initiating litigation. During this period, The U.S. Fish and Wildlife Service normally tries to resolve the issues of alleged violation of the Act. However, unless directed by court order, the U.S. Fish and Wildlife Service, the National Park Service and other cooperating agencies will continue to carry out the mandates of the Endangered Species Act and the Record of Decision and continue with preparation of plans and facilities to complete the reintroduction.

NOVEMBER 1994
RESOURCE TEAM ESTABLISHED FOR WOLF RESTORATION

Since the decision to restore wolves to Yellowstone National Park and central Idaho was announced on June 15, 1994, much work has occurred toward beginning the transplant of wolves from Canada to Idaho and Yellowstone this fall. In order to help structure the planning and completion of the myriad of tasks that need done, the park has formalized a resource team, using the Incident Command System commonly used for wildfires and other major incidents. The resource team was approved by the park's Resource Council (an extension of the Superintendent's squad of senior staff) on October 11.

The incident operation, named "Wolfstock," has the following objectives:

1. Plan and implement integrated actions to restore a gray wolf population to Yellowstone National Park.
2. Top priorities are the safety and welfare of personnel associated with this project and the safety and welfare of wolves.
3. Immediate focus will be site preparations, information management planning, and security planning.
4. Additional priorities are: close coordination between operations sections, providing information of actions and progress of project to all park employees, providing for close coordination with cooperating agencies, providing opportunities for public information to the extent that it does not compromise other critical objectives, minimizing ef-

fects on other resources, and minimizing disruption of other park operations.

The Incident Commander is Wayne Brewster, Deputy Director of the Yellowstone Center for Resources. Sections and their Chiefs include: Planning—Joy Perius: responsible for coordination, resource advice, written and photo documentation, arranging volunteers. Logistics—John Mack: responsible for managing supplies, facilities, ground support, communications, medical needs, carcasses to feed wolves while in holding pens. Finance—Melissa McAdam: responsible for authorizing and tracking funds, employee timecards, processing claims for injury or lost property, and procurement of needed supplies and equipment.

Operations—Mona Divine. The Operations Section is subdivided into Branches responsible for the following components: Information—Marsha Karle: responsible for media liaison, staff and public education. Site Preparation—Mark Johnson: responsible for planning, preparation, and construction of holding pens at three already established sites in northern Yellowstone. Wolf Management—Mike Phillips: responsible for handling, monitoring, and care of wolves during and after reintroduction. Security/Site Monitoring—Michael Keator and Bundy Phillips: responsible for planning and securing sites prior to and during reintroduction. Air Operations—Dick Bahr: responsible for air support to the operation.

The team includes staff representing nearly all park divisions (Resources, Interpretation, Maintenance, Resource Operations & Visitor Protection, Administration) and the Superintendent's Office (Public Affairs). In addition to the Section and Branch Chiefs listed above, numerous persons have been assigned areas of responsibility, and many others will be assisting as needed during the planning and implementation of wolf restoration.

The Information Branch has initiated this newsletter primarily to provide park staff with one means of getting periodic updates on the project. Other education efforts include interpretive programs given inside and outside the park, distribution of a wolf education curriculum for school groups, development of a site bulletin and/or addition to the park newspaper addressing wolf restoration, providing media opportunities, and answering special information requests. The Information Branch includes Cheryl Matthews of the Public Affairs Office, Sue Consolo Murphy and Norm Bishop from the Yellowstone Center for Resources, and Tom Tankersley, Matt Graves, Sandi Snell-Dobert, and Ellen Petrick-Underwood from the Division of Interpretation. If you have questions about the project, we encourage you to contact one of these sources.

October Progress Report

On September 29 and 30, the park helicopter was used to fly fencing materials and plywood security boxes into the first of three temporary holding pen sites on the northern range. A group of media representatives were escorted to the site on the second day, and provided an opportunity to get pictures of the operation as well as interviews with several park staff involved in the project. During the first half of October, fire cache staff continued transporting materials into the second and third sites, while maintenance crews began assembling the fence panels. As of October 14, two of the holding sites were essentially completed, and assembly work was ready to begin at the final site.

The holding areas will be temporarily closed to public use and travel from now through the period of wolf occupancy. However, guided visits to the wolf pen areas are available to park staff prior to the middle of November. If you are interested, please call the Public Affairs Office at 344-2013 for more information. Priority will be given to those individuals who will be providing information to park visitors about the project as part of their official duties.

Media interest in the reintroduction of wolves to Yellowstone is escalating daily. The Public Affairs Office is receiving about a dozen wolf-related media calls each day. As with all media contacts, please refer any wolf-related media calls to the Public Affairs Office (either Marsha Karle or Cheryl Matthews).

We are planning for a large event the day the first wolves are brought into Yellowstone from Canada. This could occur by the last week of November. The media will only be able to see the wolves being driven into the park; the actual placement of wolves in the pens will be covered by a media "pool" videographer. The park will also have a 16mm filmer and a still photographer on site to capture the event for archival purposes. A media center will be established in the Mammoth area and media will be provided with experts and officials to interview and videotapes of the placement of wolves in a pen. Opportunities for employees to see the videotapes will also be made available. If you have any questions regarding how media coverage will be handled, please contact the Public Affairs Office.

The wolves, each in its own shipping container, ready to be loaded aboard the plane at the Jasper-Hinton airport. NPS photo by Mark Johnson.

DECEMBER 1994
WOLF CAPTURE AND TRANSLOCATION FROM CANADA

Alberta and British Columbia authorities have chosen two general areas for removing wolves for translocation to Yellowstone and central Idaho. These areas fit the criteria of having adequate numbers of wolves, having elk and deer as primary prey, and having similar landscape as habitat.

The area chosen in British Columbia is located approximately 470 miles north of the U.S.-Canada border. Operations will be based out of the small town of Fort St. John. Forest cover in the area is sparse enough to permit helicopter darting of wolves, a technique familiar to local Ministry of Environment and Parks personnel. They believe desired members of wolf packs can be removed in a safe, humane, and cost-effective manner. Wolves from the Fort St. John area are expected to go primarily to Yellowstone, because members from discrete packs are more likely to be captured, thus the relationships between individual wolves are more likely to be known. Having knowledge of the wolves' social relationships is important in order to reduce the level of stress experienced by wolves in the acclimation pens in the Lamar Valley; unrelated (or unfamiliar) wolves placed together in a 1-acre enclosure would probably fight.

A cooperative agreement for covering translocation costs is being developed between the U.S. Fish and Wildlife Service and the British Columbia Ministry of Environment and Parks. The area chosen in Alberta extends over an area of 160 miles and stretches northwest-southeast along the eastern front of the Rocky Mountains. Operations will be based out of the towns of Rocky Mountain House and Hinton. Since this area is characterized by substantial tree cover, darting from helicopters will probably not be an effective capture method. As a result, snaring will probably be the capture method of choice in this province. Because of forest cover, it is more likely that radio-collared wolves will not be observed during telemetry flights. As a result, less is expected to be known about the social relationships of wolves captured in Alberta. Thus, it is likely that wolves captured in Alberta will be translocated to and released in the central Idaho wolf recovery area.

Radio collars are being placed on wolves in both areas one to three weeks prior to initiating captures for translocation. Pre-collaring is designed to simplify capture of wolves for translocation. It will also permit follow-up monitoring by the Canadians to assess the impact of wolf removals, and will allow some disease screening to ensure that wolves selected for reintroduction meet the "disease-free" criteria established by U.S. and Canadian veterinarians. Additionally, pre-collaring may facilitate capture of wolves for reintroduction initiatives in subsequent years.

As of November 13, two wolves (a 95 pound male and a 82 pound female) had been captured, radio-collared, and released in Alberta. Unfortunately, the male was shot and killed (legally) on November 14.

Prior to initiating capture of wolves for translocation, U.S. Fish and Wildlife Service staff will construct temporary holding facilities (i.e., kennels) where the wolves will be confined until transport to the U.S. The kennels will measure 12' long, 6' wide, and 6' high. They will be situated in a secure area where access will be strictly limited. An aluminum transport box (along with bedding material) will be placed in each kennel so that the wolves can avoid inclement weather and visual contact with people during those rare occasions when people are present in the area.

Prior to transport to the U.S., each wolf will be given a thorough physical exam and outfitted with a radio-collar. This ensures that, barring an unforeseen event, the wolves will not have to be handled in Yellowstone Park prior to being released into the wild.

To ensure the safety and health of the wolves, a veterinary staff will monitor the wolves during capture, confinement, and transport; and be on hand to help ensure the health and welfare of the wolves while in acclimation pens in Yellowstone.

Current plans indicate that wolves will be transported from Canada to the U.S. via a U.S. Forest Service "Sherpa" aircraft. Loading and departure from Canadian sites will likely occur during early morning in order to get wolves to Yellowstone and central Idaho before darkness. Aerial transport will involve stops in Calgary, Alberta, and Great Falls, Montana, in order to clear both U.S. and Canadian customs.

Since wolves will not be acclimated to release sites in Idaho, releases to the wild will be conducted before those for Yellowstone. As a reminder, wolves transported to Yellowstone will be maintained for 6 to 8 weeks in pens in the Lamar Valley prior to being released. It is hoped that the 6 to 8 week acclimation period will predispose the wolves to restrict movements to the Lamar Valley. Even though the acclimation period will probably prompt some wolves to remain within the confines of Yellowstone Park, it would not be seen as unusual for some of the animals to exhibit wide-ranging movements during the first few months after being released. "Realistic expectations" concerning wolf restoration must take into account the fact that wolves are capable of travelling considerable distances in short periods of time. Accordingly, realistic expectations must include an expectation of the unexpected.

Setting Realistic Expectations for Wolf Recovery

If all goes as planned, by December 1994 up to 15 wolves will be residing in acclimation pens in the Lamar Valley. After releasing the wolves in early 1995, we will tackle the difficult task of documenting how the animals respond to their new environment. Although some will behave predictably, others will not. The National Park Service and the Fish and Wildlife Service anticipated this uncertainty and designed the recovery effort so that about 15 wolves would be reintroduced every year for 3 to 5 consecutive years. This approach ensures that a population of wolves will be restored to Yellowstone, but the uncertainty of individual animal behavior remains. Accordingly, it is important that we maintain realistic expectations concerning the fate of individual wolves.

Because the future of the hoped-for population will rest on the shoulders of the wolves translocated from Canada, we gave much consideration to how to best maintain these animals before releasing them. Transport boxes, acclimation pens, and shelter boxes were all specifically designed to ensure that the wolves experienced minimal stress during transport and confinement. Additionally, an "acclimation period" protocol was developed that ensures that the wolves receive the best possible husbandry and veterinary care.

The critical test for the wolves will begin after they've been released. Even though Yellowstone is superb wolf habitat, colonizing a new environment will be a challenge. It is reasonable to expect that about 20% of the wolves will die without contributing to population growth. This level of mortality is similar to levels experienced by other wild wolf populations. With normal reproduction, even in the presence of 20% mortality, by 1999 the wolf population should be growing at an annual rate of about 22%. Accordingly, by 2002 the Yellowstone area should support a "recovered" wolf population (i.e., a population that consists of 10 breeding pairs that have been present for 3 consecutive years).

While it is realistic to accept uncertainty and wolf mortality as part of the restoration process, it is also realistic to believe that the restoration program is destined to succeed. Yellowstone supports an adequate prey base for wolves, and the National Park Service is deeply committed to wolf restoration. The plan that has been developed for restoring wolves will work, and in the near future the howl of the wolf will once again echo through the forests and valleys of the Yellowstone ecosystem.

Plans for Park Information and Media Center Proceed

The Public Affairs Office continues to be inundated with wolf-related calls and requests for information, both from the media and park staff. In response to employee inquiries, three opportunities were provided to visit one of the pen sites. Each guided visit was well attended, and John Mack, who led all three, was pleased with employee participation and questions. Currently, no additional visits have been scheduled.

A primary goal of the Information Branch and "Operation Wolfstock" is to keep park staff informed of the progress of the wolf reintroduction. Plans are underway to establish an information area in the hallway of the Administration Building at park headquarters. The area will be used to post current information and pictures of the wolf project. Additionally, there will be opportunities available for employees to see video footage of the first major event—the day the first wolves are brought to the park.

If desired, a representative from the Information and Education Branch will travel to interior park locations to update field staff.

Every major television network anticipates being in the park to cover the return of wolves to the park, and Secretary Babbitt has expressed an interest in being here for the event, as has George Frampton, Assistant Secretary for Fish & Wildlife & Parks. A media center will be established at the Mammoth Rec Hall. Locating the media center away from the headquarters building is also designed to minimize the disruption of other staff in the workplace. The center will be used for news conferences and as an area for news media to work from and do interviews with park managers. The media center will be operational during this first event for a 4–5 day period.

JANUARY 1995
LEGAL ACTION RESULTS IN DELAY OF OPERATION WOLFSTOCK

In a not unexpected action, the Wyoming Farm Bureau et al., represented by the Mountain States Legal Foundation, has followed up on their notice of intent to sue to stop the reintroduction of wolves into Yellowstone and central Idaho. Following the publication of the final rule for designation of reintroduced wolves as a "nonessential-experimental population" in the Federal Register on November 22, 1994, attorneys entered into discussion with representatives of the United States Attorney's Office. The discussions resulted in a stipulation that was filed on November 29, 1994, in U.S. District Court for the District of Wyoming. Defendants in the case are Bruce Babbitt, Secretary of the Interior, et al.

The parties reached a stipulation concerning the Farm Bureau's (the plaintiff's) motion for a temporary restraining order to halt the reintroduction of wolves from Canada into the United States. The defendants agreed not to import any wolves into the U.S. before January 1, 1995, and to provide the plaintiffs with portions of the administrative records related to wolf reintroduction. The Farm Bureau agreed to file their motion for a preliminary injunction and to provide copies of the motion and any supporting information to the government on or before December 9, 1994. Both parties agreed to file lists of potential witnesses on or before December 16, and to suggest that a hearing on the plaintiff's motion be scheduled on December 21, or as soon thereafter as possible.

The U.S. District Court judge scheduled a hearing in Cheyenne, Wyoming on December 21, 1994. The stipulation stated that both parties would make an effort to complete the hearing within one day, and the government has asked that a decision on the motion for the preliminary injunction be issued on or before January 1, 1995.

In Alberta, Canada, representatives of the U.S. Fish and Wildlife Service have been working with area residents and Canadian government representatives to capture, radio-collar, and release wolves from at least six packs. If the court denies the plaintiff's motion for an injunction, the collared wolves can be tracked for recapture. The telemetry information may be useful in helping locate and capture additional pack members for relocation into Yellowstone and central Idaho. If the court issues an injunction, the reintroduction would be postponed until the issue is resolved. Here in Yellowstone, preparations for the reintroduction continue to occur so that all is ready. The three reintroduction pens are complete, and arrangements for transporting wolves into the pens have been worked out. Park staff have used mules and bobsleds for hauling equipment into the release sites. Handlers report that the stock and the sled are working well as a quiet, light-impact mode of transportation. Fifteen commissioned rangers hired to provide 24-hour security for wolves during the acclimation period have received training previously outlined as necessary for the operation. At present they are being assigned other patrol duties back at their summer duty stations or, in the case of those seasonals not hired from Yellowstone's summer staff, being used in other projects.

The Information and Education branch of Operation Wolfstock continues to make ready for a potential media event and for a variety of environmental education programs and briefings for the staff and public.

FEBRUARY 1995
WOLF RESTORATION BEGINS IN YELLOWSTONE

In mid-January, fourteen wolves arrived in Yellowstone National Park as part of a long-planned restoration effort. The wolves are being held in pens for an acclimation period prior to a planned release in approximately six weeks.

In November, as the capture of wolves from Canada was beginning, the American Farm Bureau Federation had filed a legal request to halt the reintroduction efforts. The United States entered into a legal agreement with the plaintiffs and capture efforts ceased pending the outcome of a hearing held in U.S. District Court in Wyoming on December 21–22, 1994.

Wolves were transported in their shipping containers from the road to the acclimation pens by mule-drawn sleigh; for the remainder of the winter and early spring, as long as there was sufficient snow, meat was taken to the pens using the same sleighs. NPS photo by Jim Peaco.

On January 3, 1995, U.S. District Judge William Downes denied the request for an injunction to block the return of wolves to Yellowstone and central Idaho. The judge said the American Farm Bureau Federation and Mountain States Legal Foundation failed to prove that ranchers around the park would be irreparably harmed by the return of wolves. On subsequent days, the U.S. Fish and Wildlife Service reinitiated efforts to capture wolves from the wild in Alberta in cooperation with local authorities. Wolves were trapped by several methods, including snares set by local trappers and by darting from helicopters.

Meanwhile, Yellowstone's Incident Command (ICS) Team proceeded with planning for the transport and stocking of wolves into the park. Personnel needed for the operation were alerted to be ready to report for their assignment with 48 hours notice from the USFWS staff in Canada. Word came at 4:15 p.m. on January 10 that wolves captured in Canada would be flown to the U.S., clearing customs in Great Falls, Montana. The first shipment included eight wolves for Yellowstone and four for the central Idaho release. A transport convoy left the park at approximately noon on Wednesday, January 11, anticipating pickup of the Yellowstone wolves from Missoula, Montana that evening. The convoy's schedule called for return to the park early on the morning of January 12. The plan was to place the wolves in acclimation pens in the Lamar Valley area later that same morning.

Media interest in the wolves' arrival was high. Staff from the park's Public Affairs Office set up a Media Center in the Rec Hall behind the Mammoth Hotel to provide information to interested press and others, as only a small group of pre-selected representatives would form the media "pool" to view the wolves' release into their acclimation pens.

Yellowstone's Superintendent Finley hosted an all-employees' meeting on Wednesday afternoon, and at the end of the typical workday (for many, but not all folks) staff went home still expecting "Operation Wolfstock" to proceed according to plan. Secretary of the Interior Bruce Babbitt and USFWS Director Mollie Beattie were enroute to Yellowstone to participate in the arrival event.

In the early evening hours, park staff received word that the 10th Circuit Court of Appeals in Denver had issued a Temporary Administrative Stay in order to study the pleadings submitted by the Farm Bureau Federation in appeal of the decision issued by Judge Downes in Wyoming. The stay was issued through 5 p.m. on Friday, January 13, during which time the court would also hear information submitted by the Department of Justice on behalf of the government in support of continuing with wolf restoration. Calls went out to ICS team members to reconvene in the Superintendent's Conference Room to assess the changing situation.

The "Sherpa" airplane carrying twelve wolves, tended by two veterinarians, one from Idaho Fish and Game and one from Yellowstone National Park, was already airborne from Hinton and Edmonton, Alberta. The plane was expected to arrive in Great Falls, Montana, to clear U.S. Customs at about 9:30 p.m. Wednesday evening. No one on the plane was aware of the issuance of the Temporary Administrative Stay.

Meanwhile, the park's transport convoy had arrived in Missoula and was powering up humans and vehicles for the return trip. An unexpected change in the schedule became necessary when park staff received word that the plane carrying the wolves could not fly beyond Great Falls, Montana that evening due to limitations on the numbers of hours a pilot can fly in one day. When the transport convoy checked in, they were told to finish dinner and drive on to Great Falls and pick up

Bringing the first wolf to the Crystal Creek acclimation pen: left to right, Yellowstone Wolf Project Leader Mike Phillips, Maintenance Foreman Jim Evanoff, U.S. Fish and Wildlife Service Director Mollie Beattie, the wolf, Yellowstone Superintendent Mike Finley, and Secretary of the Interior Bruce Babbitt. NPS photo by Jim Peaco.

their cargo. USFWS and park officials were advised that they could proceed with bringing the wolves into the U.S., but that the wolves could not be "released"—even from their shipping containers—until the Circuit Court released the Temporary Stay. Government attorneys consulted with USFWS and park staff about the effects of keeping the wolves in the 2' × 3' × 4' aluminum shipping containers for up to two additional days, and planned to be in court Thursday morning, January 12, to file an emergency request that the Circuit Court review the appeals and lift the stay by the end of the day.

The wolves and their escorts landed safely in Great Falls and cleared customs without difficulty. In the wee hours of Thursday morning, the transport crew proceeded to bring the eight Yellowstone wolves to the park, and the expected arrival time was revised to be between 7:30 and 8:30 a.m. As dawn broke over the Arch marking the historic North Entrance to Yellowstone, a small crowd of photographers began to gather, positioning themselves to get the best shot of the arrival.

At about 8:15 a.m., Secretary Babbitt arrived along the entrance road and made a brief statement about hoping that the process of wolf restoration could continue as planned. Just prior to the convoy's arrival on Front Street, the Gardiner School let the children out to line the entrance road to see the arriving wolves. Teachers and park interpreters explained that the wolves were inside shipping containers carried inside a horse trailer, so that they would not be visible. Nevertheless, the children seemed aware that this was a historic event, and several commented that they enjoyed the break from the normal school routine!

Several park ranger vehicles preceded the horse trailer carrying the wolves, and several others came behind. The convoy moved slowly through the Arch at about 8:40 a.m., and continued to park headquarters at Mammoth, where fresh drivers were exchanged for those exhausted by their 21-hour drive across Montana. The Secretary, Superintendent Finley and his entourage, and the media pool continued out to Crystal Creek, where the first wolves would be placed into a holding pen. Already located at the trailhead was a sled, which was hitched to a team of mules that hauled three shipping containers in each of two loads approximately 1/2 mile to the pen. Onlookers had to walk or snowshoe to a previously selected observation point on the hillside approximately 300 yards above the pen.

Park staff, the Secretary, and Ms. Beattie helped carry the wolves from the sled into the pen where, unfortunately, they could not yet be released as no word had come from the Court of Appeals. At about 1:30 p.m., most of the entourage returned to Mammoth, where the Secretary and park officials held a press conference expressing joy for the historic return of the wolves while voicing concern for their welfare while being confined to the shipping containers. The wolf Project Leader and his crew continued out to Rose Creek where they carried two wolves into that pen.

Just after 6:00 p.m. on January 12, park staff received word that the 10th Circuit Court had lifted the stay, paving the way for the wolves to be immediately released into the one-acre holding pens. Park officials moved immediately to begin preparations for releasing the wolves from the shipping crates. At approximately 8:15 p.m., park biologists headed back to the pen sites. They opened the containers in the Crystal Creek pen at approximately 10:25 p.m. on Thursday evening, and after 20 minutes, none of the wolves had yet emerged from the containers so the biologists left. At approximately 12:35 a.m. on Friday morning, January 13, the biologists opened the two Rose Creek containers, and as they

The Crystal Creek group, getting used to their new surroundings shortly after their arrival from Canada. NPS photo by Jim Peaco.

were leaving the site, saw one of the wolves emerge from the container and find her way across the enclosure, running in the moonlight.

On Friday morning, Secretary Babbitt, Mollie Beattie, and the media pool were again escorted to the observation site overlooking the Crystal Creek pen, where they were able to photograph and observe the wolves for about one hour. Five of the six wolves were outside their containers; the one that was not was checked by project biologists and determined to be in good health. One of the wolves had received a minor laceration during the capture operations in Canada, but had ripped out some of the sutures in the corner of its mouth and was bleeding. Mike Phillips, Project Leader, netted the wolf and injected it with a tranquilizer. He and Doug Smith, project biologist, carried the animal to the 20'x 20' holding area on one side of the pen, where veterinarian Mark Johnson re-sutured the animal's wound. Three of the other wolves stayed at the opposite end of the enclosure from the park workers, and moved constantly back and forth along the fence line. After determining that the Crystal Creek wolves were doing well, the biologists proceeded on to Rose Creek, where those wolves were also running in the pen, adapting to their new surroundings.

On several occasions in the next week, biologists took additional food (road-killed ungulates) to the wolves and observed that all were eating well and looked healthy. In Idaho, the first four wolves finally had been released from their containers directly into the woods on the Salmon River Road approximately 50 miles north of the town of Salmon. While the wolves were moving, they were not covering dozens of miles daily as some persons had predicted. Meanwhile in Alberta, Canada, efforts were proceeding in an attempt to provide additional wolves for both Idaho and Yellowstone.

By the evening of Tuesday, January 17, capture crews had twenty-one more wolves for possible transport to the U.S. Eventually, four of these wolves were radio-collared and released near their capture sites, which will help biologists study the effects of removing animals from some of the region's packs. Yellowstone prepared to accept six additional animals (five pack members, plus one adult male to be placed with the adult female and her pup already in the Rose Creek pen).

A transport convoy left the park in mid-afternoon on Thursday, January 19, but this time had to journey only to Bozeman, where the wolves arrived by plane. The wolves were driven to the Lamar Station where they were held overnight in their shipping containers inside the Lamar barn. In an expedition similar to, but smaller than, that of the previous week, five of the wolves were transported by mule-drawn sled to the Soda Butte pen where they were released at about 10:30 Friday morning, January 20. A small group of regional media representatives watched the containers being taken to and inside the pen; all but the project biologists left the area before the containers were opened.

One wolf came out of the shipping crate immediately, but the others did not emerge while project biologists were present. The biologists subsequently proceeded to take a single adult male wolf to the Rose Creek site. Since this wolf was not from the same pack as the adult female and pup already placed in that pen, biologists watched carefully as the male and the female tentatively met. Within a short time it appeared that the pair had assessed and accepted each other, and monitoring during the following week indicated that all 14 Yellowstone wolves were eating well and socializing.

States, Congress Debate Measures Related to Wolf Restoration

On January 18, members of the Idaho legislature voted not to approve the wolf management plan prepared by the State and approved by the Fish and Wildlife Service. Another vote is expected by next Thursday.

TABLE. Yellowstone's Wolves—A quick run down of the wolves in each of Yellowstone's three holding pens. [Editor's note: This table has been updated and expanded based on information that was not available at the time this issue of the Wolf Tracker *was completed.]*

Crystal Creek

Wolf no. and sex	Age	Weight at capture (lbs.)	Color
004M	adult	98	black
005F	adult	98	light gray
002M	pup	80	black
003M	pup	77	black and silver
006M	pup	75	black
008M	pup	72	gray

Rose Creek

Wolf no. and sex	Age	Weight at capture (lbs.)	Color
010M	adult	122	light gray
009F	adult	98	black
007F	pup	77	gray

Soda Butte

Wolf no. and sex	Age	Weight at capture (lbs.)	Color
012M	adult	122	black
013M	adult	113	gray
011F	adult	92	gray
014F	subadult	89	gray
015M	pup	no data	black

Under the special regulations prepared by the USFWS, which took effect in November 1994, once wolf management plans are completed for each state, the states and tribes would implement and lead wolf management outside the boundaries of national parks and wildlife refuges within federal guidelines. If the plan approved by the State of Idaho is not acceptable to the Fish and Wildlife Service, the Service continues to be responsible for management of wolves in Idaho. In the interim, Idaho Fish and Game will continue to monitor released wolves.

On January 19, a Wyoming state legislative committee approved a bill to put a $500 bounty on wolves that stray from Yellowstone National Park, where the federal government transplanted eight Canadian wolves. The bill also would require the state to pay lawyer's fees for anyone charged with violating the Endangered Species Act by killing a wolf. The bill has not yet been taken up by the full legislature. The Governor of Wyoming sent a letter to the Secretary of Interior requesting that the Yellowstone wolves remain in the enclosures until resolution of all pending legal actions, development and approval of their state management plan, and assurance of future Federal funding.

On January 22, the *Baltimore Sun* reported that Colorado's legislature was considering a bill requiring state permission for reintroduction of endangered species into Colorado.

On January 26, U.S. Representative Don Young (R-AK) scheduled an oversight hearing on wolf restoration to Idaho and Yellowstone NP in Washington, D. C.

MARCH 1995
WOLF PROGRESS REPORT: LIFE IN THE PENS

As of February 24, 1995, all 14 of Yellowstone's wolves are faring well. At first this seems like a rather mundane report, yet it isn't. Wild wolves have seldom been held in captivity, so some worry was warranted. Captivity took getting used to as all three groups of wolves were confused by the fence, and initially tried to get out. They paced the fences, dug at the bottom, bit the chain links, and jumped high trying to escape. Eventually all groups adjusted to their temporary captivity; they have ceased fighting the fence, and seem to be tolerating their temporary captive existence.

After this unavoidable period of adjustment, park biologists have tried to make the captivity as stress-free as possible for the wolves. This includes very limited access to the pens, brief, twice weekly feedings of road-killed ungulates (elk, deer, bison, or moose), and security rangers operating at a distance. The wolves are fed about 15 lbs of ungulate/ wolf/day, or, since this measurement includes bone, about 10 lbs of meat/wolf/day. This is a more robust diet than normally occurs in the wild just to insure that they are getting adequate food in a confined situation.

What the wolves do most is pace along the fence. Each group has their favorite part of the pen—the furthest area away from the door—and frequent pacing has produced a concrete-like path on the snow. Other activities include resting, eating, and playing. The most frequent play activity in all three pens is raven chasing as the ravens descend on the

The wolves were fed a variety of road-killed meat, mostly elk and deer, which was transported by sleigh to each of the three pens twice a week. Otherwise, they were left undisturbed by human visitors, except for security patrols by rangers, who stayed a considerable distance from the pens. NPS photo by Jim Peaco.

provided carcasses. Wolves and ravens know each other well in the wild and wolves, especially pups, seem to enjoy trying to catch a raven. In the wild it has been observed that they are occasionally successful at it. Another play behavior observed includes pups parading around the pen carrying bones in their mouths, quite humorous for the security rangers to watch from a distance.

Each group of wolves seems to have its own distinct personality and has been behaving somewhat differently than the others. The Crystal Creek wolves calmed down more quickly, and the alpha female of this group consistently begins feeding 10–20 minutes after the carcasses are brought in and the feeding crew has left. The Rose Creek male, one of the largest Yellowstone wolves, is one of the boldest. No other wolf circles us in the middle of the pen as we deliver the carcasses. He is never so bold as to come close, but seems to like checking the door behind us. He will often sniff at a carcass before we leave. Of the three groups, the Soda Butte wolves took the longest to become somewhat tolerant of their con-

Wolf 10M, the large male placed in the Rose Creek acclimation pen, was eventually killed outside the park, but not before fathering a litter of eight puppies. NPS photo by Jim Peaco.

finement. They also exhibit more dominance behavior upon our entry to their pen. A whimper or whine is heard, for instance, as an adult disciplines a sub-adult. This behavior usually subsides after feeding. Also, this group is the only group to venture into their wood security boxes (dog houses). In fact, the older blue-black male retreats to his security box every time we feed; if need be he'll run by us to get inside.

A pleasant, unexpected behavior of the wolves has been their howling. Most biologists doubted that the wolves would be comfortable enough to howl in the pens, but all groups have. According to coyote researchers in the Lamar Valley, the local coyotes have been howling more since the wolves showed up; maybe in response, the wolves were motivated to advertise their presence. Security rangers report hearing each group howl six or seven times, commencing approximately one week after each group was placed in their respective pens. For the rangers who have heard them howl, it has been a real treat. One entry from the security rangers' log book reads: "a truly incredible sound-not eerie or evil sounding- but with such forlonging [sic] sadness . . . to be hearing this sound to such a backdrop of moon and stars—alone." If these wolf howls are compensation, then the rangers are being duly rewarded for conscientious 24-hour security and their efforts in observing and noting certain wolf behaviors when possible. Their work reminds us of how many people are involved with wolf restoration in Yellowstone.

The most significant behaviors the rangers report indicate signs of breeding. The breeding season for wolves is in February. While feeding, wolf biologists have noted signs of estrus (blood) on the fur of the Crystal Creek female. Security rangers have corroborated these observations by noting her receptiveness to the alpha male, and by spotting a very distinctive behavior associated with breeding—averting her tail. In short, she moves her tail to the side in front of the alpha male. One ranger lost sight of the Crystal Creek pair for approximately 40 minutes while the pair was in tree cover. While the adults were obscured from view, a younger wolf sat looking into the trees, cocking his head from side-to-side.

Although not proof of breeding, we suspect that such activity may be occurring. The other pens are not as visible as the Crystal Creek pen, but signs of possible breeding activity have been reported from both Rose Creek and Soda Butte, and the alpha female at Rose Creek came to us in proestrus. Although we did not suspect successful breeding behavior to occur this year, we are cautiously optimistic; pups this year would be a great way to begin wolf restoration in Yellowstone.

Park Discusses Wolf Release and Monitoring
With Neighboring Agencies

During the week of February 13, 1995, Yellowstone National Park, at the request of the U.S. Fish and Wildlife Service, hosted a variety of biologists and managers who came to discuss current and future plans for wolf recovery in the Yellowstone area. Approximately 40 people met for two days, including representatives from the U.S. Fish and Wildlife Service (USFWS), the U.S. Forest Service, the Idaho Department of Fish and Game, the Wyoming Department of Game and Fish, the Montana Department of Fish, Wildlife and Parks, and Animal Damage Control

(ADC). Ed Bangs, USFWS Montana Wolf Recovery Coordinator, reviewed the Canadian capture operations and the transport of the wolves to Yellowstone and central Idaho. Park staff updated attendees on the status of the wolves and plans for post-release monitoring (which are discussed in the following article.)

Several well-known biologists instrumental in planning for wolf restoration, including Dr. Steven Fritts, Northern Rocky Mountain Wolf Recovery Coordinator; Ed Bangs, and Dr. L. David Mech, NBS Wildlife Research Biologist, were among the visitors with whom park staff discussed plans for release of the 14 wolves now temporarily penned on the park's northern range. The intent of the "soft release" technique employed in wolf restoration to Yellowstone is to acclimate the wolves to their new surroundings and reduce the likelihood that, upon release from the holding pens, they will disperse widely or attempt diligently to travel toward their home range in Canada. However, like the "hard release" technique employed in the central Idaho wolf recovery area, there are no guarantees that either experiment will have the desired results.

For wolves, breeding generally occurs in January-February, and wolves have a 63 to 65-day gestation period. Wolves do not use dens for shelter year-round but only for the female to bear and raise pups, from approximately April to June. As reported in the previous article, signs of potential breeding activity have been observed in each of the three holding pens in the Lamar Valley, though this will not necessarily result in successful pup production this spring. In planning for the wolves' release from their pens, biologists have discussed the advantages and disadvantages associated with holding the wolves during breeding season.

Breeding season increases social tension within wolf packs. Despite their apparent good health, continued feeding, and tolerance to the holding period, this stress, combined with the effects of temporary captivity, could affect their breeding activity. Conversely, keeping the wolves penned during this time could enhance the pair-bonding and reduce the chance that wolf pairs or groups will split apart once released. Females, if pregnant, need a few weeks to select and prepare a den site, which is likely to be on a rocky slope near a source of water. There should be no shortage of potential den sites in the Yellowstone recovery area.

Due to the increased stress that wolves may be experiencing during breeding season, and in preparation for the release, the employee and media opportunities to observe the wolves have ceased.

Interested NPS employees and media selected by lottery were offered an opportunity, in groups of five persons escorted by one member of the Information and Education group, to watch the wolves during twice weekly feedings. Observation was done from a preselected site approximately 300 yards above the wolves, and only at the Crystal Creek pen. The last employee opportunity was February 28, and the last media visit was March 3. Staff and media were presented with information on wolf behavior and encouraged to use the extended viewing opportunity to focus on wolf recognition, as such lengthy viewing may be rare once the wolves are roaming freely.

The decision on when to release Yellowstone's wolves from their pens is being considered on a day-to-day basis. At this time, the wolves continue to feed well and are making few attempts to dig or climb out of their holding pens. Project biologists continue to monitor their health and behavior, and see no signs of serious injury to the animals. However, if aggressive intraspecific activity is observed such that might seriously injure one or more animals, a decision could be made to release the wolves immediately. Another concern is the potential for human and wolf safety as bears begin to emerge from their dens; adult male grizzlies in Yellowstone are consistently observed to emerge in mid-to late-March.

Ultimately, the behavior of the wolves will determine when they are released. The Incident Command Team has outlined plans to manage the human aspects of the wolf release. A media center may be set up again at the Mammoth pavilion, but no one will be at the pens, so no one will be able to view the release. Tentative plans call for biologists to ski into the pen sites, lock the gates open, and immediately leave the area. Biologists have considered whether or not to leave ungulate carcasses around the pens just prior to the release, but there is some doubt as to how long any carcass left would remain untouched by other scavengers. Also, the wolves may disperse in any direction and may travel a considerable distance away from their pen site, making it unlikely that carcasses would be used by the wolves, as intended.

Plans also call for minimizing public use restrictions while giving the wolves the best opportunity to settle into Yellowstone. The 24-hour security around the pen sites will continue for a while, dependent on wolf movements near the pens. Adjacent to each of the three sites a "No Stopping" zone will be posted for approximately four miles along the Northeast Entrance road; this restriction will take effect just prior to the wolves' release and be maintained no longer than necessary. The zones will take advantage of natural breaking points; for example, the no stopping zone near the Crystal Creek pen will end at the Lamar Canyon, allowing visitors to continue to park and use the Slough Creek ski trail (weather permitting).

Although the immediate post-release period will be a period of the highest uncertainty for the wolves (and their watchers), in general, very few human use restrictions are expected to be necessary during wolf restoration. The only specific human use restriction likely to be used on a recurring basis, as outlined in the plan and EIS for restoration of wolves to central Idaho and Yellowstone, is a limit on human access within approximately one mile of den sites between April 1 and June 30, if intrusive human activity would put the den and pups at risk. It remains to be seen whether, once released, any of the groups of wolves penned this winter in the Lamar Valley will stay and establish territories in or near Yellowstone National Park.

What Happens After Release? Wolf Monitoring in Yellowstone

Most of the controversy surrounding wolf restoration focussed on the idea of bringing wolves back to Yellowstone. Should it be done, how will it be done, and what administratively is necessary? Now that the program is underway here and in central Idaho, we must focus on what will happen after the wolves are released. Monitoring the wolves will help us both evaluate the success of the restoration efforts and will provide basic population information so that wolves can some day be recovered in the northern Rockies.

What basic population information on Yellowstone wolves will we need to know? Most studies of animal population dynamics gather data on total population size, reproduction, mortality, and age and sex structure. We will be interested in the same data.

The Final Environmental Impact Statement on wolf restoration (FEDS) defined three wolf population levels of management concern. The plan called for reintroducing wolves to Yellowstone and central Idaho unless a population defined as two breeding pairs each successfully raising two young for two consecutive years existed. Furthermore, the FEDS stated that no private or public land use restrictions would be developed solely for wolf recovery (except at release sites during reintroduction) after six breeding pairs of wolves were established in an experimental area.

Recovery of the northern Rocky Mountain wolf would be considered when the Yellowstone, Idaho, and Montana recovery areas have ten breeding pairs (total of 30 breeding pairs) of wolves established. Hence, it is obvious why we need data on total population size and reproduction, but data on mortality, age and sex structure also pertain to wolf population management.

Besides population monitoring, we will need to have information on wolf movements. Do wolf packs range entirely within Yellowstone, move in and out, or live completely outside the park? For wolves that leave the park, will they travel far enough to leave the designated recovery area? If so, and if there are potential or actual conflicts, then they could be captured and returned to the park. We recognize the need to allow wolves the opportunity to travel and go where they want, but there are places where wolves will be undesirable, from the standpoint of potential land-use conflicts and for the security of the wolves.

Another measure of how well wolves are doing is how much they are eating. Wolves will likely kill elk most often with other prey species (i.e. deer and bison) taken opportunistically (they may have to learn to kill bison as they have not seen them before). How often will wolf packs make kills? If an average sized pack (5–7 wolves) kills at an interval of 3–5 days, they will be very well fed; a kill rate exceeding ten days would indicate the wolves might be having trouble finding food. This is unlikely in Yellowstone. Knowing what kinds of prey wolves kill will also be valuable: Will they kill mostly elk? What are the ages and sex of the animals they kill? And will wolves consume all of the animals they kill or will they leave some? These are questions aimed at determining how well wolves fit back ecologically into the Yellowstone ecosystem.

Fitting back ecologically will not just be examined from the point of view of the prey, but also from the standpoint of the other carnivores already here. Coyotes, foxes, mountain lions, and bears will be the animals of primary concern; although there are other carnivores here, these are the most likely to be affected by wolf restoration. Because we will be concerned with wolves, these other animals will hopefully be studied by other researchers as we study the wolves. We are curious to learn whether there will be interactions between these animals at wolf kills. If so, how will they occur? Will one animal usurp a carcass from another, or will other predators merely wait until the wolves leave the carcass? These kinds of observations and others will be recorded as we monitor the wolves, although the park staff's primary function is to track the success of wolf restoration, not research wolf behavior or interactions between wolves and other prey or predator species.

The activities discussed above will be our priorities. While we do this, however, it will be possible to do other things. Following wolf movements will allow us to map territories and determine size and juxtaposition to other wolf territories. This information will allow us to ask questions such as: How do wolf movements relate to human activity, roads, and elk distribution? What areas or habitats are important to wolves?. The park GIS system should be a great aid in achieving this objective.

Other parts to our wolf monitoring plan include gathering wolf feces in summer to learn more about food habits, inspecting wolves and their feces for parasites and disease, evaluating wolf genetics and health by gathering blood samples, and determining how best to handle a wolf if necessary. Weather or winter severity (snow depth, temperature, forage availability for elk) will also concern us. We will probably not gather these data ourselves, but rely on other systems already in place, or on new research, because winter severity will affect wolf/ungulate relations.

How will all of this be done? Our primary methodology will be radio tracking, mostly from fixed-wing aircraft, but when we can, we will track wolves from the ground. Every wolf brought to Yellowstone has been fitted with a radio collar to allow us to follow them. Indeed, wolves are too elusive and range too far for any other monitoring method to be useful. Having radio collars on wolves will be so important that wolves born in Yellowstone will need to be captured and collared so we can obtain data from them important to the above objectives; however, collars will not be placed on pups until they are substantially grown.

So much has gone into bringing wolves back to Yellowstone, but our task is far from complete. Failure to monitor the wolves after they are released would be a major oversight in this first-ever experiment in major carnivore restoration. It may take years for us to evaluate its success. In the process, we expect to learn a great deal about wolves and, perhaps, other components of the Yellowstone ecosystem.

Donations to the Wolf Recovery Effort

In June 1994, the Secretary of the Interior approved the restoration of wolves to Yellowstone National Park and central Idaho. This momentous decision, the result of twenty years of research, debate, and compromise, only reflects the results of all the opinion polls: the American public is overwhelmingly in favor of returned wolves to Yellowstone and central Idaho.

This is a remarkable conservation milestone. It is the first time anywhere in the American west that a large carnivore has been brought back, on purpose. The work, conducted under often extremely difficult conditions, will be scientifically complex and logistically challenging, but the rewards, in public fulfillment, in education, and in our scientific knowledge, are immeasurable. The park has received numerous calls from individuals wishing to make private contributions to this historic program.

[*Editor's Note: Since the* Wolf Tracker *was published, donation addresses have changed. Donations can be made either to the Wolf Education and Research Center, P.O. Box 3832, Ketchum, Idaho, 83340, which has an agreement with the U.S. Fish & Wildlife Service for raising and using funds for wolf restoration, or the Yellowstone Wolf Recovery Fund, Yellowstone Association, P.O. Box 117, Yellowstone Park, WY 82190.*]

Legal Actions Contesting Wolf Restoration Continue

Several lawsuits contesting aspects of the wolf restoration plan have been filed. The American Farm Bureau Federation, which lost its attempt for a preliminary injunction to halt the transport of wolves from Canada to Yellowstone and central Idaho, continues to pursue its case against the reintroduction program. The Urbigkits, interested citizens from Pinedale, Wyoming, have also contested the decision on the grounds that wolves of a different subspecies, *Canis lupus irremotus*, remain in the greater Yellowstone area, and might be affected by the reintroduction of another subspecies from Canada. The Sierra Club Legal Defense Fund has contested the aspect of the plan that calls for experimental nonessential designation of the wolves in central Idaho, because this could threaten wolves that have naturally re-colonized Idaho and received full protection under the Endangered Species Act. U.S. District Judge William Downes, who heard the Farm Bureau's first request for an injunction in Cas-per, Wyoming last December, is reviewing documents related to all three cases.

APRIL 1995
WOLVES ROAM FREELY IN YELLOWSTONE

At 3:45 p.m. on Tuesday, March 21, 1995, Yellowstone's Wolf Project Leader Mike Phillips and Northern Rocky Mountain Wolf Recovery Co-ordinator Steve Fritts opened the gate of the Crystal Creek acclimation pen to begin the release of gray wolves into the wilds of Yellowstone. By that time, the Crystal Creek group of six wolves (four young males and

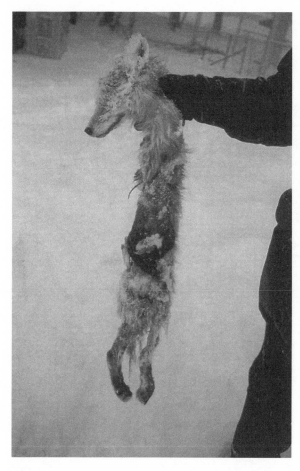

The first known predation in Yellowstone by the new wolves was a red fox that somehow got into the Soda Butte pen site and was killed and partially eaten. NPS photo by Jim Peaco.

an adult male and female), had been acclimated for 69 days, since January 12. Approximately 25 lbs. of meat was placed near the gate inside and outside of the pen to prompt the wolves to explore outside of the pen. Despite high levels of anticipation on the part of human wolf–watchers, who remained out of sight to monitor wolves using remote sensing devices, the wolves remained in the pen all night.

Park superintendent Mike Finley had decided, in consultation with park staff, that no media or VIP entourage would accompany the release crew. The release, and the period immediately afterward, would be the time of most stress for the wolves and that additional excitement at that time could cause the wolves to bolt in response to human activity. A no–stopping zone was established along the park's northeast entrance road

National Biological Service wolf ecologist L. David Mech (left) prepares deer meat while Yellowstone Wolf Project Biologist Doug Smith cuts hole in the Crystal Creek acclimation pen to encourage the wolves to leave. NPS photo by Jim Peaco.

for several miles in either direction from the release site. The areas around the pens remained closed to public access.

In anticipation of the release day, park staff had placed several devices on site to help monitor the wolves' activity in the early stages of release. Rangers installed motion detectors to monitor movement through the open gate of the pen. Photographers from Busch Productions, who have an agreement with the park to provide film footage, installed remote cameras to photo–document initial activity through the gate. And since all of Yellowstone's wolves are wearing radio-collars, biologists could remotely monitor the animals' movements by telemetry. Yet throughout the day following the opening of the first pen, none of the devices detected any movement out of the gate.

In response to public questions about the wolves' lack of movement, Phillips said, "This is perfect . . . exactly what we wanted. We wanted them to come out on their own terms and explore . . . We just have to be patient." There was also considerable discussion about whether the wolves recognized the gate—which had been used twice weekly by biologists to enter and place food inside the pen—as an opening to freedom or only as an area of less safety and comfort to the animals.

On Wednesday, March 22 at 4:45 p.m., biologists locked open the gate of the second acclimation pen at Rose Creek. Rose Creek had been temporary home to three wolves; an adult male and an adult female from different packs, and a young female from the same pack as the adult female. The females arrived in the park as part of the first transport from Canada, along with the Crystal Creek wolves. The male had been placed in the pen following the second shipment of wolves to Yellowstone, which arrived on January 20; thus his acclimation period had been 62 days. No movement was detected from the Rose Creek pen until early in the morning of Thursday, March 23, when the motion sensor indicated that something had moved across the opening. Telemetry readings, which cannot detect movements over very small distances, indicated that the Rose Creek wolves were either still in their pen or just outside throughout that day.

Also on March 23 at about 3:45 p.m., the biologists returned to the Crystal Creek pen, having decided to cut a second 4' × 10' opening on the "back side" of the pen in an area away from the gate where the wolves had spent much time. Renowned wolf biologist L. David Mech had suggested that because the "front door" was so associated with humans, the wolves might not exit through the open gate.

In fact, Phillips pointed out that the wolves' behavior demonstrated that they had not become habituated to humans during their acclimation; tamed and zoo wolves commonly gravitate toward a gate or entrance instead of avoiding it. While project biologist Doug Smith added that "we never would have predicted this," all agreed that this was truly turning out to be a very "soft release," as intended. The soft release method is designed as much as possible to limit the degree of human stimulation at the actual release, and let the wolves take their time to explore their new, wild surroundings.

During a windy spring snowstorm on Friday, March 24, wolf activity started to pick up. Beginning just after 9:00 a.m., the motion sensor–which had been moved to the opening cut in the Crystal Creek pen–recorded activity six times that morning, and four additional times throughout the afternoon. Meanwhile at Rose Creek, the motion detector indicated some activity between 1:45 a.m. and 9:06. Since telemetry signals continued to indicate that the Rose Creek wolves were in the vicinity of the pen, biologists approached that site to cut an additional opening similar to that at Crystal Creek. However, as they approached the pen in the mid-afternoon, they saw the adult male wolf several hundred yards outside the pen. He howled from a distance of 100–200 yards, and the crew immediately left the deer carcass they were carrying and departed the area. They had observed the adult female still inside the pen; the female pup was not visible during that short time. For the next several days, sensors and observation from long distances with binoculars and spotting scopes indicated that the wolves were staying close to both the Crystal Creek and Rose Creek pens, but that there was some movement in and out.

On Monday, March 27, at 4:01 p.m., biologists cut a 6' × 10' hole in the third acclimation pen at Soda Butte. The five Soda Butte wolves (two adult males, an adult female, a subadult female and a subadult male) had been penned for 64 days, since January 22. A deer carcass was left in the fence opening, but the wolves did not exit their pen that day or the next.

On Wednesday, March 29, biologists received a report that a wolf was traveling east along Soda Butte Creek at about 8:15 a.m. Ground tracking revealed that the subadult male from the Soda Butte group was south of his release site; the other four Soda Butte wolves were radio-located on the western slopes of the Thunderer, northeast of their pen. On the same day, tracks in the snow indicated that the Rose Creek wolves had approached within approximately 300 yards of the Lamar Ranger Station, then the wolves turned around and traveled north out of the range of ground telemetry. Biologists thus moved up toward the release site to inspect the carcass of a bull elk; they determined that it had been killed by a predator, possibly the wolves.

The first aerial monitoring flight for wolves occurred on Thursday, March 30. The Crystal Creek wolves remained near their pen. The Rose Creek wolves were located in the Buffalo Creek drainage, in the Absaroka-Beartooth Wilderness of the Gallatin National Forest, some 7 miles north of the Yellowstone Park boundary. The entire Soda Butte group was located southeast of their release site near the Lamar River. During ground tracking, biologists found an elk calf that had been killed and partially consumed by the Soda Butte group.

Mike Phillips, Doug Smith, and Dave Mech examine a wolf-killed elk.

Friday, March 31 was the first time the Crystal Creek wolves were monitored at any distance from their pen. While one young male remained in the pen, the other five wolves were seen bedded in a snowfield on the southern slope of Specimen Ridge. Later that day while biologists worked to cut another hole in the fence, the last wolf left through the first opening and howled, presumably to help him locate the other wolves in his group.

During the early days of April all three groups of wolves continued to explore their new surroundings. The Crystal Creek wolves were located on Amethyst Mountain and in the Calfee Creek and Cache Creek drainages. At last report, the subadult male remained by himself, and had moved west to the Yellowstone River.

After spending 4–5 days in the Buffalo Creek drainage, the Rose Creek wolves moved back inside the park. The adult pair were monitored apart from the young female, who was located near the Crystal Creek pen. The adult male and female were last located in the Cache Creek drainage, several miles west of the Crystal Creek wolves.

On April Fool's Day, aerial observation revealed that a grizzly bear was on the kill that the Soda Butte wolves had apparently made the day before. The wolves were subsequently monitored on the slopes of Mt. Hornaday and Druid Peak, several miles from their release site.

Monitoring from the air and ground will continue as necessary. While preliminary results indicated that the acclimation period has attenuated the wolves' tendency to home toward Canada, the next few weeks are critical, because that tendency may yet surface. Nonetheless, project biologists are encouraged with results so far.

Park operations should be little affected by the presence of the newly–released wolves. The only no–stopping zone that had been temporarily in effect for approx. 4 miles along the northeast entrance road in the vicinity of the Crystal Creek pen was lifted on April 4. The pen sites remain closed to public access for the present, as some wolves have periodically been monitored near the enclosures. Also, the electric fences designed to deter other wildlife from approaching and damaging the wolf pens need to be secured and marked to alert people they are electrified prior to the areas being open to public use. This will occur in the next few weeks. A high degree of curiosity among park employees and visitors about the wolves' movements and activities will be addressed by periodic news updates, press releases, employee newsletters, and electronic bulletin boards.

Judge Denies Urbigkit's Motion for Preliminary Injunction

While wolf restoration proceeds on the ground in both Yellowstone and central Idaho, legal challenges continue to be addressed in the courts. On January 30, 1995, James R. and Cat Urbigkit of Pinedale, Wyoming filed a motion for a preliminary injunction against the release of wolves. They alleged that the Defendants (Bruce Babbitt, Secretary of the Interior, et al.) failed to use all methods to conserve naturally occurring gray wolves in the designated areas, particularly the Greater Yellowstone Area. They alleged that the final rules, promulgated by the U.S. Fish and Wildlife Service to manage wolves, and the Final Environmental Impact Statement were arbitrary, capricious, an abuse of discretion, and in violation of the Endangered Species Act and NEPA. The plaintiffs claimed that introduction of a non–native subspecies of wolf would negatively impact wolves that they believe already exist in the area by contaminating their gene pool and competing for their habitat.

In a decision issued in U.S. District Court in Casper, Wyoming on March 19, 1995, Judge William Downes denied the plaintiffs' motion. Judge Downes wrote that plaintiffs "submitted precious little evidence in support of their assertion that the wolves existing in Yellowstone are of a distinct subspecies different from the wolves scheduled to be released by the Defendants." Nor, he wrote, did plaintiffs provide sufficient evidence to show that a unique gene pool is threatened, or that harm, even if supported by scientific evidence, would be immediate. Therefore, the plaintiffs failed to prove that they would suffer the "immediate irreparable harm" that must be demonstrated prior to granting a preliminary injunction, according to previous rulings by the Tenth Circuit Court.

MAY 1995
WOLVES CONTINUE EXPLORATORY MOVEMENTS

Throughout April, the fourteen wolves released in Yellowstone National Park (YNP) made exploratory movements in and around northern Yellowstone and park biologists monitored wolf movements as weather permitted. Monitoring flights were conducted twelve times between April 7–May 1, 1995; the animals' movements are summarized below:

Crystal Creek Group—Six wolves (adult male and female; 4 subadult pups) were acclimatized in a pen at Crystal Creek. Throughout the first half of April, the wolves remained inside YNP, mostly in the Lamar River drainage. Generally, the adults and three of the younger wolves roamed together, while one young male was most often observed by himself and close to the release site. During a flight on April 11, the solitary subadult appeared to have killed a malnourished elk calf by himself. He confined his movements to the Lamar and Soda Butte drainages. In the latter half of April, the rest of the Crystal Creek group moved eastward outside the park, first into the Shoshone National Forest (NF) and then into the Custer NF northeast of the park, approximately 55 miles from Crystal Creek. Then, near the month's end, the five wolves retraced their route back toward Yellowstone, and by May 1 were back in the Lamar Valley not far from their release site. The young male who had remained mostly by himself throughout the month was observed bedding with the rest of his group on the slopes of Specimen Ridge.

Soda Butte Gorup—This group of five wolves (2 adult males, adult female; 1 subadult male and 1 subadult female) have been located together during all monitoring attempts to date. In early April, they were not far from their release site in the northeastern part of Yellowstone NP, and were located in association with several ungulate kills. An early kill was an elk

319

calf, but on April 18 biologists inspected a cow moose killed by this group. The moose appeared to be 10 or more years old but did not appear to be malnourished, and a grizzly bear had also fed on the moose carcass. By the third week of April, the Soda Butte group had moved northward outside the park, approximately 30 miles from their release site. Their movements were fairly restricted within the Absaroka-Beartooth Wilderness in the Custer NF, where as of early May they remained.

Rose Creek Group—Three wolves had been penned at Rose Creek (adult male and female; 1 subadult female). As the month began, the adult pair had separated from the younger female, and all had returned to the park from an early foray northward into the Absaroka-Beartooth Wilderness. By the second week of April, the adults had again moved north of the park, while the subadult remained by herself, mostly within Yellowstone's boundary, for the entire month. During a flight on April 13, she was observed within 1/2 mile of a predator–killed elk, but biologists could not at that time confirm that she had made the kill. The pair of adults remained outside the park, and inclement weather prevented biologists from closely monitoring their movements during the third week of April. However, by April 24, the pair was located in the vicinity of Red Lodge, Montana, approx. 60 miles east of their release site. (See article below for follow-up.)

The movements exhibited this month are characterized by project biologists as not atypical; they probably represent exploratory behavior on the part of the wolves. Preliminary results indicated that the acclimation period did attenuate the wolves' homing desires and abilities; early movements were restricted to fairly small areas near each release site, and the wolves generally continued to travel together in groups. Early evidence also clearly demonstrated that wolves were killing elk, even those young wolves who were apart from the rest of their pen–mates. Project biologists have documented at least 7 ungulate kills by the wolves; 5 elk calves, 1 bull elk, and 1 cow moose.

It is unclear why most of the wolves began widening their travels during their third week of freedom, although it appears significant that all exploratory movements were in a northward direction. As of May 1, however, 7 of the original Yellowstone wolves were inside the park, 5 were north of the park in the Absaroka–Beartooth Wilderness area, and 1 remained near Red Lodge, Montana.

One Yellowstone Wolf Missing, Believed Killed

During a routine monitoring flight on Wednesday, April 26, 1995, Yellowstone National Park biologists received a "mortality" signal from the collar of the adult male wolf from the Rose Creek group. A mortality signal occurs if the collar is stationary for at least 4 hours, indicating that either the collar is no longer carried by the animal, or the animal is not moving and possibly dead. The monitoring crew notified the U.S. Fish and Wildlife Service's (USFWS) Helena office of the signal and position on the map. During the flight, the adult female from the Rose Creek group was also radio-located in the area.

Thursday morning, April 27, park biologists located the signal by air and USFWS biologists retrieved the radio-collar used in monitoring the reintroduced animal. The radio-collar was located east of Red Lodge, Montana; the animal itself was not in the area. The condition of the collar indicated it may have been physically removed rather than having slipped off the animal.

USFWS personnel, in cooperation with local law enforcement officials and Montana Department of Fish, Wildlife and Parks officers, are continuing an investigation into the disappearance of the adult male wolf, one of the 29 wolves relocated from Canada into Yellowstone NP and central Idaho. The reintroduced wolves are protected under a special rule in the Endangered Species Act. This special rule, referred to as reintroduction of nonessential, experimental populations, allows private landowners or their agents to kill a wolf if it is found in the act of maiming or killing livestock. The USFWS reports that there has been no sign of such an attack. The special rule also requires landowners or their agents to report any such incident within 24 hours, and no such report has been made.

A reward of $1,000 is being offered by the USFWS, $5,000 by Defenders of Wildlife, and $5,000 by the Audubon Society for information leading to the arrest and conviction of any individual or individuals responsible for taking the wolf. All information provided will be kept in the strictest confidence. Anyone with information should contact the USFWS agents in Billings, Montana (406-247-7355); Cody, Wyoming (307–678–7604); or a local fish and game officer.

Rose Creek Female Gives Birth Near Red Lodge, Montana

On May 3, USFWS biologists confirmed that the adult female from the Rose Creek group had given birth to a litter of pups on private land near

Red Lodge, Montana. The female had restricted her movements for a week or more, during the same period in which her missing mate's collar was discovered. Upon field investigation, biologists observed 7 or 8 pups still with their eyes closed, with mother and pups appearing to be in good condition.

Under normal conditions all members of a wolf pack assist the alpha female in caring for pups. The alpha male provides food for the female while she stays with the pups until weaned, at about age 6–10 weeks. Since the Rose Creek male is missing and presumed dead, she has no other wolf to assist her in obtaining food for either herself or her pups. As it would be very difficult for her to successfully raise the pups alone during this early phase, USFWS biologists will bring in carcasses and leave them at a safe distance from the wolves.

The pups were not observed in association with a dug-out den, but were seen in a somewhat protected area above the ground. This is unusual, but biologists believe that perhaps the Rose Creek female was waiting for the male to return, possibly to continue the search for a den site, when she was forced to give birth. Because the next few weeks are critical for the survival of the pups, the USFWS will continue to monitor the condition of the Rose Creek female and her offspring.

JUNE/JULY 1995
WOLVES SETTLING INTO LIFE IN THE
YELLOWSTONE ECOSYSTEM

Wolves from two of the three packs brought to Yellowstone and released in late March appear to be settling into life in the ecosystem, killing prey as needed to survive and interacting with other native wildlife. Somewhat in defiance of predictions, wolves have been relatively visible to persistent observers in the right locations during May and June. Biologists continue to monitor the movements of the wolves by ground and aerial telemetry as well as by remote observation when possible, and report the following:

Crystal Creek Group—This group of six wolves (adult male and female; 4 yearling males) has remained in the Lamar Valley area of the park, and has provided most of the visitor opportunities to observe wild wolves in Yellowstone in 1995. One or more of this group of wolves have also been observed interacting with elk, bison, coyotes, and grizzly bears. In June, a series of observations over the course of several days suggested that the wolves were digging out active coyote dens in what could be a demonstration of interspecific competition between members of the two canid species. Wolves have been observed chasing (and occasionally being chased by!) elk and bison, which calve in the riparian zones and adjacent sagebrush-grassland slopes of the valley. A number of visitors and park staff have observed grizzly bears and wolves interacting over carcasses of elk calf kills. To the casual observer it is not always apparent whether there are clear "winners" or "losers" in these interactions; some of them suggest play behavior between subadult bears and subadult wolves, in which the predators alternately appear to "win" possession of the carcass for a short period of time, only to be displaced from or abandon the carcass a short time later.

One park biologist observed an early-morning interaction between a sow grizzly with two two-year-old cubs and five of the Crystal Creek wolves. The bears moved out of the tree cover into a meadow where the wolves were resting in the sun. Off and on for a period of more than an hour, the bears and wolves remained in fairly close proximity (within approximately 50–100 yards of each other), moving tentatively back and forth toward each other. The adults of both species appeared to stand their ground and keep their distance slightly more than the subadults. No kills were apparent in this interaction. After a while, the wolves resumed lying in the grass, some 100–150 yards from where they were first seen, as the grizzly bears moved back into the woods.

Naturalist Rick McIntyre, who came to Yellowstone to focus on interpreting wolves in 1994 and again in 1995, has estimated that more than 2600 persons have seen wolves thus far this spring in the Lamar Valley.

Wildlife watchers are advised to stay along the road, parking in designated pullouts well off of the main road corridor when looking for wolves and other park wildlife. Binoculars and spotting scopes will greatly enhance viewing opportunities. While it is possible to recognize the adult wolves largely by coloration, visitors might enjoy trying to distinguish adults from subadults by differences in their size or behavior as well.

Soda Butte Group—The five wolves (2 adult males, adult female; 1 yearling male and 1 subadult female aged 1–3) have remained not far from their release site in northeastern Yellowstone NP, staying mostly in the Absaroka-Beartooth Wilderness area north of the park. Park biologists found it compelling that the adult female remained within a 2–3 mile area for more than six weeks during the typical denning season; how-

Memorial Day weekend in Lamar Valley witnessed numerous "wolf jams," as many park visitors watched the wolves hunting, playing, and otherwise going about their daily routines. NPS photo by Jim Peaco.

ever, the terrain and cover seldom allowed aerial observers to see these wolves during monitoring flights. Finally, on June 16, Wolf Project Leader Mike Phillips observed one black pup with one of the female wolves in the Absaroka-Beartooth Wilderness. The large male was not seen or heard during this flight. The three other wolves were just north of the park boundary. Biologists originally suspected that more pups could have been born, however, subsequent monitoring has not turned up any evidence of additional pups.

Rose Creek Group—Of the three wolves released from Rose Creek (adult male and female; 1 yearling female), the younger female has remained on her own, ranging in and outside the park boundary. On April 26, 1995, the adult male wolf's radio-collar triggered a mortality signal, and the animal was subsequently determined to have been illegally killed. On May 3, USFWS biologists confirmed that the female had given birth to a litter of eight pups on private land near Red Lodge, Montana. Under normal conditions all members of a wolf pack assist the alpha female in caring for pups until weaned, at about age 6–10 weeks. However, the

One of Wolf 9F's three-week-old pups on May 18, 1995, when the mother and her litter were flown back to the park from near Red Lodge, Montana. NPS photo by Douglas Smith.

Rose Creek female had no pack members to help her raise her newborn pups. On May 7, the skinned-out carcass of the Rose Creek male, its head missing, was discovered by a hunter. On May 15, USFWS agents executed a search warrant on property owned by Chad McKittrick of Red Lodge, and found the cape and skull of the wolf. McKittrick has been charged with violation of the Endangered Species Act for killing the alpha male wolf. The trial has been set for October 1, 1995, in Billings, Montana.

After extensive deliberation by USFWS and NPS wolf biologists and other wolf experts, the decision was made to move the female and her pups back to temporary confinement in the Rose Creek pen inside Yellowstone National Park. "The area where she had the pups was not the best for them to learn how to be wolves," said USFWS wildlife biologist Ed Bangs. "With the added stress associated with single parenthood, this was not the most desirable of situations." The area in which the Rose Creek female gave birth was near houses, working ranches, hotels, restaurants, and other human-related establishments. "We had to make a

Mike Phillips and Yellowstone Park Wildlife Veterinarian Mark Johnson examining one of Wolf 9F's pups on June 26, 1995. All the pups were given a variety of vaccinations and other treatments in preparation for their release in the fall. NPS photo by Douglas Smith.

decision—were their chances better here or in the park? We went with the park," Bangs said.

On May 15–16, traps were set for the adult wolf; once trapped, biologists planned to find and capture the wolf pups by hand. At about 4 a.m. on Thursday, May 18, the female was captured in a trap that turned out to be very close to the den. It took another six hours after the female's capture before the den was discovered; the mother had moved the den from the original site. Biologists used telemetry equipment and common sense to find the den, said YNP biologist Doug Smith. Each of the pups appeared fit with their eyes wide open. The female, caged in a small dog kennel, and her eight pups were helicoptered to Yellowstone and taken immediately to the one-acre Rose Creek pen. The pups weighed approximately five pounds each, and their eyes had just opened. The litter was half male and half female. Waiting for them in the pen were chunks of deer and bison meat. The wolves are being fed three times each week. Access to the penned wolves has been extremely limited.

On June 26, park biologists did make a foray into the pen to vaccinate the pups. While it is not in keeping with NPS policy to capture and handle free-ranging wildlife just to vaccinate them, park staff view this situation differently. Since the Rose Creek wolves are in captivity due to human-caused circumstances that have hampered their ability to survive in the wild, it behooves us to protect them from diseases just as it is our responsibility to feed them while in temporary captivity. The pups were vaccinated for parvovirus, canine distemper, leptospirosis, parainfluenza, and infectious canine hepatitis. They were also given Ivermectin for internal and external parasites, and treated for tapeworms. The pups were too young to be vaccinated for rabies, but the plan is to give them rabies vaccine as a precaution prior to their release, even though rabies has never been identified in Yellowstone Park or Park County, Montana. Project veterinarian Mark Johnson reported that the pups were given physical examinations and all looked very healthy; the adult female looked in good condition as well.

Initial plans were to keep the wolves in the pen at least until weaned. Some biologists believe that the wolves will have the best chance of survival if released this fall when the pups are more fully grown. After further consultation with numerous wolf biologists, the consensus is to hold the Rose Creek wolves until late summer, at which time the decision on when to release the wolves will be reevaluated. It is likely that the young wolves will be radio-collared prior to their release, to allow biologists to continue to monitor their movements and survival rates as these animals disperse into Yellowstone to join the other wild wolves in the ecosystem.

AUGUST/SEPTEMBER/OCTOBER 1995
ROSE CREEK WOLVES RELEASED FROM ACCLIMATION PEN

On October 11, the Yellowstone wolf restoration team released female #9 and her pups from the acclimation pen at Rose Creek, where they had been held since May 18.

Number 9's mate had been killed near Red Lodge, Montana, and in late April she whelped eight pups there. In the absence of the male, and without other adult pack members to support her and the pups by bringing food to them, female #9 and her pups were at risk. Subsequently, the decision was made to trap her and the pups and to hold them at the Rose Creek acclimation pen, where they could be fed and isolated from threats to their safety and where the pups could mature to the point that they were competent to survive even if some accident killed their mother.

With more than one adult wolf in a pack, wolf pups are led from the den 8–10 weeks after birth to a series of rendezvous sites, where they are tended through the summer by their mother and another pack member, a "baby-sitter." Other members of the pack hunt and bring food to the pups and the wolf tending them. With the Rose Creek wolves, park biologists took over the food–gathering function, bringing road–killed deer, elk, moose, and bison to the wolves.

On July 29, a windstorm blew two trees down across the fence of the Rose Creek pen, smashing two of the panels and creating holes in the fence. On July 31, biologists discovered the damage and observed that all eight pups were outside of the pen, while the adult female was still inside. From signs at the scene, the pups apparently were going in and out of the pen at will. Early the next morning biologists returned to the site and found three pups had gone inside the pen on their own.

It was decided to try to capture the other pups using non-invasive techniques; this resulted in one pup being caught in a kennel trap. Four of the pups were outside the pen, but staying in the immediate area.

After discussion with the U.S. Fish and Wildlife Service, it was decided to use #3 padded leghold traps to try to capture the remaining pups, since the non–invasive techniques had only yielded one pup in several days of trapping. Three pups were caught with the leghold traps and put inside the pen. Later, the pups went back out through one of the holes in the fence, leaving four of the pups outside the pen.

Subsequently, the wolf crew fixed all of the holes in the pen, and trapping efforts resumed. However, by now the pups were "well-educated" about the traps and only one pup was caught. For the next six weeks biologists brought food to the wolves: the female and five pups inside, and three pups outside the pen.

On October 9, wolf biologists and the park veterinarian visited the pen to administer a second series of vaccinations to the pups: shots for parvovirus, rabies, tuberculosis, and distemper. They also fitted the pups with radio collars. The team found six pups in the pen. Apparently one pup had scaled the fence, which was built with an interior overhang to prevent exit but not entry.

On October 11, the wolf team removed a panel and released the wolves from the Rose Creek pen. Biologists had planned a mid-October release, but that was hastened by observation of a grizzly bear in the vicinity of the pen. The bear was probably attracted to the food that had been left for the wolves. To avoid potential dangerous confronta-

The swift growth of the pups is revealed in this October 9 photo of Mark Johnson (left) and Doug Smith carrying one of the Rose Creek pups to a processing area for radio collaring. NPS photo by Jim Peaco.

tions between the bear and the wolves, the wolves were released a few weeks earlier than planned.

Another surprise greeted the wolf team on October 11. Earlier that morning, cinematographer Ray Paunovich and his sound man Colin Phillips, who met the team at Lamar to film the release, had observed and filmed the two black pups outside the pen showering affection on a gray wolf and howling with it. They assumed the gray wolf to be female #7, a female born to #9 in 1994 and captured with #9 in Canada and held in the Rose Creek pen until late March. Number #7 had dispersed from the mated pair and had been living on her own in the northern portion of the park. Wolf Restoration Team Leader Mike Phillips switched through the radio frequencies of the wolves' collars on his receiver and found that the gray wolf was not female #7 but male #8, a member of the Crystal Bench group. Number #8 had been roaming apart from the rest of the Crystal Bench group in recent weeks and had last been located alone near the Grand Canyon of the Yellowstone River.

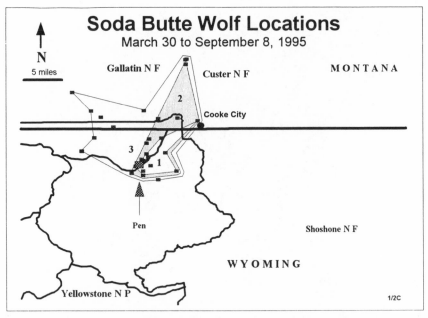

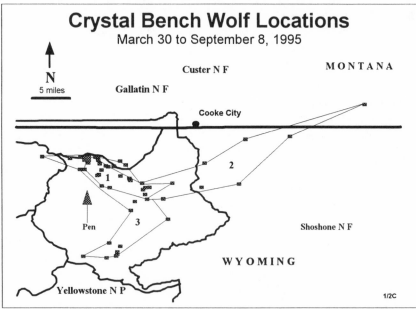

The movements of the various wolf groups in the first few months of freedom tended to divide into three stages, indicated on each map by the numbers 1, 2, and 3. Stage 1 is an initial period fairly near the release site, stage 2 is a time of wandering and exploration, and stage 3 is a period of what may be movements

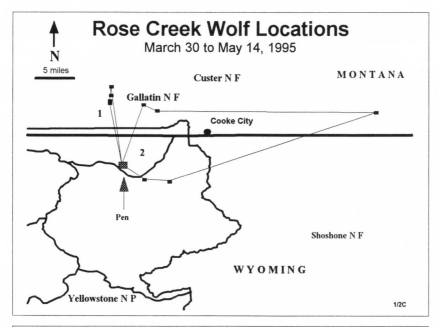

Rose Creek Wolf Locations
March 30 to May 14, 1995

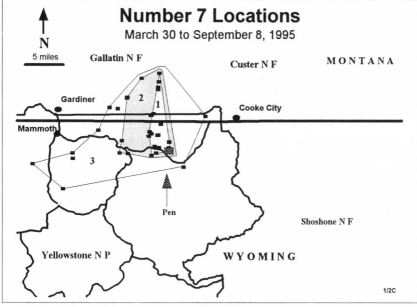

Number 7 Locations
March 30 to September 8, 1995

within a familiar and successful home range. Number 7 is the female yearling from the Rose Creek pen, whose movements during her first six months of freedom were almost entirely independent of any other wolf. Maps by James Halfpenny, courtesy of the Yellowstone Wolf Project.

On October 13 at 11:30 a.m., all of the Rose Creek wolves were located two miles east of the pen site. It is assumed that they came out early that morning. As of October 19, the Rose Creek wolves were seen, along with male #8, on Bison Peak; the Crystal Bench wolves (minus male #8) were seen halfway between Specimen Ridge and Pelican Valley; and the Soda Butte group were located in the Slough Creek drainage. Subadult female #7 was located on Electric Peak, in the northern portion of the park.

Is "Soft" Release of Wolves in Yellowstone Working?

What are the criteria for success in restoring wolves to Yellow-stone? How are we doing? So far, returning wolves to their old home by capturing them in Canada, holding them for several weeks and releasing them on–site using soft ("delayed") release seems to be working.

The advantage of a nonessential, experimental wolf reintroduction was discussed in Appendix 16 of the *Final Environmental Impact Statement, The Reintroduction of Gray Wolves to Yellowstone National Park and Central Idaho*. It responded to concerns about effects wolves might have on human activities: grazing, hunting, and land use.

But, what are the prospects for success in restoring wolves to Yellowstone? Commenting on the EIS in 1993, 16 wolf biologists, whose combined wolf experience totals 220 years, said:

"We believe it is a practical plan that meets the needs of state governments and local residents while facilitating prompt, effective, and economical wolf recovery."

Some indicators of the success of the project since the wolves were released from the pens last March are:

- The wolves have settled where their presence isn't a problem – near the acclimation sites. They didn't try to home for Alberta the moment they were allowed out of the pens, and, after a few weeks of exploration, the wolves have settled down in the park and nearby wilderness areas.
- Two of the three groups have stayed together.
- There has been no indication that handling and feeding the wolves increased their tolerance of humans.
- The acclimation and release process did not disrupt the wolves' breeding cycle. Two of the three groups produced litters, and a female in the third group exhibited breeding behavior.

332

On August 25, the First Family visited the Rose Creek pen site as part of a visit to Yellowstone Park. As biologists hold the wooden shelter box's lid open, President Clinton and daughter Chelsea look in at the pups, while (left to right) the White House photographer, a Secret Service Agent, Mrs. Clinton, and family friend Rebecca Kolsky look on. NPS photo by John Varley.

- When the Rose Creek female and her pups showed up in a place that was undesirable both for their safety and for the comfort of livestock producers, they were airlifted back into Yellowstone. That demonstrated not only the efficiency of radio collars but also the ability and determination of managing agencies to respond to potential conflict situations.
- The young female from the Rose Creek pen has shown that she can live independently, and she may find a mate this winter. Another potential disperser, Number 2 from the Crystal Bench group, early demonstrated his ability to kill elk by himself.

In summary, we can evaluate this year's progress toward a successful restoration effort by the facts that the wolves have settled where their presence isn't a problem, near the pen sites where they were acclimated to Yellowstone. If the wolves end up living in those areas permanently—setting up home ranges or territories there—that's successful. They have remained together as functional units, reproduced, and have not interacted in ways that conflict with human interests. We have demonstrated management control of wolves "out of bounds." Further, many park visitors have enjoyed seeing the wolves.

A Letter from the Field

For the second summer, I worked in Yellowstone as a seasonal naturalist, specializing in interpreting the park's wolf reintroduction program.

During the 1995 season, I spoke to over 40,000 park visitors about wolves and found overwhelming support for the wolf project. Out of the 40,000 contacts, only a tiny handful of visitors expressed any opposition to the program. Many of those people changed their mind after hearing details of the plan. In my twenty years of experience in national parks, I have never seen such a high level of visitor support for a park service program.

Many people doubted that the wolves would be visible to tourists. I personally had 138 wolf sightings this summer and estimate that at least 4,000 park visitors saw the wolves. These sightings significantly enhanced the popularity of the wolf project.

I found, as predicted, that the presence of wolves is a great boon to the local economy. Gift shops in nearby towns did a great business in wolf–related items. The Roosevelt Lodge gift shop, the store closest to the wolves, reported a 44% increase in sales this year, an increase the manager attributes mainly to the presence of the wolves.

In summary, I can report that Yellowstone's wolf reintroduction program enjoys overwhelming support from park visitors.

Rick McIntyre

When the gates to the pens were opened in late March, the wolves' behavior was monitored intensively and the surprises and education (for people if not for wolves) began immediately. As the first week of wolf freedom recedes into the past, the anxiety and excitement of that time may eventually be difficult to understand. But keep in mind that there was simply no way of knowing what was going to happen, what it might mean for the immediate welfare of the wolves, and what it might mean for the long–term prospects of the wolf recovery program. Suspense and tension were high, and a lot was at stake. Though the language is restrained and professional, the report on the first week reflects that mood.

MEMORANDUM

Date: 6 April 1995

From: Mike Phillips, Yellowstone Wolf Restoration Project Leader Doug Smith, Yellowstone Wolf Restoration Biologist
To: Agencies and Individuals Interested in Wolf Restoration in Yellowstone National Park
Subject: Status of Wolf Restoration Project from 21 March – 6 April 1995

This is the first status report concerning wolf restoration in Yellowstone National Park. We apologize for the delay in preparing and distributing this report but fieldwork kept us from tending many other administrative chores as well. We appreciate your patience. We intend to prepare and distribute subsequent reports about every 7 days for the next few weeks, unless events dictate more frequent preparation and distribution.

SOURCE: Memorandum as given at beginning of chapter, Yellowstone Center for Resources files.

To promote clarity, information is presented for each group of wolves which are referenced by the name of their acclimation site.

We determined wolf movements via ground and aerial radio–tracking, motion detecting devices installed near the pens, and direct observations.

Crystal Creek Group (wolves 002M, 003M, 004M, 005F, 006M, and 008M)

Tuesday, 21 March

The gate of the acclimation pen was opened at 1545 h. By this time the wolves had been acclimated for 69 days (01/12/95–03/21/95). Food was placed near the gate inside and outside of the pen to prompt the wolves to explore the opening and exit the pen. However, as of 2359 h the wolves had not exited the pen.

Wednesday, 22 March

Wolves remained in the pen throughout the day.

Thursday, 23 March

As of mid-day the wolves were still in the pen (about 45 h after gate was opened). To promote their departure, from about 1545-1600 h we cut a hole (4' × 10') in a panel of the pen in an area where the wolves spent much time during the acclimation period. As of 2359 h the wolves were still in the pen.

Friday, 24 March

The motion detecting device indicated that something passed through the hole at 0914 h (17.25 h after the hole was cut). The device registered similar movement 8 more times from 1017 h–1401 h. During the afternoon we determined from observations and ground tracking that some wolves were inside the pen while others were either inside or just outside the pen.

Saturday, 25 March

During early morning we determined from observations and ground tracking that the wolves were inside or just outside the pen. From 1500–1530 h we observed five canids southeast and southwest of the pen. However, we were not able to confirm that these animals were wolves rather than coyotes because of the distance over which the observation was made (about 2 miles).

Sunday–Monday, 26–27 March

From observations and ground tracking we determined that the wolves were inside or just outside the pen.

Tuesday, 28 March

At 1300 h we observed five wolves in the pen. Through radio–tracking we determined that the 6th wolf was either inside or just outside the pen.

Given that the wolves had not yet definitely exited the pen we decided to enlarge the exit hole. We arrived at pen about 1330 h and determined from tracks that the wolves had at some point in the past exited the pen. Additionally, in response to our presence the 6th wolf howled from outside the pen. Given that the wolves were going and coming from the pen we did not enlarge the exit. We left about 30 lbs. of deer meat and quickly departed the area. While hiking back to the trailhead we determined that 1 wolf had wandered at least 0.3 miles from the pen and investigated a winter-killed bull elk. We were unable to determine if the wolf fed on the carcass.

There was no change throughout the remainder of the day as the wolves remained inside or just outside the pen.

Wednesday–Thursday, 29–30 March

From observations and ground tracking we determined that the wolves remained inside or just outside the pen.

Friday, 31 March

During the telemetry flight we observed all the wolves, except 002M, bedded in a snowfield a few miles south of the pen.

To promote 002M's departure from the pen, we enlarged the original exit hole and cut another. While we were completing the second hole, 002M walked out the original hole and up the hillside to the south. Within 3 min of departing the pen we heard 002M howl, probably in an attempt to determine the whereabouts of the rest of his group.

Saturday, 1 April

During the telemetry flight we observed all the wolves, except 002M, just south of Amethyst Mountain, or about 7 to 8 miles from their pen. In contrast, we located 002M near the pen.

Sunday, 2 April

During the telemetry flight we located all the wolves, except 002M, about 13 miles east of their pen. We located 002M near the pen.

Monday, 3 April

During the telemetry flight we located all wolves, except 002M, about 16 miles east of their acclimation pen. We located 002M about 2 miles south of the pen.

Tuesday, 4 April

During the telemetry flight we located all the wolves, except 002M, about 13 miles east of their acclimation pen. We located 002M about 4 miles west of the pen.

Wednesday–Thursday, 5–6 April

We did not determine the location of the wolves because inclement weather prompted cancellation of the telemetry flights.

Rose Creek Group (wolves 007F, 009F, and 010M)

Wednesday, 22 March

The gate of the acclimation pen was opened at 1645 h but the wolves remained in the pen throughout the remainder of the day. 007F and 009F had been in acclimation for 70 days (01/12/95–03/22/95), whereas 010M had been in acclimation for 62 days (01/20/95– 03/22/95).

Thursday, 23 March

The motion detecting device indicated that something moved through the hole at 0621 h. We determined from ground tracking that the wolves were either inside or just outside the pen throughout the remainder of the day.

Friday, 24 March

From 0145–0906 h the motion detecting equipment indicated movement through the gate of the pen and the telemetry equipment that all the wolves were in the vicinity of the pen.

Since it was possible that some or all of the wolves had not yet departed the pen, we decided to cut an exit hole similar to the one we provided the Crystal Creek wolves. As we approached the pen we saw that 009F was still inside while 010M was about 300 m outside the pen (howling at us). Radio–tracking allowed us to determine that 007F was either inside or just outside the pen. We left a deer carcass and hiked back to the trailhead. Because 010M and perhaps 007F had exited the pen through the gate, we did not cut an exit hole.

Saturday, 25 March

The motion detecting device registered movement through the gate throughout the day. We determined from ground tracking that the wolves were near the pen.

Sunday, 26 March

We determined from ground tracking that the wolves remained inside or just outside the pen throughout the day.

Monday, 27 March

We determined from ground tracking that 010M and 007F were inside or just outside the pen. From 1015 – 1045 h we observed 009F in the pen.

We also observed a bull elk that died about 0.3 miles north of the pen.
Tuesday, 28 March

We determined from ground tracking that the wolves were inside or just outside the pen.
Wednesday, 29 March

At 1200 h we received no radio signals from the wolves which indicated that they were not in or near the pen. Accordingly, we hiked to the pen to inspect the area. Tracks indicated that the wolves traveled south to within about 300 yards of the Lamar ranger station before turning north and traveling out of monitoring range. Inspection of the bull elk indicated that it had been killed by a predator a few days earlier. It is possible that the elk was killed by one or more of the wolves.
Thursday–Sunday, 29 March–2 April

During telemetry flights we located 007F, 009F, and 010M about 15 miles northwest of their pen which placed them about 8 miles north of the park boundary.
Monday, 3 April

During the telemetry flight we determined that the Rose Creek wolves had returned to the park. We located 007F about 4 miles south of the Rose Creek pen and 009F and 010M about 11 miles southeast of the pen. 009F and 010M were within 3 miles of the Crystal Creek group.
Tuesday, 4 April

During the telemetry flight we located 007F about 0.5 miles north of her pen and 009F and 010 about 7 miles southeast of their pen.
Wednesday–Thursday, 5–6 April

We did not determine the location of the wolves because inclement weather prompted cancellation of the telemetry flights.

Soda Butte Group (wolves 011F, 012M, 013M, 014F, and 015M)

Monday, 27 March

At 1601 h we released the wolves by cutting an exit hole (6' × 10') in the east end of the pen. The wolves had been in acclimation for 67 days (01/20/95–03/27/95). Although they fed on deer that we left in the hole, they had not left the pen by the end of the day.
Tuesday, 28 March

We determined from ground tracking and observations that the wolves were still in the pen.
Wednesday, 29 March

At about 0815 we received a report of 1 wolf traveling east across Soda

Butte Creek. We determined from ground tracking that all the wolves, except 015M, were about 3 miles northeast of their pen. In contrast, 015 appeared to be about 4 miles south of the pen.

Thursday, 30 March

During the telemetry flight we located all the wolves about 4 miles southeast of their pen. By following wolf tracks leading away form the pen we discovered an elk calf that the wolves had killed.

Friday, 31 March

During the telemetry flight we located all the wolves about 6 miles northeast of the pen.

Saturday, 1 April

During the telemetry flight we located all the wolves about 2 miles north of their pen.

Sunday, 2 April

During the telemetry flight we located all the wolves about 2 miles north of their acclimation pen.

Monday, 3 April

During the telemetry flight we located all the wolves about 0.5 miles from their pen.

Tuesday, 4 April

During the telemetry flight we located all the wolves about 2 to 3 miles north of their pen.

Wednesday–Thursday, 5–6 April

We did not determine the location of the wolves because inclement weather prompted cancellation of the telemetry flights.

Preliminary results indicate that the acclimation period has attenuated the wolves' homing behavior. However, the next few weeks are critical because that behavior may yet surface. Nonetheless we are excited about the future because the wolves are traveling as groups and are restricting movements to a relatively small area.

Epilogue: The Long View

Historical research suggests that Yellowstone hasn't had a healthy wolf population for about 120 years, and hasn't even had a reported pack of wolves for 60 years. That's a long time for an ecologically complex place like this to be deprived of one of its foremost evolutionary engineers. But neither evolution nor individual animals are predictable, and so what we've started by bringing back a few wolves doesn't instantly straighten out whatever harm we did so long ago when we destroyed their ancestors. Maybe 120 years from now, Yellowstone managers will be able to look back on this project and make some meaningful judgments on the ecological and spiritual consequences of what we've done today. For the moment, all we can do is give ourselves a little credit for having the belated decency to right such a long-standing wrong, and pray for puppies.

John Varley
Director, Yellowstone Center for Resources

SOURCE: The NPS Electric Courier, March 22, 1995, Vol. 1, No. 5.

Suggestions for Additional Reading

This book contains material from many important published sources. If you want to read more, start with those. The following list of additional sources is not comprehensive, as the literature of the wolf is quite large and is growing larger at an amazing rate. Most of these titles are about wolves, but a few are about related topics, especially the history of wildlife management in Yellowstone National Park.

Allen, D.L. 1979. *Wolves of Minong: their vital role in a wild community.* Boston: Houghton Mifflin Co. 499 pp.

Cahalane, V.H. 1939. The evolution of predator control policy in the national parks. *J. Wildl. Manage.* 3:229–237.

Carbyn, L.N., ed. 1983. *Wolves in Canada and Alaska.* Canadian Wildlife Service Report Series 45. 136 pp.

Carbyn, L.N., S.H. Fritts, and D.R. Seip. In press. *Ecology and conservation of wolves in a changing world.* Edmonton: Canadian Circumpolar Institute.

Cook, R.S. 1993. *Ecological issues on reintroducing wolves into Yellowstone National Park.* Denver: Scientific monograph NPS/NRYELL/NRSM–93/22. 328 pp.

Curnow, E. 1969. The history of the eradication of the wolf in Montana. M.S. Thesis, Univ. Mont., Missoula. 99 pp.

Fischer, H. 1995. *Wolf wars, the remarkable inside story of the restoration of wolves to Yellowstone.* Helena: Falcon Press. 183 pp.

Haines, A. 1977. *The Yellowstone story.* Boulder: Colorado Associated University Press. 2 vols.

Harrington, F.H., and P.C. Paquet, eds. 1982. *Wolves of the world.* Park Ridge, N.J.: Noyes Publishing. 474 pp.

Houston, D.H. 1982. *The northern Yellowstone elk, ecology and management.* New York: MacMillan. 474 pp.

The Yellowstone Wolf

Keiter, R.B., and R.T. Holscher. 1990. Wolf recovery under the Endangered Species Act: a study in contemporary federalism. *Public Land Law Review* 2:19–52.

Lopez, B.H. 1978. *Of wolves and men.* New York: Charles Scribner's Sons. 309 pp.

McIntyre, R. 1995. *War against the wolf.* Stillwater, Minnesota: Voyageur Press. 480 pp.

Meagher, M.M. 1973. *The bison of Yellowstone National Park.* Washington: National Park Service Scientific Monograph Series No. 1. 161 pp.

Mech, L.D. 1970. *The wolf: the behavior and ecology of an endangered species.* Garden City, N.Y.: Natural History Press. 384 pp.

———. 1988. *The arctic wolf, living with the pack.* Stillwater, Minnesota: Voyageur Press. 128 pp.

———. 1991. *The life of the wolf.* Stillwater, Minnesota: Voyageur Press. 120 pp.

———. 1991. Returning the wolf to Yellowstone. Pages 309–322 in R.B. Keiter and M.S. Boyce, eds., *The greater Yellowstone ecosystem.* New Haven: Yale University Press. 428 pp.

Milstein, M. 1995. *Wolf: return to Yellowstone.* Billings. 96 pp.

Murie, A. 1940. *Ecology of the coyote in Yellowstone.* Washington, D.C.: U.S. Government Printing Office. 206 pp.

Peterson, R.O. 1977. *Wolf ecology and prey relationships on Isle Royale.* N.P.S. Scientific Monograph Series No. 11. 210 pp.

Schullery, P. 1992. *The bears of Yellowstone.* Worland: High Plains Publishing Company. 318 pp.

Strauch, T.B. 1992. Holding the wolf by the ears: the conservation of the northern Rocky Mountain wolf in Yellowstone National Park. *University of Wyoming College of Law Land and Water Law Review* XXVII(1):33–81.

Tucker, P. 1988. Annotated gray wolf bibliography. Denver: U.S. Fish and Wildlife Service Region 6. 117 pp.

Wright, R.G. 1992. *Wildlife research and management in the national parks.* Urbana: University of Illinois Press. 224 pp.

Young, S.P., and E.A. Goldman. 1944. *The wolves of North America.* New York: Dover. 632 pp.

Acknowledgments

$\mathbf{M}$y understanding of Yellow-stone wolf history and recent developments is the result of my own historical research and reading plus what I have learned from many other people, especially Aubrey Haines, Douglas Houston, Mary Meagher, John Varley, and Lee Whittlesey. Ed Bangs, Norm Bishop, Wayne Brewster, Hank Fischer, Bruce Hampton, Alice Levine, Mike Phillips, Doug Smith, John Varley, and Lee Whittlesey provided countless helpful suggestions and criticisms of the manuscript at various stages. Sarah Broadbent, Ursula Weltman, and Lori Wilkinson were of great assistance in converting older documents into usable word processing files and in other editorial logistics.

Most important, I acknowledge the authors of the material in this book. That this large a volume represents such a small part of what has been written about the wolves of Yellowstone is some indication of how these animals demand our attention. In the case of recent authors (especially in Part II), their institutional affiliation at the time they wrote their material is given.

P.S.

About the Author

P aul Schullery is the author, co-author, or editor of more than 20 books on nature, conservation, and outdoor sport, and contributing author to 12 others. He has worked in Yellowstone as a ranger-naturalist, park historian, and senior editor of the Yellowstone Center for Resources. His other Yellowstone books include *The Bears of Yellowstone, Yellowstone Bear Tales, Mountain Time, Old Yellowstone Days,* and *Yellowstone's Ski Pioneers.* He has written for many technical and popular publications, including *BioScience, The New York Times, The Encyclopedia Britannica Yearbook of Science and the Future, National Parks, American Forests,* and *Outdoor Life.* Paul is an affiliate professor of history at Montana State University, and an adjunct professor of American Studies at the University of Wyoming.

Index